The Significance of
Religious Experience

The Significance of Religious Experience

Howard Wettstein

OXFORD
UNIVERSITY PRESS

Oxford University Press is a department of the University of Oxford.
It furthers the University's objective of excellence in research, scholarship,
and education by publishing worldwide.

Oxford   New York
Auckland   Cape Town   Dar es Salaam   Hong Kong   Karachi
Kuala Lumpur   Madrid   Melbourne   Mexico City   Nairobi
New Delhi   Shanghai   Taipei   Toronto

With offices in
Argentina   Austria   Brazil   Chile   Czech Republic   France   Greece
Guatemala   Hungary   Italy   Japan   Poland   Portugal   Singapore
South Korea   Switzerland   Thailand   Turkey   Ukraine   Vietnam

Oxford is a registered trade mark of Oxford University Press
in the UK and certain other countries.

Published in the United States of America by
Oxford University Press
198 Madison Avenue, New York, NY 10016

Library of Congress Cataloging-in-Publication Data
Wettstein, Howard K.
The significance of religious experience/Howard Wettstein.
    p.   cm.
ISBN 978-0-19-984136-3 (hardcover : alk. paper); 978-0-19-022675-6 (paperback : alk. paper)
1. Religion—Philosophy. 2. Experience (Religion) I. Title.
BL51.W3743   2012
210—dc23   2011036817

*For my teachers, Rabbi Aharon Lichtenstein
and Rabbi Moshe Chait, z"l,
and for Rabbi Mickey Rosen, z"l,
from whom I learned so much.*

Contents

Acknowledgments

I am grateful to many people for comments, reactions, passing remarks that made a difference, examples of one or another aspect of religious virtue, and a million other things. Although it is a bit terrifying to list people for fear of omitting a name that should by no means be omitted, it is important to acknowledge people who were especially helpful in thinking through the issues discussed here:

Robert Adams, Joseph Almog, Antonio Capuano, Brian Copenhaver, Rabbi Yehoshua Engelman, John Fischer, Harry Frankfurt, Yehudah (Jerome) Gellman, Charles Griswold, Richie Lewis, Jeff Helmreich, Chip Manekin, Richard Mendelsohn, Jack Miles, (the late) Philip Quinn, Mark Ravizza, (the late) Rabbi Mickey Rosen, David Shatz, Josef Stern, Bernie Susser, Eleonore Stump, Barbara Wettstein, Nicholas Wolterstorff, Mark Wrathall, Larry Wright, Linda Zabzebski; finally the folks who over the years have attended the Philosophy Conference at the Hartman Institute in Jerusalem. Thanks to Katharine Henshaw for invaluable editorial assistance.

Prior Publication

The following papers appear in this volume by permission

"Awe and the Religious Life" appeared in *Midwest Studies in Philosophy*, volume 21, 1998, with comments by Philip Quinn and Eleonore Stump. A different version appeared in *Judaism*, volume 47, 1998.

"Terra Firma" appeared in *The Monist*, volume 78, 1995.

"Theological Impressionism" appeared in a slightly different version under the title, "Doctrine," in *Faith and Philosophy*, volume 14, 1997. The current version appeared in *Judaism*, volume 49, 2000. Still another version, "Religious Poetry and Religious Doctrine," appeared in David Shatz, ed., *Philosophy and Faith*, 2002 (McGraw Hill).

"Against Theology" appeared in Robert Eisen and Chales Manekin, eds., *Philosophers and the Bible*, 2008 (University Press of Maryland).

"The Significance of Religious Experience" appeared in *The Modern Schoolman*, volume 86, 2011. Reprinted in *Conversations: The Journal of the Institute of Jewish Ideas and Ideals*, 2011.

"Against Theodicy" appeared in *Proceedings of the Twentieth World Congress in Philosophy*, volume 4, 1999. Reprinted in *Philosophia*, volume 30, 2003. Another version in *Judaism*, volume 50, 2001.

"God's Struggles" appeared in Michael Bergmann, Michael Murray, Michael Rea, eds., *Divine Evil?: The Moral Character of the God of Abraham*, 2011 (Oxford University Press).

"Coming to Terms with Exile" appeared in H. Wettstein, ed., *Diasporas and Exiles: Varieties of Jewish Identity*, 2002 (University of California Press). Closely related versions appeared in A. K. Sahoo and B. Maharaj, eds., *Sociology of Diaspora*, 2007 (Rawat Publications—Jaipur, India), and in M. A. Erlich, ed., *Encyclopedia of the Jewish Diaspora*, 2009 (ABC-CLIO, LLC).

"Forgiveness and Moral Reckoning" appeared in *Philosophia*, volume 38, 2010

"Ritual" appeared in the *Routledge Encyclopedia of Philosophy*, 1998.

The Significance of
Religious Experience

1

Introduction

Recent times have seen the advent of a new atheism. A number of writers have weighed in—philosophers, scientists, literary people—individuals with little sympathy for traditional Judeo-Christian-Muslim religion with what they see as its metaphysical and epistemological pretensions. Even worse, from their point of view, are ethical pretensions that stand in contrast with a highly spotty ethical history. I share many of their concerns, and yet I count myself among the practitioners of traditional religion. My return to Jewish religious life some twenty years ago was a response to a hunger for meaning, one to which life in the academy was, while not irrelevant, not quite adequate.

Since that time I have been on something of a mission, to understand what to make of religion—its truth, its mythological dimension, its monumental ethical successes, and equally monumental failures—and of the fact that while my orientation in philosophy is naturalistic, I find myself powerfully drawn to religious life. The essays in this book represent my attempt to come to terms with the matter.

My inspiration and direction in this project derive from multiple and very different sources, some philosophical, some religious, others somewhere in between. On the philosophical side, there is the sense that philosophy should have something to say about the large issues in human life. Religion—more generally the domain of the sacred—is a prime candidate, one that did not receive much attention during the heyday of analytic philosophy.

A second factor, at once a kind of constraint on how to think about religion (and everything else), is the naturalism of which I spoke. The term "naturalism" nowadays brings to mind various trends—reductionist, eliminativist—that are not hospitable to religion. My kind of naturalism is quite different. One needs to return to the American naturalists of the first half of the twentieth century to get the flavor of what I have in mind, to philosophers like James, Dewey, and Santayana—thinkers who took religion seriously as a central human concern. Historically, my naturalism resonates with that of Aristotle, hardly a reductionist or eliminativist, and Spinoza.

Of the American naturalists, George Santayana played a particularly important role for me. Santayana writes about religion, most directly in *Reason in Religion*, in a way that is difficult to characterize. Not a supernaturalist, he is hardly a conventional believer, indeed an atheist in that term's most precise (metaphysical) meaning. At the same time, he appreciates religious life so deeply that he appears to inhabit its fringes.[1] God himself is perhaps puzzled about where exactly to locate Santayana—so I have thought only half-jokingly: an almost-insider of independent spirit or an appreciative outsider.

An even more profound philosophic influence was Ludwig Wittgenstein,[2] himself deeply reverent of religious tradition but never quite able to make personal contact. I avoided Wittgenstein's work for years, a reaction to his seemingly indulgent writing and the cliché-ridden discourse of many of his followers—too much easy talk of language games, meaning as use, forms of life. Some thirty years ago, however, I forced myself to engage with Wittgenstein's work, primarily as a challenge to my developing views in the philosophy of language. I had the impression—I came to see it as a misimpression— that Wittgenstein represented a radical alternative to the orientation I found so attractive. Alternative or not, it quickly became clear that I was in the presence of rare philosophical depth. Clearly I had much to learn here. And my thinking about language—more generally about philosophy and beyond—has never been the same. In *The Magic Prism*,[3] I sought to bring Wittgenstein to bear on the late twentieth century debate in the philosophy of language. In the present context, Wittgenstein makes occasional appearances. But

---

[1] With Catholic roots, Santayana is of a very different sensibility than Dewey, whose roots are Protestant. Dewey had no use for religious institutions, with their "historical accretions." See his *A Common Faith*, (Yale University Press, 1934).

[2] Philosophical compatibility, like friendship, is hardly transitive. Indeed, it is almost amusing, or in the borderland between amusing and painful, to imagine Santayana and Wittgenstein in dialog. I am profoundly grateful to Wittgenstein's writings for what feels like a deepening my understanding of philosophical things generally.

[3] Oxford University Press, 2004.

throughout this book, I am trying to think through religious commitment in a way that reflects what I have learned from him.

Abraham Joshua Heschel[4] served as a kind of mentor-in-print. Heschel's work sits between philosophy, poetry, and religious literature; he is perhaps best thought of as a philosophical poet of the religious life. During my first sojourn in religious life during my twenties, I was too rigidly analytical to appreciate Heschel, or indeed to read poetry. Upon reaching an age accessible to my Jungian shadow, poetry opened up to me. It was as if I was graced with a new form of perception, as if suddenly I had taste buds in my fingertips. And with poetry came Heschel. He too makes occasional appearances in the chapters here. But his spirit pervades.

It would be difficult to exaggerate the role of religious literature per se: the Hebrew Bible, the Talmud, and the subsequent tradition of commentary. From this oceanic corpus, I have learned more than I can say. Most important for the development of the view I articulate here is the Talmudic era interpretive tradition of *Midrash/Aggadah*, commentary that ranges from speculative filling in of missing pieces in the biblical narrative to parable, homily, even humor.[5]

Biblical narrative, parable, and the like, along with *Midrash/ Aggadah*, are, in the Jewish context, as close as one gets to theology—until the Middle Ages with its full-blown philosophical theology. And this earlier "theology" is largely literary in genre, much closer to the arts than to the doctrinal theology of the medievals. The stark contrast between the earlier and later modes of theology came as a shock to me; they represent very different approaches. Indeed I'm inclined to think that they fail to engage a single theological project. They appear to emerge from distinct religious sensibilities.

I turn now to the essays that constitute this book. "Man Thinks, God Laughs," chapter 2, is an autobiographical entry point into the philosophical work of the volume. The domain of the personal and that of the philosophical are, for me, much closer than one might suppose. The chapter is a brief exploration of how my work in

[4]See especially his *God in Search of Man: A Philosophy of Judaism* (Farrar, Straus, and Giroux, 1976).
[5]These two genres share the characterization in the text. Collections of *Midrash* are organized as commentaries on the biblical texts that they elucidate. *Aggadot* appear interspersed with legal materials in the Talmud. They are often not keyed to any particular biblical text but take up theological issues connected with the legal discussions or with the general project of the Talmudic tractate in which they appear.

philosophy conspired with a variety of human factors to induce a second look at religious life, abandoned many years earlier.

"Awe and the Religious Life," chapter 3, emerged from my transition from a Santayana-like appreciation of religion to residence inside traditional religious life. My reentry has required some refurbishing of the living quarters. It has been a labor of love—not without its rough spots—to see how I am to make sense for myself of a religious outlook that is conventionally understood in ways with which I cannot connect. The ordinary religious idioms, expressive of a distinctive way to approach life, have great appeal for me. The question has been what those idioms come to. And if they come to something quite different than ordinarily assumed, what happens to their initial, straightforward appeal? (Answer: It remains. But that is a long story.)

One point of difference concerns the contrast between my naturalism, already mentioned, and the more conventional supernaturalism. And then there is my emphasis on the earlier literary theology that I have mentioned, something I want to champion, and the contrasting philosophical style of theology that has become virtually normative.

The latter approach places doctrinal belief at the very heart of a religious outlook. And yet the Hebrew Bible knows of no concept like our concept of belief.[6] If belief is not focal, what is? Standing in awe of heaven, in awe of God are the relevant biblical idioms. Affective matters, like awe and also love, constitute pillars of the relationship between people and God, pillars of religious life.[7]

Such affective matters, as opposed to metaphysical beliefs, are basic to the sort of religious way to which I am drawn. And when I speak of things like awe and love, I mean to speak not of mere feelings but of attitudes realized in the life of the agent. One who loves and stands in awe of God is one whose life exemplifies such ways, albeit imperfectly. Nor should one suppose that such modes of living—I have referred to them as affective—do not have a cognitive dimension. One does not simply feel awe or behave in an awe-inspired fashion. One stands in awe of God.

---

[6] See especially chapters 2 and 7. But the point is discussed and emphasized throughout the volume.

[7] It occurs to me now, as opposed to what I say in the essays collected here, that it is probably best to say that the Bible has no expression for "religious outlook," since in the biblical purview, God is about as controversial as the weather. In the biblical imagination, awe and love are best thought of as focal in religious life, that is, in the sort of life appropriate to a world in which one stands, willy-nilly, in a relation to God.

Philosophy of religion in the twentieth and twenty-first century has not attended much to concepts like awe, love, and gratitude, though things seem to be changing in this regard.[8] The primary philosophical focus has been religious metaphysics and epistemology.[9] In Chapter 3, I begin my project of exploring these relatively neglected attitudes along with the distinctive conception of human flourishing that makes them focal. My focus is awe, itself a surprising constellation of humility and elevation (how do these go together?). I had hoped to write about love next, but the topic proved too difficult. It is a topic on which I am at work as I finish this volume.

Though the focus here is awe, there is also a kind of undercurrent obsession with the role of metaphysics. In this essay, I do not reject the metaphysical project as wrongheaded; I argue that religious life is viable in the absence of settled metaphysical beliefs. I do so by directing attention to other domains of human reflection and knowledge in which we get along quite well in the absence of clarity about what is in some sense fundamental.

Mathematics constitutes a striking example. Who is going to question the integrity of mathematics just because its epistemological and metaphysical underpinnings are less than entirely understood? Imagine the folly of first trying to solidify the metaphysical and epistemological foundations of mathematics, this as a preliminary to and justification for mathematical practice.

My attitude to religion and religious practice has similarities to the case of mathematics. I am entirely confident about them. This is not to say that religion is for everyone, or that I cannot understand those to whom it does not speak. And my confidence is in part predicated on my leaving open the foundations, if that is what they are. Of course, intellectual responsibility mandates that I say much more about my claim to confidence—about why and how religion makes sense. This is the burden of the entire volume, and I address it directly in chapter 7.

To say that we should not start with metaphysical questions or, even more radically as I am now inclined to suppose, that the usual supernaturalist religious metaphysics provides a misleading picture of what the game is all about, is not to diminish the central role

---

[8] There are exceptions, e.g., the work of Eleonore Stump, who has devoted a great deal of attention to love and related affective matters. See, e.g., her APA presidential address and her recent masterful (and heavy) volume, *Wandering in Darkness: Narrative and the Problem of Suffering* (Oxford University Press, 2011).

[9] Another focus has been theodicy, the critique of which is central to my project. See chapters 8 and 9.

of God in religious life. (Compare mathematics: the centrality of numbers, sets, and the like does not depend upon a person's metaphysical views, or lack of them.) At the heart of religious life are awe and love for God.[10]

"Terra Firma," chapter 4, aims at clarifying my sort of philosophical naturalism, distinct from other views known by that name. Indeed, "religious naturalism," my overall outlook in this book, will seem to many an oxymoron. In chapter 4, I illustrate my kind of naturalism with examples from epistemology, the philosophy of mind, and the philosophy of religion. The focus of the chapter is what I see as Wittgenstein's kindred naturalism, specifically as exhibited in his treatment of our talk of pain.

Central to Wittgenstein's way in philosophy is a wariness about philosophers' handling of noun phrases. We learn as children that nouns refer to—I can almost hear the words—"persons, places, and things." It can seem a harmless philosophical rendering of this grammatical truism that the use of noun phrases entails "ontological commitment" to their referents. Talk of souls would then presumably involve commitment to the supernatural; talk of abstract things like meanings, numbers, and propositions would entail commitment to a realm of nonnatural abstracta; and talk of pain would involve a commitment to mental states or events.

One of Wittgenstein's strategies was to explore the natural history, the evolution, of the sorts of phrases in question: nouns like "soul," "meaning," "number," and "pain." Understanding this evolution and clarifying what these phrases are doing for us, supposes Wittgenstein, may well render the usual metaphysical posits less attractive, even otiose. Needless to say, the matter is subtle and complex and deserves extensive exploration. My aim in chapter 4 is the exploration of one suggestive case of the general phenomenon, the case of pain vocabulary.

Chapter 5, "Theological Impressionism," returns to religion per se and represents what was for me an important step, trying to sort out the nature and relative centrality of, and the relation between, religious imagery and religious belief. The title of the chapter reflects the fact that the primary religious works—the Hebrew Bible, Talmudic literature—speak of God impressionistically. Their mode of description is as remote from definition as poetry is from mathematics.

---

[10] And not only toward God; the sort of religious outlook I am drawn to makes central awe, love, and (related attitudes like) gratitude toward one's fellows, toward the universe, toward life.

The contrast is with the classical picture of religion from medieval times to the present: religious life as living atop a system of refined doctrine.

My anti-doctrinal outlook is (for only some readers) less shocking in the context of a Jewish religious sensibility than with others because of the centrality of practice in Jewish religious life. Still, religious practice without religious thought would yield a mere shadow of that life. In denying philosophized doctrine a central place, I thus have much work to do articulating the role of religious thought on my approach. "Theological Impressionism" constitutes a beginning.

Chapters 6 and 7, "Against Theology" and "The Significance of Religious Experience," represent my most recent treatments of the philosophic fundamentals implicated in religious commitment. Chapter 6 begins with a look at the history of theology. Think of the Israelite religious tradition, as represented by the *Tanach* (the Hebrew Bible), as having progeny: first Rabbinic Judaism, then Christianity, and then Islam.

In the beginning—in *Tanach*—the dominant forms of talk about God were poetry, poetically infused narrative, parable, and the like. When talk of God[11] undergoes something of a genre transformation, from literary to philosophical, God's *properties* and His *perfections* (omniscience, omnipotence, ethical perfection, and so forth) along with doctrinal propositions take center stage. In *Tanach*, and dominantly in the oral tradition reported in Talmudic literature,[12] God's *roles* are central: creator, judge, ruler, teacher, even lover, friend, and the like. That roles are emphasized as opposed to properties highlights the contrast between the literary and philosophical. And when God's properties are mentioned in the earlier tradition, they are typically ethical properties anthropomorphically characterized: long suffering, quick to forgive, and the like. The philosophical turn is evident first in late Christianity,[13] then in Islam, and then in Jewish tradition[14] for those living in Islamic civilization.

[11] This is as opposed to "talk to God" (as in prayer), a very different matter. Jewish liturgy retains much of the poetic and narrative character of *Tanach*.
[12] This tendency is continued in the early New Testament. The omni-properties seem unknown in much of *Tanach*.
[13] Philo was an early Jewish philosophically minded thinker, but his approach failed to have much sway among the Rabbis.
[14] I avoid the term "Judaism" whenever I can. It is the "ism" suffix that irks. I suggested in a talk on the subject in Jerusalem that we speak instead of Cosa Nostra ("our thing"), but my suggestion has not yet taken root.

This genre transformation is hardly a matter merely of style. Its enormous importance is related to the coming (and lasting) dominance of doctrine—theoretical propositions about the universe, now seen as being at the heart of religion—and to our very way of thinking about religious people as "believers." Its influence extends to how we conceive religious practice. Maimonides, at his most philosophically bold, surprisingly seems to attribute limited value to the ordinary modes of Jewish religious life: prayer, rituals, Talmudic learning.[15] The arch religious moment, he suggests, is one spent in solitary and specifically philosophic reflection on divinity. Wittgenstein warned that philosophers tend to reinterpret subject matters in ways amenable to philosophical treatment. The transformation I have been exploring seems a paradigm.

If one uses the term "theology" for the earlier reflections on divinity, theology becomes a literary frame for religious practice, a way to emphasize and enhance the moral and spiritual significance of religious life, a way to add to the power of that life to edify and transform. This is a dramatically different enterprise than philosophical theology with its theoretical aim of providing a metaphysical underpinning. What emerge from philosophical theology (and persist to this day) are what have always seemed to me heroic epistemological constructions, these by way of shoring up, justifying, rationalizing the metaphysical commitments.

The local aim of chapter 7, "The Significance of Religious Experience," is a critique of William James's argument for the existence of God from individual religious experience. As developed by a number of twentieth-century philosophers of religion, James's argument constitutes one of the latest attempts to supply epistemic foundations. I am as skeptical of this modern proof for God's existence as I am of the traditional ones.[16]

A more general and perhaps important aim of this chapter is an exploration of the power and significance of religious experience. If such "gifts to the spirit" (James) fail to provide the makings of a demonstration of God's existence, what do they provide? What are we to make of the striking and powerful experiences reported by so many, representing different traditions and outlooks? Here, the

[15] See the last chapters of his *Guide For the Perplexed*.
[16] This is not to deny that the various arguments for God's existence appeal to genuine and important features of experience that are by no means irrelevant to the power and meaning of religion, like the order and beauty of the universe, the character of religious experience, and the like.

thought of the mystic, St. Teresa of Avila, as articulated by Rowan Williams, proves helpful.

The chapter concludes with a still more general concern: how does one make sense of religious commitment? Some twentieth-century analytic philosophers of religion have tried to square the circle, to emphasize belief in supernaturalist metaphysics and argue that somehow, such belief is as plain as common sense. One way has been to emphasize the power of skepticism. Swinburne argues, for example, that skepticism about common sense is so powerful that the principles one needs to defeat it are sufficient to justify religious belief. Such an approach seems doubly dubious because it grants skepticism such power and denies the intuitive gap between belief in the supernatural and common sense.

James, although he has a hand in encouraging such thinking, emphasizes religious experience. Following this side of James's thought, even deemphasizing religious belief, I want to think about making sense not of a theoretical position but of a form of life, in some sense more plain and intuitive than in Wittgenstein's use of that expression.

There is, however, a strong connection here to Wittgenstein. My approach parallels his more general reflections on "making sense" (and the transition in thought that he recommends) in *On Certainty*. His focus is the concept of knowledge; his aim, to set the concept of *knowing* at a distance from skeptical concerns, their defeat, and the like. Details aside, his aim is twofold (at least). First, to show that certain philosophical projects are off the mark, inappropriate—the project of defeating the skeptic, or that of providing a non-question begging intellectual justification of our ways. Second, to explore the naturalness of our ways in the world. I am trying to move our thinking about religion in a parallel direction.

The essays discussed so far focus on "first philosophy." It has seemed to both defenders and critics that religion requires substantial metaphysical and epistemological commitments. And I mean to be taking us in a very different direction. But there is another and very different sort of issue that that has seemed paramount, one that for many closes the books on traditional religion: the problem of evil, the threat from unjust suffering. Specifically, the sheer awfulness that is so much with us presents enormous difficulties for traditional ideas about God, specifically the constellation of His goodness, knowledge, and power.

This challenge is so plain and so powerful that one might well wonder what could count as a persuasive, cogent answer. From ancient times, the best minds have been tormented by the problem, and answers one more brilliant than the next—the project dubbed "theodicy"—have been proffered.

But brilliance is one thing; plain talk another. Early in chapter 8, "Against Theodicy," I recall the wonderful Talmudic turn of phrase: the question is better than the answer(s). The question in this case is made vivid by the biblical text itself: There are myriad passages that portray God and His universe as just, and reward and punishment (even in this world) accordingly meted out. Not only does such a portrayal violate our experience, the Bible is not shy in relating stories that on the face of it are inconsistent with justice. Job is just one example. Indeed, in Isaiah (45:7) God Himself is quoted as saying that He creates both good and evil.

A response to this crucial challenge should take its cue from Psalm 146 in which God is said to be the guardian of truth. What is needed is not theoretical facility and brilliance, but rather a natural way to think about the topic, one that does not engender the sense that our naive instincts have been outsmarted.

Chapter 8, largely a reflection on Job, is a brief on behalf of na-iveté about evil and God. Marx had his own issues with religion. But his famous remark that religion is the opiate of the masses resonates when one thinks about theodicy. My aim in chapter 8—and I pursue the idea further in chapters 9, "God's Struggles," and 10, "Coming to Terms with Exile"—is the exploration of what I call non-opiate reflections of the problem of evil.

Chapter 9, "God's Struggles," derives from my concluding remarks at a conference on the Hebrew Bible at the University of Notre Dame. The conference explored passages from *Tanach* in which God seems to mandate all manner of ethical evils, such as the killing of the inhabitants of the Promised Land, including children and animals, and the "taking" (i.e., rape) of some of the women. Many of the papers by Christian philosophers proposed some form of theodicy—explaining or justifying God's mandates. This was roundly rejected by atheists for whom such moves are both alto-gether expected from religious advocates and altogether unaccept-able, a good reason (among others) to reject religion.

My talk reflected my distance from both perspectives. I began by introducing a related but even more devastating challenge to God's justice: God's treatment not of His/Israel's enemies, but of his beloved. Two heartbreaking cases are that of Job, already mentioned, and Abraham in the *Akedah*, Abraham's response in Genesis 22 to God's command to sacrifice his beloved Isaac.

My approach to these issues is first and foremost to insist on, not to fudge on, what is morally plain. God's motivation for these things is unfathomable. Referring to these ordeals as "trials," as the biblical text does, is hardly to explain their lack of ethical awfulness. Carl Jung, in an inspired if irreverent moment, said that the Accuser (a heavenly roaming prosecutor called "Satan" in the text of Job, but not to be identified with the Satan of Christian tradition) represents God's insecurity about Job's love. Does Job really love God? Would he remain loyal when pushed to the very edge, robbed of all he has achieved, including his family?

What is striking about the Book of Job, and also about the *Akedah*, aside from God's apparent cruelty to those he loves, is the eerie quality that there is something true and profound and universal here. Thinking about Job, one can hardly resist the thought that the universe—life— takes just as it gives. And, taking the Satan story at the beginning of Job as a parable, it does so with indifference. Life's gifts are transitory, fleeting. The Spinoza-flavored quality of the Whirlwind vision, shared by God with Job, may provide solace. But it certainly does not supply answers. Job is healed without being answered.

Turning to Abraham and the *Akedah*, it is customary to see Abraham as immediately choosing to follow God's command, hastening to the sacrifice of Isaac. This would be out of character for the Abraham we meet up with earlier in the biblical text, in chapter 18, for example, when he argues with God on behalf of Sodom. As I experience chapter 22, Abraham faces an excruciating dilemma that under one description is hardly unknown to us: the universe forces a choice between our greatest loves, between alternatives each of which is not negotiable.[17] Abraham models for us a heroic response: he refuses to panic, refuses to choose between these non-negotiable alternatives, refuses to look too far into the future where he may have to make a decision. Such a glance ahead would be crippling. Instead of seeing Abraham as a willing accomplice, one can see him as holding on with his teeth both to God and to his boy, marching toward Moriah, head down. I find great meaning—moral and religious—in both Abraham's plight and his response.

In chapter 10, "Coming to Terms with Exile," I explore a non-opiate religious resolution to the difficulties posed by exile, a pervasive

---

[17]I owe to Harry Frankfurt the insight that, contrary to the understanding of many commentators, what makes the choice so excruciating is not that Abraham, if he is to follow God's command, must violate morality but rather that he must violate his love for Isaac.

theme in Jewish history and in Jewish and Christian liturgy and theological reflection. In the Jewish context, exile is both a political idea (exile from the homeland) and a metaphorical one: dislocation as a focal aspect of the human condition. In the Christian context, the metaphorical sense of exile takes prominence, the human being as fallen and in need of redemption. The shared sense of exile may be highlighted by reflection on the mythological past (Eden before the apple) and the mythological future (the Messianic era), when human existence was not, or will not be, radically troubled and confused.

The rabbis of the Talmud struggled mightily with what they saw as the exile of exiles, the destruction of the Second Temple in 70 CE and subsequent exile of the people. The talmudic comment that God went into exile with the people reveals the perceived depth, severity, and extent of dislocation. The Rabbis' self-appointed task was nothing less than reconstruction of social and religious life that was on the brink of destruction. Their quest was to develop a manual, as it were, for the successful, meaningful, and rich negotiation of life experience even when it does not go well—to take exile (in both senses) seriously, give it its due, but to use it as a sensitizing rather than stultifying force. The challenge is the darkness of life in both ordinary and dire circumstances; the project is largely non-opiate.

I say "largely" since there were also attempts at theodicy-flavored explanations of the tragedy, for example, the oft-repeated remark that the Temple's destruction/exile is a result of the rise of baseless hatred within the community. But such remarks do not have great explanatory force, as opposed, for example, to political/military explanations in terms of, say, Roman military power. Such comments have a kind of ethical/homiletical power, but that's another matter.

The Rabbinic response to the threat of cultural destruction and cosmic dislocation was largely a practical one—significant adjustments and accommodations in the absence of what had been the centerpiece of religious life, the Temple in Jerusalem. But there was a theological response as well, a largely non-opiate one, I argue. Interestingly, during the period that Christians developed a theological response at once messianic and incarnational, the Rabbis, some of whom more than flirted with their own messianism, stayed with God in heaven, as it were, but enhanced their conception of divinity hyper-anthropomorphically. God, in the *Midrash* on Lamentations, is spoken of in vivid, human ways, as a mother bird whose nest has been destroyed, as a father who has beaten and exiled his wayward sons, as one who confesses to not knowing how to mourn and asks for help from the Patriarchs. Mourning with God over the exile and over the human condition is a paradigmatically non-opiate Jewish response.

Chapter 11, "Forgiveness and Moral Reckoning," is a critical review of Charles Griswold's seminal book *Forgiveness*, and takes us in a different direction from earlier chapters. Here, my concern is to reflect on this central notion in religious tradition, as theorized in a secular mode by Griswold. The chapter derives from my participation in an American Philosophical Association symposium of Griswold's book, a symposium to which Griswold invited me in part because I would bring a religious orientation to the subject.

Most of my discussion of Griswold's theory does not presuppose a religious outlook. At the end, I return to what seem to me important aspects of forgiveness that are absent on Griswold's reading, but central if one begins with a religious perspective.

Griswold's is a classical analysis: he attempts to formulate conditions that are both necessary and sufficient for forgiveness, not in my view a formula for success. It seems to me, though, that many of his conditions are not universally applicable; indeed, they seem inapplicable to many garden-variety cases of forgiveness. Griswold's focus is on what he calls "paradigm cases of forgiveness." However, these are not paradigms in the sense of standard, central cases of our actual practice of forgiveness. They are what Griswold considers "perfect cases," paradigms in a Plato-inspired sense. They are extreme cases, where extreme moral transgressions are involved, transgressions that require various extremes of forgiveness. Such a focus may skew our thinking about forgiveness, or so I argue.

What I call *legalism* is both central to Griswold's view and of concern to me. Bernard Williams and others have objected to what they call *scientism*, the (mis)application to various domains of philosophy of modes of thought and explanation that derive from the sciences. Parallel to such scientism is legalism, the imposition of legal categories on the ethical domain. *Justification, warrant, obligation* and *duty:* are such ideas pivotal in potential forgiveness situations, as Griswold assumes? There are many examples; particularly striking was Griswold's contention that the moral community cedes to the offended party the *moral standing* to be the sole purveyor of forgiveness.

To return for a moment to chapter 7, "The Significance of Religious Experience," I note there the same legalizing tendency in epistemology: *warrant, justification, and epistemic obligation* as central notions. In both domains—ethics and epistemology—my idea is to think less legalistically. In the epistemic realm, we would do better, I think, to worry about whether we are being *responsible* in our beliefs than whether they are *justified*, the latter granting too much respect to the skeptic, or so I argue in chapter 7.

To turn to my interest in a religious perspective on forgiveness, I do not suppose that religion makes possible forgiveness of some special or superior sort. The Jewish sensibility that I inhabit domesticates forgiveness between people and God, a consequence of its domestication of love between those parties. Love is modeled, as in the Song of Songs, the Book of Hosea, and other places in *Tanach*, on love between human partners, each needing, even longing for, the other. Such intimacy—proximity as it were—makes friction inevitable; forgiveness becomes a focal virtue.

Griswold and I agree that it is important to think about forgiveness not only as an act but also as a virtue of character. I provide comments toward a model of the virtue; God as forgiving partner proves to be of assistance. My characterization of forgiveness as a virtue makes strong contact with earlier hesitations about Griswold's approach. Love, for example, plays a large role, this in place of Griswold's emphasis on moral duty as motivating the foreswearing of resentment.

Chapter 12, "Ritual," which previously appeared in the *Routledge Encyclopedia of Philosophy*, confronts a prominent perplexity about the value of ritual. There is the sense that to routinize expressions of love, awe, and worship is to mechanize and constrict these things and to evacuate them of meaning. It is indeed striking that none of the prevailing approaches to ethical theory—Aristotelian, Kantian, Utilitarian, for example—make it easy to see how ritual might figure crucially in the ethical life. Yet both ethically and spiritually, ritualized ways are seen as crucially valuable within communities of practitioners.

Perhaps I can formulate a virtue of ritualized ways in a way I could not do when I wrote the encyclopedia piece. In any long-term love relationship, the participants develop ways to express intimacy. Think of nicknames and any number of practices that will inevitably seem idiosyncratic to the outsider but which have great meaning to the participants. Now think of religious rituals as ways the community expresses intimacy with the divine. The practices do not have to make sense; they are merely our ways with God. But that is quite enough. And so, when a practitioner fails to observe the prescribed ways, she can feel a sense of letting the other party down, of not living up to her side of the relationship. Such feelings are indeed common among religious practitioners.

What I was able to point out at the time of writing the piece was the difference between a single individual's typically inarticulate expressions of gratefulness, awe, love, and the like, and expressing these things by making various passages from, say, Psalms, one's own. So traditional liturgies, for example, compare with spontaneous expressions of emotion the way Shakespeare compares with my poetry or yours. It is not as if there is no place for spontaneity. But insisting on the value of spontaneity should not blind us to the potential power of ritualized ways. This is, of course, not to deny that ritualized practice can descend into something purely mechanical.

Chapter 13, "Concluding Remarks: Religion without Metaphysics," highlights what is perhaps most distinctive and most controversial in my approach: the divorce between religion and metaphysics. One aspect is the idea that religious life can proceed in a way that is philosophically naïve, the pictures that the traditional texts encourage taken at face value. Another is the idea that religious conceptions not be seen as at the surface of an underlying metaphysical picture. Instead, religious institutions embody procedures for the encouragement and development of a unique sort of responsiveness, related but not reducible to ethical and aesthetic responsiveness.

2

Man Thinks; God Laughs[*]

A little philosophy inclineth man's mind to atheism, but depth in philosophy bringeth men's minds about to religion.

—Francis Bacon, "On Atheism"

When Bacon penned the sage epigram . . . he forgot to add that the God to whom depth in philosophy brings back men's minds is far from being the same from whom a little philosophy estranges them.

—George Santayana, *Reason in Religion*

As a young man entering college—Yeshiva College in New York City—I made my first contact with traditional Judaism. I was smitten. It was more than mere infatuation; I worked very hard at it, wrestled with it: with belief in God, with the demanding ritual life, not to speak of the linguistic (Hebrew, Aramaic) and analytical skills required for the sort of study that I came to see as at the heart of my engagement.

To speak of a love affair is to get a bit too close to cliché. Nevertheless, it feels apt. To switch metaphors, I had found a home, an intellectual and spiritual community altogether unknown to me until college. I would sometimes go home for weekends, returning

[*] The title of this chapter translates an old Yiddish epigram. It seemed appropriate to my story of religious change.

to a very different world. And although at home I could attend synagogue on *Shabbat*, the culture of the synagogue was but a dim reflection of the rich world I had found. Synagogue services were long, mechanical, boring. Returning to school was a homecoming.

My passions at Yeshiva were Jewish studies and philosophy. Philosophy was itself a new and exciting world, and it offered the essential tools—or so it seemed—to evaluate the ambitious truth claims of religion. However, there was only so much philosophy one could study at Yeshiva. This was not the case for Jewish studies, and I delayed graduating for a year in order to devote more time to Talmud, the heart of traditional Jewish learning. After five years of hard work— Talmud is something like the theoretical physics of the tradition—I was ready for the rabbinical program. I had no ambition to enter the practicing clergy. But rabbinic ordination seemed to be the way forward, spiritually and intellectually; I would worry later about how to earn a living.

Just then Bacon's "a little philosophy" reared its head. I had nagging doubts about the theological fundamentals, about belief in God, for example. There were no such hesitations about the life; its appeal remained steady. But how did I know there really was a God? How could one know? I was stricken, you might say, by philosophical conscience. Why should I pay more attention to my *feeling* that all this was true than to my neighbor's conviction that Jesus was the son of God or my former doubt that there was a God? How could one intellectually justify the basics? It seemed crucial to be intellectually responsible about something so important, indeed foundational to my life.

Religion seemed spiritually and intellectually rich but philosophically burdensome. The summer before entering rabbinical school, I was teaching Talmud in a *kollel*, a special study group, at a summer camp operated by Yeshiva University. By day I worked intensely and with great enjoyment on Talmud; by evening, I worked over (and under and through), again and again, my theological doubts. By the end of the summer, I was convinced (as much as one can be with such matters) that a just God would well understand why I could not believe.

Twenty-odd years later—in the midst of a career as a philosophy professor—I felt drawn to have another look at religion, one that eventually produced a return to traditional religious life. The reasons are complicated; it is really difficult to be clear about such acts of God, as it were. In my case, it is especially difficult to tease apart the role of philosophy from more personal factors; I suspect there is no sharp separation. I will begin with my life in philosophy and move on to the more personal.

Disappointment with academia was surely a factor. My dream had been that in philosophy—the subject matter and hopefully the profession—I would find the sort of fulfillment that I experienced with Talmud, perhaps even more so. The Talmudic subject matter was, after all, a system of law. Although pursued in a particularly profound and engaging way, the legal subject matter was not earth-shaking.[1] Philosophy, by contrast, scrutinized the most profound questions, rock-bottom foundations.

But the way philosophy was pursued during my graduate school years and in the aftermath—this was the late sixties, the heyday of classical analytic philosophy—left me cold, feeling like an outsider. I had limited undergraduate training, mostly in the history of philosophy, but more than enough to generate a love for the subject. Analytic philosophy—its vocabulary, its moves, its paradigms—was another thing.[2] And my attempts to probe were greeted with a kind of polite dismissal—polite at least some of the time. The contrast with my undergraduate experience could not have been more dramatic. In academic philosophy it seemed that competition rather than shared learning was the rule; intellectual dispute was hardly "for the sake of heaven," as it was often in the world of the yeshiva.

Things improved when I entered the workforce at the University of Minnesota, Morris, a small liberal arts college located near the Dakotas. By then I had made my way into analytic philosophy and found issues, especially about language and thought, which were indeed fundamental. And having learned from master teachers as an undergraduate, I took great pleasure in trying to create similar relationships with students.

Still, Minnesota had something of the feel of Siberia, especially to two New Yorkers (Barbara and me) straight from Manhattan. Our two children were born in Morris, population 3,500 (including the students), hardly our natural habitat. This was especially so for my wife who was the only practicing Jew within a hundred miles and was in any case eager to get back to graduate school.

---

[1] Indeed, it is one of the wonders and mysteries of Talmudic learning that the process *feels* so powerful and religiously significant, almost despite the typical subject matter, torts for example.

[2] Ironically, my dissertation and subsequent two books were about the philosophy of language, specifically the theory of reference. But it took quite a while for me to master the vocabulary, moves, and paradigms.

In an effort to move on, I took a visiting position at the University of Iowa; it proved philosophically stimulating and a good experience for the family. Subsequently, I received an NEH Fellowship and went to Stanford University. Arriving in Palo Alto, California, straight from western Minnesota, my wife and I felt that we had entered Eden. Our first dinner was a picnic in Foothill Park; we ate among deer running free.

The NEH year was extremely profitable; Professor John Perry and I found many hours to talk. I much appreciated the personal and intellectual comradeship, not to speak of the philosophical stimulation. The following year Stanford offered me a visiting professorship, and then in 1983 we departed for a new position at the University of Notre Dame, home of a fine graduate philosophy department.

In late 1988, I received a call from an old friend at the University of California, Riverside offering me a position and a chance to fulfill something of a lifelong dream: to help create a first-rate research department in which I might have flourished as a graduate student. Leaving Notre Dame meant leaving an established and congenial department. But the temptation was great. And it meant moving back to California where philosophy of language seemed to grow on palm trees.

At UCR, however, I found a deeply troubled department, with much free-floating mistrust and considerable antipathy between Analytic and Continentally oriented philosophers.[3] The painful discord prompted reflection on the limitations of my life in academia. I was and remain enormously grateful for the intellectual growth that academic life facilitated and still facilitates, and the pleasures of teaching are difficult to exaggerate. Nevertheless I found myself longing for the sort of intellectual community within which I had flourished as an undergraduate. Academia was and was not my natural home.

Robert Bly, the American poet, remarked that there are two times of "opening," times when the individual is genuinely accessible to new experiences and ways: late teenage years and mid- to late forties. The experience I just related, longing for intellectual (and for that matter, spiritual) community, occurred in my mid-late forties. Indeed Bly's "openings" represent the two times when religion became powerful for me.

---

[3]This is very much not the case nowadays. Several of us devoted ourselves to changing the culture and with significant efforts this rarity actually occurred and persists.

It was during this period that I began to read poetry, a genre with which I could not make contact earlier. As I said in the Introduction, it was as if a new, wonderful mode of perception were open, as if I suddenly had taste buds in my fingers. It is important to add that I experienced poetry as a supplement to and not a replacement for the analytical thought which remained a touchstone. This is only worth saying in the context of an intellectual climate that often sees these modes as opposed to one another. My own sense is that poetic sensibility and the analytical inclination are perfectly complimentary. The problem is with people who, perhaps understandably, find it difficult to incorporate both modes. I certainly did for quite a portion of my life.

I was in my late forties, grappling with professional life, longing for an intellectually and spiritually rich past, reading poetry, and then two other things happened, each of powerful import. First, I was invited to participate in a 1990 conference in honor of UCLA's David Kaplan, a person who had figured in major ways in my thinking and my career in the philosophy of language. The conference was in Israel, a place I had never visited and one that at least at that time I had no special interest in visiting. As a Jew, I had a special interest in the place, but found myself disaffected by the Israeli treatment of Palestinians, especially post-1967. But the conference was in honor of Kaplan, and my wife was eager for what would be our first family visit to Israel. So we took our two teenage children for what turned out to be a signal family experience.

Landing at Tel Aviv Airport on a Friday afternoon, I was stunned—on the verge of completely unexpected tears—when an Israeli customs agent wished me a *Shabbat shalom*, something between a Sabbath greeting and blessing of peace. (It doesn't translate well.) A longtime fan of *The Godfather*, I thought to myself, "This is like what Michael Corleone must have felt landing in Sicily."[4] This was followed by the rare academic conference in which I felt completely at home, and by visits with the two rabbis who were my undergraduate mentors, and were in 1990 heading institutes in Jerusalem.

One of them, Rabbi Aharon Lichtenstein, a Talmudic scholar, Harvard PhD in literature, and published scholar of Cambridge Platonism, invited my family to his home at 7:00 a.m. on a Sunday,

---

[4]Recently I related this story to faculty at the Palestinian Al Quds University and was gratified that despite their personal and political feelings, they appreciated the emotion. For the past twenty years, I have been visiting Jerusalem annually to study Talmud, and for the past five, lecturing at Al Quds.

before he headed out to his yeshiva. When I tried to thank him for all he had done for me—Talmud with him was like boot camp for analytic philosophy—his humility inserted itself; he lowered his head and changed the subject. The contrast with much of academia could not have been more stark.

Another notable Israel experience: I had lunch with a prominent Israeli philosopher who remarked, "If you want to do good for this country, go home and tell your congressman to stop supporting us unless we learn to behave." This was turning out to be quite a different visit than anticipated.

The second important occurrence was my mother's death in 1992.[5] The event was cataclysmic in ways I did not and could not anticipate. My world was shaken, and my hunger for meaning turned ravenous. And there it was, in the form of Jewish religious mourning practices. The time became a holy one, although I had no idea what this meant or where I was headed; it was a time of spiritual and personal growth borne of great sadness, edging on depression. The moments of growth were sometimes palpable, so much so that I would feel tinges of guilt. I was, after all, benefiting from my mother's death. But then the depression would hit, evening the score.

My philosophical conscience was intact despite my religious enchantment. In thinking about the cliché that "there is no atheist in a foxhole," I reflected that this was for me more about meaning than about a change in my metaphysical outlook. The comfort afforded me had no metaphysical component. I did not believe, for example, that my mother (or her spirit) was somehow now literally somewhere else. The comfort had more to do with things like feeling her presence and making relative peace with our differences. And the contribution of the religious community was substantial.

My ability to embrace religious life—by this time I felt the urge to do so—reflected my study of Wittgenstein in a number of ways. First, Wittgenstein's approach to philosophy conspired with my interest in poetry to loosen the bonds of my analytic bent. Second, Wittgenstein helped to free me from seeing religion as the medievals had: at its heart a large-scale theoretical take on the world. Philosophy, Wittgenstein taught, tends to reinterpret various subject matters, to see them in terms with which it is comfortable. Accordingly, it is not uncommon in philosophy to exaggerate the role of intellect in our lives, specifically the roles of belief and theory. I saw the medieval theology as a

---

[5] My son reminded me of the year. He said, "The reason I remember it is because virtually on her death bed she voted for Bill Clinton."

case in point. Finally, and relatedly, Wittgenstein's way of making sense of various human ways was less a matter of justifying underlying beliefs and of defeating various skepticisms.[6] An attractive picture of religion was emerging: at its heart, a special kind of responsiveness, a sensibility that needs as little intellectual justification as our responsiveness to music or art.

The relation between religious life and supernaturalist metaphysics, already mentioned in the Introduction, is for me a very delicate business, one that constantly lurks behind the scenes in this book and in my life. From time to time, it will make an overt appearance. Here I will add a few words on the topic.

In chapter 6, I discuss what I call the medieval philosophical turn. Part of my ambition in this book is to explore the implications of the older, prephilosophical biblical and Rabbinic way. I repeatedly emphasize that *Tanach* has no native concept of belief and that the "theology" of the ancients consists largely in a literary supplement to religious practice, a supplement meant to edify and instruct. However, that the ancients did not think in terms of belief does not entail that we cannot bring that concept to bear in thinking about them and their lives. Nor is it clear that their outlook was pure of metaphysics—not clear at all. No doubt some had strong views in that direction. So when I reflect on religious commitment, I neither want to claim that such metaphysical views are irrelevant nor that they are crucial. A much lighter touch is needed, one that is extremely difficult to achieve. One has to grow into it, and my project is designed to assist me, and with good fortune the reader, with just such growth.

Here is something that one should bear in mind in pursuing the question: strikingly, few if any nowadays come to religion on the basis of an attraction to the supernaturalist metaphysical picture. Imagine the strangeness of meeting someone who says that he has no feeling for religion or for religious life but on grounds of philosophical/metaphysical argument, he has come to the conclusion that some form of traditional religion is true. Maybe there are a couple of people like this somewhere. But it is not the way religious change typically occurs. For the most part, people come to religion in some sort of quest for meaning, perhaps inspired by a life crisis, perhaps by a general hunger for or interest in spiritual things. And the metaphysical picture sort of tags along.

That may not seem to be of great consequence to the philosophically uninitiated. But to those of us in the business, the idea that

---

[6]See chapter 7 in this volume and Wittgenstein's *On Certainty*.

one falls in love, as it were, and ends up with a metaphysical picture is enormously consequential. It threatens our sense of intellectual responsibility. It feels like an unstable resting place.

Now consider those who become disenchanted with religion. It is rarely the burden of the metaphysical picture that is responsible. For me, it came close to being that. But I stop short of claiming such ideological purity. Big decisions are complicated things involving layers and layers.

Coming to or leaving religious life has more in common with falling in or out of love. Alternatively, it is a bit like finding a work of literature powerful. One does or one does not. In thinking about love, or about literature, we are not tempted to bring to bear concepts like intellectual justification, proof, and the like. My sense is that these concepts are probably not particularly germane to religious change or indeed to religious commitment or rejection.

I do not mean to suggest that it is only philosophy that sees in religion a metaphysical picture. When one becomes religious, one begins to speak, to sing, in a new language, one to which the usual metaphysical interpretation is hardly unnatural. One then finds oneself "believing" things that would formerly have seemed strange. It is something like the cost of doing business—not that it seems so costly to people; more likely it will seem like a sort of new discovery.

I have been speaking about religious change, coming to religion or leaving it. What of those who grew up "inside," those for whom a religious outlook constituted part of their upbringing? Does the metaphysical picture merely tag along for them? My sense is that with most religious people, almost regardless of whether they are relative newcomers, the layers of meaning and metaphysics are interwoven and difficult to tease apart.

3

Awe and the Religious Life: A Naturalistic Perspective[1]

I. Introduction: Analytic Philosophy and the Study of Religion

That philosophy provides scrutiny of fundamentals is its great virtue, one that brought many of us to its study. Virtues and vices—theoretical no less than personal—are often intimately linked. In the theoretical domain, the linkage is evident in philosophical studies of religion, at least in those carried out in the analytic tradition. Concern with what seems fundamental—the existence of God—often has been all-absorbing, and I would argue, distracting.

There are intellectual arenas in which we get along quite well in the absence of settled doctrines about the fundamentals, the philosophy of mathematics, for example. While questions about the existence and status of mathematical entities like numbers and sets is of great interest, no one would suggest that work in the philosophy of mathematics awaits a satisfactory treatment of these basic questions. Imagine the folly of the even stronger thesis that work in mathematics itself awaits such philosophical underpinning. However, with regard to the philosophy of religion and even to religion

[1]This paper appeared in *Midwest Studies in Philosophy*, volume 21, 1998; another version appeared in *Judaism* in Fall 1997.

itself, we commonly assume that we need to attend to the fundamental questions first.

The difference is of course explained by our complete confidence in mathematical practice. Indeed, a philosophical defense of mathematics seems otiose. Moreover, we are surely more confident about mathematics itself than about any philosophical account of its nature. In the case of mathematics, the institution and its practices, we might say, are primary, the interpretation a much more dubious business.[2] Whereas with respect to religion, the institution awaits the sort of justification in which philosophers trade, or so we usually assume.

Were we confident of the power of religious practice, confident about the virtues of the life that religion facilitates, we might well be willing to treat religion as we do mathematics. It would be natural, that is, to see the institution as primary, and the justification or interpretation as of great interest, but a delicate business. Such is the view I will defend in this paper. Having great confidence in the power of religious practice and the virtues of the religious life, I will freely employ terminology central to that practice and life. The reader should bear in mind the analogy with mathematics.

Concerning my own outlook on those fundamental questions, a topic to which I return at the end of this paper, I am with those who reject belief in the supernatural. While the deniers are thus correct, they are correct on a technicality, as it were. They almost universally miss the point.

There is at the core of our religious institutions something of the first importance. This is not to endorse as true some sectarian theological doctrine, or, even worse, some general nonsectarian one. What I have in mind is in the spirit of one who thinks that, say, Aristotle's ethics hits upon features of the human condition that are fundamental, easily overlooked, and crucial to at least one way to pursue human flourishing. The analogy is perhaps especially suggestive, since, as I see it, the Western religions (and perhaps the phenomenon is more widespread) encourage a distinctive take on human flourishing, one that is tragically unappreciated in secular, including philosophical, culture. The analogy is also suggestive since I do not presume to have views about what is essential or indispensable to flourishing; only about one way that flourishing has been and might still be successfully pursued.

---

[2] I owe this way of putting the matter to Larry Wright.

A distinctive understanding of human flourishing ought to be of great interest to philosophy. Moreover, if it is in the domain of our subject to explore fundamental ideas and institutions—as we were led to believe as undergraduates—it is indeed strange that the power and character of religious institutions have been so radically under-explored. These institutions show no sign of going away, notwithstanding the views of secular messianists who see such development just around the next corner. The persistence alone might suggest to the open-minded that there is something of interest here, that religious life seems to touch something deep in us.

This is not to say that recent philosophy has ignored religion. The past few decades have seen a resurgence of interest among analytic philosophers. Often, however, such studies have been advanced in defense of theistic belief, and have not spoken to the wider philosophical community concerning the power and character of religious ideas. Nor has any distinctive approach to human flourishing been emphasized or made available. Spirituality has not been a central concern; indeed the term has been virtually abandoned to the philosophically vulgar. Needless to say, I am speaking here of the dominant trend; there are notable exceptions.

Religion in all its generality—even Western religion—is big game. Here I explore the only religious tradition I have studied—my own, Judaism. Perhaps what I say will be to some extent applicable elsewhere. This is not to suggest that it is less than controversial at home.

I have spoken of something important and right about our religious traditions, specifically about my own, something to do with an approach to human flourishing. But to say more, to say what it is that is distinctive and important is very difficult. In part, this is because such a tradition is a collection of ideas, themes, practices that touch many bases. Any attempt to say what it is "all about" is going to fail. Indeed, that such an attempt is bound to fail is reinforced by the perspective I have emphasized: We should see the institution and its practices as primary, the interpretation secondary.

Accordingly, and only partly joking, my project here is "what is it all about?" In this failing effort I take my cue from a common practice in Jewish thought: the Hebrew expression *k'neged kulam* is used to describe a principle, idea, or practice as "the most basic or fundamental."[3] In some contexts, we are told that the study of the Torah is *k'neged kulam*; in others, it is the keeping of the Sabbath,

---

[3] See glossary of Hebrew expressions at the end of the paper.

or the loving of one's neighbor. . . . Such rhetorical excess is part of my heritage.

II. What's It All About?

A. J. Heschel, in his discussion of awe and faith in *God in Search of Man*, suggests that we have overemphasized the cognitive in our thinking about religion. We have given pride of place to religious belief; we think of a deeply religious person as a "true believer." Heschel would have us shift focus from the cognitive to something more attitudinal, something more like a posture, a manner of carrying oneself, a way of facing life, the universe, God. (If God is hard for you, stick to the first two for now: a way of facing life and the universe. God will show up later in any case.)

At the heart of the religious orientation is a distinctive and natural human responsiveness.

> Awe rather than faith is the cardinal attitude of the religious Jew.[4] (Heschel, 77)
>
> In Judaism, *yirat hashem*, the awe of God, or *yirat shamayim*, the awe of heaven, is almost equivalent to the word "religion." In Biblical language the religious man is not called "believer," as he is for example is Islam (*mu'min*) but *yare hashem* (one who stands in awe of God). (Heschel, p. 77).

In Woody Allen's movie, *Crimes and Misdemeanors*, someone says of a deeply religious person that his religious sensibility is a beautiful thing, "like having an ear for music." As with music, the most primitive form of awe-responsiveness is something that almost everyone possesses. The most advanced and heightened forms may require a certain aptitude and are the products of sustained attention, training, and nurture.

To say that we have undervalued awe and given pride of place to belief, or religious faith, is not to dismiss these latter concepts. While religious belief is not treated in the present paper, faith is focal. Awe, you might say, is most fundamental, it is *k'neged kulam*, but it finds its completion in faith. We need to begin with awe, to provide it with sustained attention and nurture, to heighten our awe-responsiveness, if we are to attain faith.[5]

---

[4] All three quotations are from A. J. Heschel, *God in Search of Man* (New York, 1955). All subsequent quotations from Heschel are from this book.

[5] Here, I interpret Heschel. See Heschel, *God in Search of Man*, chapter 15, "Faith."

III. Awe

If we are to explore the idea that awe is at the core of the religious attitude, perhaps we should start with quite simple and ordinary cases of awe, experiences that are not religiously charged and that are available to all from time to time. Can we discern elements of the religious in such ordinary happenings?

Here are some examples:

1. Cases of awe at natural grandeur: the feelings of an astronaut standing on the moon, or someone powerfully moved by the night sky at the top of a mountain, or a relevantly similar ocean experience.
2. Awe at human grandeur. There are examples that seem available to everyone, given a certain openness and sensitivity: awe at the power of people to find inner resources in horrible circumstances, awe at human goodness and caring. Other examples require artistic and/or intellectual sophistication: powerful responses to great art of all varieties, or to great achievements in science, mathematics, philosophy.
3. Awe at the birth of one's children. Perhaps this is a compound of, or intermediate between 1 and 2.
4. Even more sophisticated, more rare, are other sorts of combinations of 1 and 2. For example, one at the top of the mountain, awestruck not only by the overwhelming beauty and majesty of nature, but also by the fact that humans, constructed of the stuff of the mountain, can take such a thing in, and indeed that they can feel awe at it.

Of course, reactions to such events may vary from person to person. And even if we can agree that a sense of awe is neither idiosyncratic nor unusual in such circumstances, it may still be that what you feel at such times is not, and almost certainly not quite, what I do. Nevertheless, the sorts of feelings and thoughts often engendered seem to me to have something importantly religious about them, as I will explain.

I begin with a curious duality that seems characteristic[6] of such experiences, a duality of special interest to religion. The two aspects

---

[6] I am exploring aspects that are characteristic of awe. Neither conceptual analysis, nor essential features are at issue here, only what is so usually or for the most part.

to be distinguished appear in all sorts of admixtures, with one or the other getting the focus.[7]

In the face of great power, or majesty, or beauty, one characteristically feels a sense of humility. The more intense experiences may engender not only humility but a sense of being overwhelmed. Often one feels a sense of distance between here and there, between oneself and the object of awe.[8]

Experiences of the overwhelming can sometimes diminish the agent, as in the case of almost shrunken-looking children of very powerful parents. Remarkably, awe experiences are not like this. One does not feel crushed or diminished, rather elevated, even exhilarated. At the top of the mountain, one feels a sense of great privilege; one stands tall, breathes deeply. The cabalistic concept of *tzimtzum* provides a beautiful image: creation involves God's pulling back and making room, as it were, for the world. Here, with respect to awe, it is as if God pulls back so as not to completely overwhelm. He pulls back, as it were, out of respect, to make room for the awestruck person.

When I say that that awe is *k'neged kulam*, this is in no small measure a matter of the central place played by the duality—humbled yet elevated, affirmed in one's dignity. This duality brings to mind a related, albeit distinct, duality that seems very close to the bone of the religious orientation encouraged by so much of Jewish religious life.

1. A sense of the fragility, fleetingness, finitude, and severe limitations of human life.
2. A sense of the great significance of human life.[9]

---

[7]Heschel's style is diffuse and it is difficult for me to know how much of what I say about the duality is to be found in Heschel. Surely both humility and elevation are discussed there.

[8]Humility needs considerably more attention than afforded here. To say that a person is characteristically humbled by awe experiences is not to suggest that she is "taken down a peg," although that may be true of some of the cases. My idea is that no adverse judgment about oneself need be a part of this sense generated by being in the presence of greatness. As Stephen Mitchell says, in his wonderful "Introduction" to his translation of *The Book of Job* (New York, 1987), "self-abasement is just inverted egoism. Anyone who acts with genuine humility will be as far from humiliation as from arrogance."

[9]I see this new duality as distinct from the humbled-elevated duality because I don't see a focus on the agent's limitations as essential to humility. See note 8, above.

A crucial piece of the big project,[10] you might say, is achieving a conception of human life and an approach to human flourishing—not just conceptions of these things but ways of implementing them—that provide a central role for 1 and 2, and achieve balance between them. There is a Hasidic adage that a person should carry two pieces of paper in his pocket, one that says "I am but dust and ashes," and the other that says "The world was created for me."[11]

Elliot Dorff, in *Knowing God*,[12] suggests that the idea of God is a powerful instrument for touching both bases. First, the idea suggests a contrast between us and God, and thus emphasizes human limitation, finitude, et al. At the same time, we reflect God's image. Such reflection cannot be a one-way street; reflection is reflexive. We and God must have important similarities. There is perhaps no more powerful imagery than that of people as God's reflections for underscoring human significance and dignity.

We have been exploring ordinary awe experiences for their religious content. And we have hit upon the duality, humbled but elevated, a powerful religious idea. But there is more. Awe experiences, perhaps as a consequence of the duality, characteristically engender a generosity of spirit, a lack of pettiness, increased ability to forgive and to contain anger and disappointment. To feel and behave in these ways is to feel and behave as, according to the tradition, God does. You might say that in the grip of awe, *imitatio Dei* becomes easy and natural, at least for the moment. One also typically feels a powerful sense of gratitude.

----

[10]I am conscious of using such expressions as "the big project," which might suggest that I take there to be some single project that is the Jewish one. Nothing like this is intended. My aim is to provide one take on the life encouraged by the practices.

[11]I have often thought that the really difficult trick is to get both on the same piece of paper. Maurice Friedman suggested to me that it would be better to leave them on separate sheets, maybe even in different pockets. The imagery of a single piece of paper suggests finding a way to make these consistent, in some sense, perhaps finding an inclusive principle. Perhaps what one needs is rather a kind of practical skill, the ability to negotiate experience so that at the appropriate moments one pays heed to the appropriate idea. There are other dualities for which this seems so, for which the drive for an inclusive principle seems the wrong idea. Consider the universalistic and particularistic tendencies in Jewish religious thought. An undue emphasis on either of these either loses the religious richness (overemphasizing the universalistic) or threatens all manner of ugliness (overemphasizing the particularistic). The matter seems related, as Friedman suggested, to the Aristotelian golden mean idea.

[12](Jason Aronson, Inc., 1992). Dorff mentions the Hasidic adage mentioned in the paragraph.

Turning from the affective/behavioral to the cognitive, awe experiences engender a godlike perspective, the ability to (almost) see things under the aspect of eternity, as Spinoza put it.

A friend who has no contact with institutional religion was recalling early experiences at an Episcopal retreat. He and his father were closer than ever at this retreat, even though the retreat involved remaining silent—they never spoke. Every morning they would be awakened at some ungodly hour to some "hocus-pocus." My friend says, though, that the memory remains very warm. His sense of the real content of all the hocus-pocus, the point of all of the practices, was "to organize one's life around one's better instincts." This seems to me an interesting comment about the religious life, about which there will be more later. In the present context, it is striking that those better instincts come to the fore at moments of awe.

There is at least one additional aspect to the religious content of ordinary awe experiences, one of great moment. For many people, and not only those who consider themselves religious, there is something *holy* about the objects of awe experiences—childbirth, a great symphony, the Grand Canyon. There is, moreover, a feeling of horror associated with the thought of destroying such objects, events, and so on. To do so—even to allow such a thing—would be sacrilege.

Although it seems natural to invoke concepts like *holiness* and *sacrilege* in contexts like these, it is difficult to know how much to make of this. Perhaps such concepts make essential reference to the religious, and so the use of them by secularists is always derivative, in scare quotes, as it were. Maybe so. Still, it seems significant that the terms seem apt.

I want to linger a moment with the concept of *holiness*, one that seems to me as difficult as it is crucial to Judeo-Christian, as opposed to (philosophical) Greek, thinking about human flourishing. Even from a traditional religious perspective, the concept is very difficult to explicate.[13] What emerges, though, indeed strikingly from our survey of ordinary awe experiences, is that awe may furnish us with an entry point into this difficult topic. For as the examples suggest, where there is awe, there is holiness. It is as if awe were

---

[13]I once posed the question to one who had lived the religious life and had thought about such things for many years. We know something, I was told, of how to attain holiness; much less about what exactly one has attained.

a faculty for discerning the holy. This seems an important topic for further exploration.

The experiences explored so far may not be felt or identified as religious by the agent; they do not pertain specifically or explicitly to God. However, they are, as I see it, the originals, the primitive cases of religious responsiveness. This is not to say that they are the paradigm cases; paradigm cases identify themselves as religiously significant.

IV. Awe, Fear, Mystery

A bit more about awe, specifically its relation to fear and mystery, before we turn to its relation to faith. The Hebrew word that Heschel translates as "awe" is *yirah*. In biblical Hebrew, the word sometimes means "awe," sometimes "fear," and sometimes has the quality of both awe and fear. In contexts in which *yirah* is seen as a great virtue, awe needs at least a good deal of the emphasis. Despite some of the standard translations, it is far from clear why simply being frightened of God is supposed to be of great ethical value, or why such fright is so admirable as to be considered "the beginning of wisdom," as we are told that *yirah* is in Psalms. That awe of heaven is a great virtue, or that it is the beginning of wisdom, is quite another matter. There is a passage in the Jewish morning liturgy to the effect that a person should always stand in *yirah* of heaven in private as well as in public. The suggestion is a powerful one, but much of its power seems lost if "fear" gets all the emphasis.

Awe and fear have an important connection, one that is perhaps underscored by the occurrence of a single Hebrew word, *yirah*, that incorporates both aspects. Many awe experiences, insofar as they involve powerful natural or spiritual forces, involve an element of fear. Indeed, the aspect of fearfulness grows with the intensity of the experience. Think here of the extremes: being present when worlds collide, as it were, or, as in the Bible, meeting God face to face, where a misstep can be fatal. Even when we consider relatively tame examples, like the awe of heaven with which one is to approach life quite generally, a bit of fear may not be far off. The more intensely one feels such awe, the more one feels himself to be in God's presence, the closer one is to at least a tinge of fright.

To allow myself some rank speculation, it seems plausible to suppose that awe, as something separable from fear, shows up relatively late on the human scene. One imagines primitive religiosity to involve a greater admixture of fear in awe experiences. As Heschel sees it, quite plausibly, by the time of the Hebrew Bible, awe takes center stage.

Another idea whose connections to awe are well worth exploring is that of mystery. "In awe and amazement the prophets stand before the mystery of the universe," writes Heschel. Nor is it just the prophets. We often feel awe at things that seem beyond our comprehension, childbirth for example, or the birth of ideas or art.

But how essential to awe is a lack of comprehension? To suppose that it is essential is to suppose that sufficient understanding precludes awe. This does not seem correct. On the contrary, one's appreciation of grandeur might well be enhanced by greater understanding. In my more midrashic moments, I like to think of God as in awe of His creation. Moreover, the heavens declare the glory of God, and not only to creatures who do not understand. The angels, perhaps lacking in the freedom to make bad choices, but possessed of perfect understanding, nevertheless stand in awe of the Creator. (Admittedly, my intuitions about angels are corrigible. . . .)

Nevertheless, it would be a mistake to dismiss the connection with mystery. For one thing, the connection is widely felt, and this should give us pause. Let's come at this from a different direction.

Heschel, in discussing concepts like awe and wonder, sometimes speaks of what he calls "radical amazement." A rich source of examples of the sort of thing Heschel has in mind is Annie Dillard's *Pilgrim at Tinker Creek*,[14] a book that opens a window on Dillard's distinctively heightened sensitivity and provides many masterful descriptions of awe at nature. Dillard's examples are particularly interesting since they are not restricted to aspects of nature that are friendly to us and our projects. One sort of recurrent example involves constellations of the exquisite and the horrendous. After one such description, of waves of sharks in a feeding frenzy, rising from churning waters, she writes, "The sight held awesome wonders: power and beauty, grace tangled in a rapture with violence." She concludes, "We don't know what's going on here."

Dillard encourages us to wonder about what we are to make of such a world. How, one wants to know, are such things—fill in your own examples of constellations of the exquisite and the dreadful—possible? This sort of question—or the state of mind that issues in

---

[14] Reprinted in *The Annie Dillard Reader* (New York, 1995). The quotations are from page 287.

the question—does not essentially pertain to constellations of beauty and horror. Heschel mentions another sort of example, a person struck by the wondrousness of existence who asks why there is anything at all, why there is something rather than nothing. There are, of course, many sorts of examples in which one is awestruck, amazed, and cannot make sense of what one has experienced.

Two things seem striking about such questions in such contexts. First, it is very difficult to know what to make of them, what exactly they ask. Second and related, a perfectly rational, sensible, sensitive person, faced with such a question, may not feel the force of the question. She may not know what the questioner is talking about. And the questioner may well be hard-pressed to explain. Next time you are overwhelmed with the wondrousness of existence, ask your colleague who occupies the next office in the philosophy department why there is something rather than nothing.

Of course, if your colleague shares your sense of awe, or if you can instantaneously generate it, she will understand the question, at least in the sense that she understands the urge to ask it. She will share the feeling that "we don't know what's going on here." So whether or not one feels the force of the question seems to depend upon whether one shares a sense of awe. But the question's content remains dark.

The trouble is with such questions is that it is difficult to characterize the gap in one's understanding that prompts them. What is it exactly that we do not understand, and what would count as an answer? One's puzzlement, for example, is not for a lack of empirical information. Even empirical omniscience would not bridge this sort of cognitive gulf. Perhaps, then, what one is missing, what one seeks, is some other sort of information, news from another realm. If one knew enough about the spiritual realm, perhaps, one would then understand how it is all possible. One would then know what is going on here. I want to suggest, on the contrary, that our discomfort is of another sort, that the mystery associated with awe does not concern a lack of information.

It seems significant that we are as apt to ask what these things mean—existence, the constellation of exquisite beauty and ugly, wanton destructiveness, childbirth, and so on—as we are to ask how they are possible. Nor do we distinguish these questions very sharply in such contexts. I want to suggest that such questions do two things. First, they themselves are a kind of expression of wonderment—they give voice to the awe. Second, they reflect the powerful sense that the subject is beyond one's comprehension, but not in the sense that one lacks information that would bring the matter into clear view. The problem is rather that one is dazed, confused; one cannot come to terms with the thing, wrap one's mind around it.

An idea of Wittgenstein's about philosophical quandaries may be suggestive here.[15] "I don't know my way about," is for Wittgenstein a kind of general form of philosophical question. Of course, this is not how we put our philosophical queries. Instead we may ask how various things are possible, empirical experience, for example. But the discomfort, thought Wittgenstein, is not for a lack of information. It is that we are lost, in over our heads.

There are of course differences between philosophical worries, as Wittgenstein saw them, and our awe-inspired sense of not knowing what is going on. Indeed, Wittgenstein's idea was that with respect to philosophical questions, we might well come to learn our way about; we might work our way out of the confusion. (But not by providing the usual sorts of solutions. A deeper understanding of the relevant domain, Wittgenstein supposed, would render the original puzzle irrelevant.) With wonderment, however, the phenomenon of being in over our heads is, unlike that of being in the grip of a distorting philosophical conception (and also unlike that of lacking information), not remediable. We do not (or should not) even want a remedy.

The cognitive dissonance signaled by "how is it possible?," the sense that we are in over our heads, is easy to confuse with, or attribute to, ignorance of information. In other contexts, after all, wonderment prompts a perfectly appropriate request for information. Woody Allen's *Sleeper* concerns a kind of modern-day Rip Van Winkle who awakens after several decades to the wonders of modern gadgetry including, notably, an *orgasmitron*. "How do these things work?," is both natural and appropriate. Such amazement is the mother of science, and it takes considerable sophistication to know when there is an explanation to be had, and when, on the contrary, one need rest with the amazement. The sophistication in question is a kind of philosophical discernment available to the public. Which is not to say that it is readily available even to the philosophically trained. It is a kind of practical wisdom, where the practice is an intellectual one.

Mystery, then, is closely related to awe, where mystery is understood in terms of wonderment and the sense that we are in over our

---

[15]I owe to Larry Wright the connection with Wittgenstein.

heads. I am not sure whether to think of mystery as a necessary condition for awe, so much as a concomitant. But it is an important idea in the neighborhood.

V. From Awe to Faith: From the Primitive to the Paradigm

Awe is relatively rare in our lives, and strikingly transitory. This would appear to make it a strange choice for what is *k'neged kulam*. One would naturally assume that what undergirds the religious outlook would need to have broad and sustained impact on our lives.

It is here that the concept of the *y're shamayim*, one who stands in awe of heaven, comes to the fore. What is distinctive about the *y're shamayim* is not merely a distinctive object of awe, an explicitly religious object. Also distinctive—and my focus for the present—is the steadiness that the *y're shamayim* has achieved. Awe, while not a constant companion, has become characteristic of everyday experience. It is not only a question of frequency. The *y're shamayim* lives in the presence of awe, a kind of background condition against which he carries on.

Nor is it only awe that has become characteristic and habitual. With awe come the godlike tendencies to feeling and behavior, the perspective *sub specias aeternitas*, the gratitude. Moreover, since awe engenders a sense of the holy, to characteristically feel awe is to be confronted by the holy in all sorts of unlikely places. The *y're shamayim* lives quite a different life than those of us for whom awe is both rare and transitory.

This is pretty astounding. It's very difficult to even imagine such a person. How might one go about configuring such a life? One can, so to speak, put oneself in the path of awe. But a single-minded quest seems futile, self-defeating, in a word, quixotic.

Perhaps what makes the whole thing so hard to imagine is that we are thinking about a kind of quick transition, a quick fix. What could I do to turn my life into that sort of life? Instead, perhaps we should think about something much more slow and painstaking, something more like character development.

Seeing *yirat shamayim* as the product of character development helps, but the whole business is still pretty astounding. It remains difficult to imagine how we would affect such character development. It is here that religious practice makes an invaluable contribution.

I can perhaps best explain what I see as the role of religious practice by contrasting religion with philosophy, or at least with what I take to be an important aspect of what we do in philosophy. As I am envisioning the philosophical project, one confronts questions that are beyond the pale of normal good sense, questions with respect to which it is very difficult to bring good sense to bear. So far perhaps this is uncontroversial. More controversial is the idea that a philosopher need do no more, and can do no more, than bring good sense to bear. The long-term project is one of seeking increasingly natural ways to think about the hard questions. Philosophers tend to think that there must be much more to it, that there may be many natural ways to pursue such questions, and that what is needed is some principled way to decide between the proposed answers. Sometimes, perhaps there are a number of such natural approaches. But we tend to lose sight of just how very difficult it is to find thoroughly natural ways to think about philosophical things.

Religion, by contrast, is not in the business of bringing plain sense to bear on a distinctive question or range of questions. I don't mean, of course, that there is no common sense exhibited in the tradition; there is, and in many ways. But there is so much else. One need not point to especially strange-seeming practices—for example the prohibition concerning wearing garments of certain mixed fabrics—or arcane theological doctrines. Even more typical and reasonable-seeming religious practices—traditional Jewish Sabbath observance, for example—are not what common sense would have naturally suggested.

To say that religion is less a matter of good sense than is philosophy is not to denigrate it. One cannot get from A to B, from where we are to *yirat shamayim*, by simply thinking hard on the matter—not that this is a bad idea. What religion seeks to achieve requires something more. It requires more in the way of equipment than individuals have been granted. What is required, you might say, is God's help. It comes in the form of inherited practices of some thousands of years standing, practices that conduce to *yirat shamayim*. How exactly they do so is as interesting a matter as it is difficult. Nor should we assume that only *these* practices could do so. Still, such a gift of tradition is striking, itself awe-inspiring.

This gift is dramatized in the fiction of Chaim Grade, twentieth-century Yiddish poet, novelist, and author of short stories.[16] Despite

---

[16] See, for example, Grade's *Rabbis and Wives* (New York, 1982).

Grade's own misgivings about traditional religion, his heroes are
often people who have achieved such character transformation as
a product of deep and sustained engagement with the religious
tradition.

In the next section, I will turn to how the religious tradition
might pull off such magic, but for the moment, I want to focus on
this idea of developed religious character. I propose—and there are
such suggestions in Heschel—that we see *faith* as involving,
although not wholly exhausted by, the sort of character transformation, the sort of generalization of awe, that we have been discussing.
Heschel writes,

> There is no faith at first sight.
> Faith does not come into being out of nothing, inadvertently,
> unprepared, an unearned surprise. Faith is preceded by awe.

Faith, to paraphrase Wittgenstein's remarks on understanding, is not
the sort of thing that occurs in a flash. This is not to say—to continue the parallel with Wittgenstein—that a datable occurrence
cannot be the felt onset of faith, or of an increase or intensification
of faith. To deny that faith can occur in a flash is rather to emphasize
the antecedents, the long and difficult business of character development. Nor can faith be achieved by a single person, and occur only
once in the person's life—I am getting carried away with the Wittgenstein analogy. The necessary character development is the product of socialization and training; it is a product of engagement with
religious practice.

Clearly this is not to think of faith as an unearned gift of grace,
unless one means by this phrase to underscore the sense that no
amount of hard work can furnish a guarantee of the hoped-for result.
Nor is it to see faith as what gets religious practice and the religious
life off the ground, as it were. Faith is rather a virtue that is the outcome of engagement with such practice and such a life.

Alasdair MacIntyre, in a lecture at the University of Notre
Dame, characterized an ancient Greek outlook on institutional ar-
rangements and their characteristic virtues. A young person joins
the community of mathematicians, or philosophers, or poets, and
grows, develops specific virtues, by his participation in the practices
of the community. Associated with different institutions may be
different virtues, characteristic capabilities that are particularly
emphasized, particularly relevant to the practices. In just such a
respect, I see *yirat shamayim*, awe of heaven, and the faith in which

yirat shamayim plays so large a role, as characteristic virtues of Judaism.[17]

VI. Yirat Shamayim *and Religious Practice*

To attain the heightened responsiveness of the *y're shamayim* is of course quite a feat. Indeed, the more one thinks about what is involved, the more enormous the task appears. What is called for is a substantial change of orientation, a deepening of wonder, of appreciation, and of one's character. Effecting such change is intrinsically difficult, and external factors often make it more so. The frailties and limitations of one's fellows often inhibit their support for such development. And the distractions, discouragements, frustrations, and sufferings of the human situation only increase the difficulty.

How then is such character development and sustenance possible? What are the tools by which the tradition facilitates *yirat shamayim*? The tradition employs a multiplicity of such tools. The sampling of *yirah*-inducing practices delineated below may, of course, have other consequences for the religious community and the religious life. Indeed, the finding of meanings and purposes in such traditional practices needs to respect what I emphasized above, the primacy of practice, and the delicacy of interpretation. Interpreting the practices is in some ways like interpreting poetry. New and different meanings emerge—certainly against the background of continuities—sometimes from day to day, and certainly from generation to generation.

---

[17]*Faith*, as I'm using this notion, is quite different than *belief*. (As noted, religious belief is not treated in this essay. This is not to say that the notion is unimportant or anything of the like.) Faith is not a matter of assent to, or conviction about, propositions. Interestingly, the Hebrew word usually translated as faith, *emunah*, has quite a different feel from *belief*. *Emunah* conveys commitment, trust, a steadiness in affirmation, and perhaps even something like a sense of living in the presence of God.

Buber, in "Two Foci of the Jewish Soul" (an address given in 1930 and collected in his *Israel and the World*) writes

"Faith," should not be taken in the sense given to it in the "Epistle to the Hebrews," as faith that God exists. That has never been doubted by Jacob's soul. In proclaiming its faith, its *emunah*, the soul only proclaimed that it put its trust in the everlasting God, *that he would be present* [Buber's italics] to the soul, as had been the experience of the patriarchs. . . .

A. Study

The practice sometimes said to be the most fundamental, another *k'neged kulam*, is study of the tradition. Indeed, "study" is not adequate, for this word fails to convey the intensity of intellectual engagement. Jewish liturgy says of the words and teachings of the Torah, "For they are our lives and the length of our days, and with them we are engaged [or on them we meditate] day and night." For millennia, in fact as well as in fiction—Grade's protagonists, for example—Jewish heroes often have been saintly figures who are giants of scholarship. Jewish tradition awards a central place to what one might call the culture of learning, a rich and fascinating topic that can only be touched upon here.

It is significant that traditional rabbinic education makes little room for theology. One's time is given largely to Talmudic study, the theoretical physics, as it were, of the tradition, and to the study of the later codifications of the law. The Talmud is itself multifaceted and rich in theological ideas and suggestions, but rabbinic education emphasizes the theoretical study of the legal code, a code that encompasses Jewish life quite generally, from civil law to religious practice. The rabbi is an expert then, not necessarily or primarily in theology, but in the practices—both their details and their legal-theoretic analysis—that constitute the life of the community.

This description of rabbinic education may elevate learning in a kind of consequentialist way. Study alone makes one an expert on the character of the practices. Indeed, the practices come to life when one has struggled with their details and meanings. But study is revered not only for its products. Such intense encounter with God's word, as understood and developed by the tradition, is seen as among the highest forms—if not *the* highest form—of religious engagement. The Jew prays that his/her eyes may be illuminated—"luminous" is perhaps an even better translation—with Torah. Spinoza, in the context of his own conception, spoke of the intellectual love of God, an idea that is deeply rooted in Jewish tradition.

The tradition distinguishes *yirat Ha'shem*, awe of God, from *ahavat Ha'shem*, love of God, the other crucial component of the religious attitude. That we speak of learning as the intellectual love of God indicates that learning, while it serves the development and sustenance of *yirah*, has other salutary effects. Clearly, though, participation in such a culture of learning is instrumental in the transition to *yirat shamayim*.[18]

B. Blessings

Traditional practice includes ritualized blessings that one makes on all sorts of occasions, on eating and drinking, on smelling fragrant spices, herbs, plants, on seeing lightning, shooting stars, vast deserts, high mountains, a sunrise, the ocean, on seeing trees blossoming for the first time of the year, on seeing natural objects (including creatures, even people) of striking beauty, on meeting a religious scholar, on meeting a secular scholar, on seeing a head of state, on hearing good news, on hearing bad news.

As a younger person, such blessings seemed to me burdensome. Indeed, who could remember all the relevant occasions, not to speak of the relevant formulas? Heschel suggests that the practice of saying such blessings is training in awe. One develops the habit, before so much as sipping water, to reflect and appreciate. In addition to the blessings' training function—practicing *yirat shamayim*—blessings also function as reminders. Ordinary living is distracting, and such reminders assist us in maintaining focus. Finally, the blessings serve as expressions of awe and of gratitude for all of us, from the novice to the *y're shamayim*.

In addition to occasion-related blessings, there are blessings specific to the performance of other mandated practices: before study, for example, or before donning a prayer shawl, or hearing the shofar, the ram's horn. Crucial in the formula of such blessings is reference to God's having sanctified us by means of the practices, the commandments. Such blessings encourage focus, indeed a reverential focus, on the activity one is about to undertake. They also invite reflection on the specific practice as one in a system of such practices.

C. Prayer

Robert M. Adams, in his essay, "Symbolic Value,"[19] reflects on the course of an ordinary day. Adams points out that our days are filled with activities that are rather disconnected with the deep values

---

[18] One should not conclude that *yirat shamayim* is the sole property of the intellectually elite. There is much in traditional practice that conduces to developed religious character even in the absence of the theoretical physics of the tradition, in the absence of the highest or deepest level of Talmudic learning. Indeed, there are all sorts of levels of study. The threat of elitism in traditions that so emphasize learning needs further discussion.

[19] *Midwest Studies in Philosophy,* Volume XXI (1997), pp. 1–15.

that give meaning and shape to our lives. We academics, for example, go to department meetings, committee meetings, grade papers; we spend significant time on the upkeep of our homes, autos, and so on. Even with respect to activities closely related to what gives meaning, we are all too human, our motives are mixed, our successes only partial. Prayer, says Adams, offers a wonderful opportunity, to spend daily time focused upon our deepest values, to think about them, praising those who exemplify them, expressing heartfelt desire for a genuine and lasting improvement in the human condition. Declaring oneself to thus be for the good, as Adams puts it, is psychologically reinforcing and spiritually centering.

My initial reaction to reading Adams' piece was a powerful sense of an important void in our culture. This is not to say that what is lacking is necessarily something religious, that religion is the answer for everyone. But finding time, making a place, for some such activity seemed of immense importance, and by and large, we do not do any such thing. Prayer may be only one answer, but it is at least that. For one who has made *yirat shamayim* one's project, prayer is indispensable, in part just for Adams' reasons.

Traditional Jewish prayer is a thrice daily activity. If what is at stake is the development of pervasive awe with its affective, perspectival, and behavioral concomitants, then timing is of the essence. Too much prayer would be counterproductive; too little would miss opportunities. Three times a day may seem excessive, but it grows on one, particularly in connection with the great difficulty in keeping one's eye on the ball in the face of ordinary experience. It is as if an omniscient being brought His attention to bear on the question of how often such *yirah*-seeking but distractible creatures would need a period of reflection and reminder.[20]

Traditional Jewish prayer is not only thrice daily, it is fixed prayer. The central portions of the three services are either identical or very closely related. Such repetition and fixety raises a question, perhaps *the* question, about ritual. It is certainly not clear that it was fixed prayer of which Adams wrote, nor is fixed prayer the only or obvious answer to the felt need that Adams articulated. Indeed it is sometimes suggested, and tempting to suppose, that to so regularize expressions of awe, gratitude, and the rest, is to constrict them, ultimately to demean them. And whatever one thinks of the

[20]Actually the thrice daily structure is understood by the tradition to be a rabbinic innovation, as opposed to a God-given injunction.

ritualized blessings discussed above, at least the blessings are appropriate to one's current experience.

We should remember, however, the magnitude and ambition of the project of facilitating *yirat shamayim*. While fixed prayer can and does degenerate into mechanical, unthinking, unfeeling performance, it offers great opportunities. Some of the usual translations notwithstanding, Jewish liturgy is a compilation of passages of literary magnificence. That such literature, Psalms, for example, has survived the ages is a tribute to its expressive power, its ability to articulate and illuminate religious experience. To engage regularly with such literature—not merely to read the words but to declare them, to wrestle with them—is to occupy oneself with the project. Encounter with literature of such power, first thing in the morning for example, encourages the regularization of attitudes to which the literature so ably gives voice. Indeed, ritualization turns out to be a great virtue: we need not wait until the appropriate experiences present themselves.

Ritualized prayer has another distinct advantage over spontaneous prayer. Spontaneous expressions, for example, of awe—and who would deny that these have a place?—are limited by the expressive capacities of the agent. How many among us are up to the challenge of summoning words adequate to powerful experiences and their concomitant thoughts and emotions?

Ritualized prayer does indeed present challenges of its own. The challenge is presented not by the repetition but rather by the difficulty, the sheer hard work, involved in summoning up the thoughts and feelings appropriate to such literary magnificence. The founder of Hasidism, the Ba'al Shem Tov, is reputed to have said that it would be easier to deliver two advanced Talmudic lectures than to offer a single *amidah*, a fixed prayer of a few pages.

D. Rhythms

As we saw in the discussion of thrice daily prayer, a refined sense of rhythm and timing are important to the project. The tradition shows great sensitivity not only to the rhythms of the day but also to that of the week and the year.

The idea of *Shabbat*, the Sabbath, is crucial to the tradition's sense of rhythm and timing. The story of the seven days of creation has it that God, who could have been portrayed as considerably more remote, as more exclusively contemplative for example, seems quite involved with the project, giving serious attention to detail. He does not make a move, as it were, until He has pronounced the prior work to be good. What emerges is a conception of six days of creative engagement with the world, then a period of withdrawal, rest, celebration of the creative achievement, and spiritual renewal. It is as if one is being told to find something important to do with the six days, something one will want to celebrate. Further, one should make time to celebrate, and to renew, to "re-soul," as the unusual biblical word, *va'yinafash*,[21] may suggest.

Shabbat is a day of involvement with family and immediate community, but it is also a day in which one has, we are told, an additional soul, a day of enhanced spiritual capacity. The withdrawal provides time to reflect, and the spirit of the day encourages reflection on the wonder of creation itself, and on the wonders provided by one's family, one's work, one's community. *Shabbat* is instrumental in the development and sustenance of *yirat shamayim*.

Turning to annual rhythm, the month of *Elul* (in the fall) is devoted to communal and individual reflection on the past year, on where we have been, on how we have done, on where we are going. The period culminates in the ten "days of awe," the last day of which is *Yom Kippur*, the Day of Atonement, a day of fasting, prayer, and profound reflection. A ritual of great power throughout *Elul* is the blowing of the *shofar*, the ram's horn. The sound is searing, eerie, almost other worldly. It conveys as no words could the call to self-examination, a call from on high.

VII. God

Yirat shamayim involves, we have seen, a distinctive object of awe as well as a distinctive steadiness. I have been focused on the latter. It is time to remark on the distinctive object of awe, God.

To pick up a theme from the beginning of this paper, as in the philosophy of mathematics with the numbers, I want to discuss God in a rather naïve way, without concern for what I called the fundamental questions of metaphysics and epistemology. If the concept has great utility in our practice, then surely it is doing important work, even if it is difficult to say what that work is. Of course, if one is convinced that the only possible work for the concept violates naturalism, then naturalistic scruples may encourage the rejection of the whole package, no matter how attractive it may be otherwise. I will return to this matter below. But first I want to naively pursue God's role in all of this.

---

[21] Exodus 31:17.

Although my previous discussion of the practices has not emphasized the role of God, God is central to each of them. Indeed, that this is so has much to do with the effectiveness of the practices in conducing to awe as a steady state. Prayer, for example, at least in the context of traditional Judaism, is prayer *to God*, not simply an expression of values. Indeed, traditional Jewish prayer becomes more powerful, more effective in facilitating generalized awe, if one experiences prayer as a thrice daily audience with God. Similar remarks apply to the blessings—grateful acknowledgments not only of God, but to God.

Another domain of practice, one that is not the focus of this essay but that surely deserves mention, is that of ethics. That persons reflect God's image and that it is of the utmost importance to become more perfect reflections are ideas at the core of the Jewish ethical attitude and practice. Such ideas have all sorts of implications for our project. Here is an example: Prosaic-seeming encounters with, or reflections on, these divine facsimiles—including ourselves—become occasions for awe, albeit sometimes tinged with irony. Not only are we more apt to be awestruck by others, we are more likely to treat them with reverence.

I said above that the *y're shamayim* lives in the presence of awe, that awe constitutes a kind of background condition for his ordinary experience. I could have said that he lives in the presence of God, and that God's presence constitutes the background condition. It is of course not merely God but a certain attitude or stance toward God that is essential and that informs the life of the *y're shamayim*.[22] For those of us in process—and of course no one has completed the process—feeling God's presence *in this way*, at least from time to time, is enormously effective in moving us toward something more like a steady state.

Earlier, in section III, I provided some examples of "ordinary awe," conceived as primitive cases of the religious. Jewish tradition moves us from the primitive cases to *yirat shamayim* by means of a system of practices. We have now seen that God is very much implicated in the practices; indeed God is key to the way that Judaism

[22]While *yirah* is not the only component in the relevant attitude, it is an essential component. As Heschel remarks, "Forfeit your sense of awe, . . . your ability to revere, and the universe becomes a market place for you." (p. 78). In the spirit of Heschel's remark, we might add that without awe, even with theistic beliefs galore, one still lives within the confines of a marketplace, albeit one with a unusually wide range of commodities.

seeks to effect the transformation. It is crucial for the project, as conceived, that there be an object of worship, an instantiation of human excellences; a fount of creativity who loves and gives freely and generously of that love, one who loves justice, honesty, and integrity, and who is at the same time big on forgiveness. Such a conception affords not only an object of worship but also a model for us. And not only a model but a partner in our projects, both local and global projects like that of bringing justice to the world.[23]

VIII. Naturalism

Although "fundamental" questions like that of God's existence are not the focus here, I will conclude with a comment on the matter. I wish to challenge the view, accepted by theists and atheists alike, that the sort of religious life I have described, with God at its heart, involves commitment to the supernatural and thus the denial of naturalism. To dispute what seems so obvious is a tall order, and I will return to the question in future work.

Let's begin by considering a traditional theist who is, for want of a better word, non-fundamentalist in her interpretation of certain parts of scripture, for example the story of the garden of Eden, or of Noah and the ark, or of the six days of creation. Let's focus on creation. With regard to the six days, perhaps she reinterprets talk of "days"; biblical "days" are extended periods, maybe eons. Another possibility, one in which I am particularly interested, is that she grants the words their ordinary meanings—"day," as she reads the creation narrative, refers to a twenty-four hour period as it always does—but she understands the story to be something like a parable or an allegory. (The reader should ignore many of the suggestions of the term "fundamentalism." I want this expression only for its suggestion that biblical passages are to read as factual descriptions. "Literalism" will not do here, or would be confusing, in light of the fact that our "non-fundamentalist" understands the biblical words in their plain, everyday senses; she does not reinterpret the words, attributing to them new meanings.)

---

[23]I leave for another occasion discussion of a very important theme, that in the Hebrew Bible and much of rabbinic tradition, God seems to have limitations, perhaps even a dark side. He loves, and so needs that which he loves, he is sometimes wrathful, sometimes regrets things he has done or created (including us), perhaps plays favorites (as among the children of the patriarchs, for example), subjects his creatures to various tests (including that of Abraham being commanded to offer up Isaac), and so on.

The biblical rendering of creation, on her view, is not a factually correct account of origins. That is not its aim, so to speak. The story as it stands—without reinterpreting the words to make the sentences come out true—has profound resonance for us. It is suggestive of deep insights about the human condition and about human flourishing. This is not to say that it actually states, discursively articulates, such insights. As noted, she offers no new account of the meanings of the words.

To think of the biblical creation story in this way is not to diminish its religious centrality. The notion of Sabbath, as creative retreat from creative engagement with the world, as spiritual renewal, will be unaffected. Indeed, such a person, no less than one who reads the passage as an actual description of creation, may participate wholeheartedly in Sabbath observance. She will be able to recite, with sincerity and enthusiasm, the traditional Sabbath liturgy that includes many references to God's working six days and resting on the seventh.

One might have supposed that she would have great trouble with such liturgy, or that she ought to have great trouble with it. After all, she does not believe what it says, for example that God created the heaven and the earth in six days. Perhaps this *is* puzzling; certainly it deserves extended treatment not possible here. But such a religious outlook and practice is quite common, and it would be rash to simply rule it irrational, intellectually and spiritually out of order.

To dismiss her as religiously out of order, moreover, would be to miss the religious power of her treatment of the biblical narrative. She, not unlike one who reads the narrative as an actual account of creation, dwells in the potent imagery—God's presence hovering over the awesome formlessness; six days filled with creative activity; the separations of light and darkness, heaven and earth, land and sea; the creation of man and woman, reflections of divinity; the renewal of spirit on the seventh day. For her, of course, the story is not factually correct. But this is, to her mind, almost not worthy of mention; it is both obvious and completely beside the point, beside the religious point. The powerful religious resonances and intimations of the story are available to her, as they are to the fundamentalist, as a consequence of dwelling so wholeheartedly in the drama of creation.

Such a traditional theist exhibits a tendency toward the sort of naturalism of interest to me. This is of course not to say that her outlook is thoroughly naturalistic—she quite straightforwardly believes in a supernatural God. Let's turn to another biblical passage to help underscore the naturalness of the naturalistic impulse.

In traditional Jewish morning liturgy, before one dons a prayer shawl, a *tallit*, one recites a portion of Psalm 104 (which I translate/interpret freely to capture something of its spirit):

> My spirit bows in praise of God.
>   *Adonai*, nurturing and compassionate, *Elohim*,[24] powerful and just, in creating such a universe you have grown very great.
>   Your clothing reveals inner majesty and outer splendor.
>   Wrapped in pure light, you stretch out the heavens like a curtain.

This passage is very different than the creation narrative. My feeling is that it is best seen as poetry, as indicated by my arrangement of the sentences. This contrasts with the opening chapters of Genesis, which I see as a narrative description of creation, even if that description is formulated in poetic language. If I am correct about the poetic character of the Psalm—or even if not—a fundamentalist reading is not very tempting—except perhaps to a fundamentalist mystic.[25] Here a naturalistically spirited approach seems natural, usual. Again, the lack of belief in the factual adequacy of the depiction poses no threat to the religious power of the passage. One is nourished to the extent that one can inhabit the imagery of God's wearing a *tallit* of pure light and savor the sense of inner majesty and outer splendor.

Such depictions, I said above, are like parables or allegories. But neither "parable" nor "allegory" seems completely apt. What we need is a word that conveys the profound resonance and suggestiveness of a depiction or image, and implies (without being heavy-handed about it) factual incorrectness, all of this without misleading suggestions.[26] Perhaps the least objectionable expression is "myth," but this is not an altogether happy choice in light of its own associations. Until a more natural expression suggests itself, I will say that our non-fundamentalist theist sees the creation story as mythological, and that we (almost) all see Psalm 104 that way.

---

[24] See the glossary at the end of this essay for an explanation of these two names of God.

[25] One can be quite seriously mystical, I think, without being fundamentalist, without supposing that the mystical imagery correctly depicts the (or some) world.

[26] "Parable," for example, suggests a simple story illustrating a religious lesson. It's not clear that we are here dealing with such a simple story or any straightforward lesson.

If we are to use the notion of myth in this way, it is important that we resist its deflationary overtones. Because of its deflationary ring—as if its meaning were exhausted by something like "a primitive, false belief"—we are apt to reserve the category of the mythological for traditions other than our own. I mean to suggest a much more positive estimation of the mythological, and to encourage the application of the concept to our own traditions.

I turn now to the matter of a thoroughly naturalistic approach. My idea is that a thoroughgoing naturalist might approach the creation narrative, for example, in very much the same way as the non-fundamentalist supernaturalist described above. The difference—at the level of theory it is enormous, of course—is that the naturalist extends to God the sort of approach our supernaturalist applied to the six days of creation.

Like his theistic colleagues, the thoroughgoing religious naturalist dwells in the potent imagery of creation, and this makes available to him what it makes available to the theist, the same religious resonances, the same suggestiveness about the human condition and human flourishing. The drama of creation, like masterful fiction, is no less powerful, no less suggestive, for its factual untruth. Not that the creation myth is, for the non-fundamentalist, mere fiction. This story, like others that figure centrally in the tradition, is not just a story. It is our own story, our own mythology; our own both in the sense that our people figure centrally in this story (or in its continuation), and in the sense of a kind of non-exclusive ownership or possession. These stories play a crucial role in the continuity of the community over time: We have learned these stories from our parents and grandparents, and we teach them to our children. The constellation of such stories provide, or play an enormous role in providing, our moral horizons, our place, and our point in the world. The term "mythology" starts to take on an honorific aura.

The non-fundamentalist theist felt no temptation to rid her vocabulary of expressions like "the six days of creation," and so it is for my religious naturalist with expressions like "God," "divine providence," "messiah," and the rest. Not only does the traditional vocabulary figure centrally in his thinking, he insists on the traditional understandings of these words. In this way, my religious naturalism is very different than what we might call religious reductionism.

The religious reductionist wants to understand "God" as a name or description of something natural, perhaps a tendency or capacity of people or of the universe, perhaps a force for good in the world, or the sum total of such forces. An intriguing suggestion is the idea that "God" represents or encapsulates those aspects of nature that evoke or inspire awe and/or love. While I can't argue for this here, I believe that to provide a naturalistic reduction of the concept of God is to lose something, indeed a great deal, of what is important in the concept. My naturalism does not then employ any sort of reinterpretation strategy. It is the traditional terminology, as traditionally understood, that figures in the religious experience of my naturalist.[27]

Let's turn to prayer, often seen as a sticking point for religious naturalism. My naturalist's experience of the traditional liturgy, like that of other religious practitioners, is multi-dimensional. The naturalist may, like others who are serious about prayer, engage the traditional liturgy in search of the imagery's applications to, or suggestions about, the human condition. Nothing naturalistically unacceptable so far. But there is another level, one that certainly seems to threaten naturalism.

In prayer, one engages God. One speaks to God, praises God, expresses awe and love toward God, asks things of God, even confronts God. That's the problem. We need here remember how we sought to resolve the parallel problem—of course not the same problem—for the case of the non-fundamentalist supernaturalist. Given the latter's disbelief in the six days of creation, we asked, how can she utter "the six days of creation" and really mean them in the sense required for real prayer? My idea, here as there, is that one engages wholeheartedly with a mythology, the factual incorrectness of which is quite beside the point.

The idea of engaging with, dwelling in, a mythology certainly stands in need of further exploration and elaboration. One source of assistance is the study of related notions in other arenas. To fully engage theatrical experience, for example, to be genuinely moved by

---

[27]Reductionism is one of the two well-known paths of naturalism. Eliminativism is the other. In contemporary discussions of naturalism it often is assumed that a naturalistic approach to naturalistically troublesome domain must either eliminate the troublesome entities or reduce them to something naturalistically acceptable. My naturalist's relation to the eliminativist is complicated. On one hand, contrary to the reductionist, both take the troublesome discourse at face value. Both agree that the troublesome discourse is not needed for the ultimate description of nature. But my naturalist and the eliminativist seem to disagree on the consequences for the utility of religious discourse. Perhaps this is not clear, since the eliminativist might allow that the non-referring terms, "God" for example, might figure in poetry and other forms of discourse that are not his concern. Such terms do not, however, figure in the scientific description of nature. Still, my emphasis on the religious life is far from the spirit of eliminativism as we know it.

it, the audience member needs to put aside his knowledge that it is "only a play"; he needs to go with it, to feel for the characters, to share in their joys and sorrows. He needs to "suspend disbelief," to engage with the as-it-were mythology, to put aside what we might call his meta-beliefs about the performed speech and behavior. Drama seems like a fertile field for exploring the matter of serious, focused engagement with the non-factual.[28]

Drama seems implicated in the religious life in any case, even for the fundamentalist. Playing in the background of the Jewish religious life there is a drama, a poignant one, with elements of triumph and tragic defeat, and with no small measure of irony, even comedy if one is in the right mood. Some elements of the drama are the creation narrative, and the biblical histories of the world, of the patriarchal families, of the Jewish people. Indeed, the drama includes post-biblical, even modern, Jewish history. It includes projections about the future course of things, and may also include more mystical elements, the heavenly host, for example. Prominent in the drama is God, who himself plays, as it were, many roles, creator, parent, monarch, lover, judge, to name some of them. In light of his many roles, God stands in a special and quite complicated relation to human beings and specifically to the Jewish people.

Such theater quietly informs countless aspects of the religious Jew's everyday life. There are times when it assumes the foreground, as in prayer, when focused and serious. For many practitioners— perhaps most—the drama contains some fictional elements. That the existence of God is a non-fictional component is supremely important to the traditional theist. For my religious naturalist, many more key players and themes in the drama are fictional. In thus viewing the theist and naturalist as on a continuum, I do not mean to diminish or make light of the differences—my religious naturalism owes its possibility to their theoretical enormity. Drama

---

[28]The language of "engagement with a mythology" may be misleading in another way (other than, that is, the misleading associations of "mythology"). It might suggest, contrary to fact, that the naturalist experiences prayer, for example, *as* engagement with mythology, that he keeps before his mind the non-factual character of the narrative. As with theatrical experience, the moments of intense involvement are not typically moments that one is focused on the non-factual character of the drama. One "goes with" the drama and is not thinking about its fictional character. Indeed, if at a tragic moment in a play when one (an audience member) is feeling great sorrow, one is interrupted with the reminder that it is only a play, one will likely be very impatient. The fictional character of the play goes without saying, and is beside the point. This is true for the non-fundamentalist theist above, and for the thoroughgoing naturalist.

thus provides a new arena for the study of religious engagement, and its substantial role in the religious life provides another vantage point on that life, and on religious naturalism.

In this essay, I have explored what I see as traditional Judaism's distinctive take on human flourishing. What is involved is not only a conception of the good life, but a system of practices that implements the conception. The fundamental notion I've explored is *yirat shamayim*; the ideal practitioner is the *y're shamayim*, whose stance is one of generalized humility and elevation with all the affective, behavioral, and cognitive concomitants. Such a life is not only a good life, but more to the point, it is also a life of holiness. The *y're shamayim*, living as he does in the presence of awe, sees holiness in all sorts of unlikely places. Being so in touch with the holy, he is himself touched by it. But the *y're shamayim* is holy in quite another sense. The character development he exhibits, the determination, the focus, the sustained hard work, indeed the success, is one of nature's most precious and awe-inspiring products.[29]

Glossary of Hebrew Expressions

Adonai	Our Lord. It is traditional to pronounce the biblical Tetragrammaton name of God as if it were the word Adonai. Adonai thus comes to be seen as a name of God rather than describing God as a lord, which is closer to the literal meaning of adonai. This name of God is often associated in the rabbinic literature with the attributes of mercy and nurture.
ahavat Ha'shem	Love of God
Elohim	Another name of God, often associated in the rabbinic literature with the attributes of power and justice.
k'neged kulam	"The most basic or fundamental," as applied to a practice, idea, or principle

[29] Talks which eventuated in this paper were given at the University of California–Riverside, Stanford University, Pomona College, the University of California–Irvine, and San Diego State University. I am very grateful to discussants at these sessions. I am especially grateful to my commentators, Philip Quinn and Eleonore Stump, and to Andrew Eshleman, Joel Gereboff, Ernie LePore, Andy Reath, and Georgia Warnke for helpful comments on earlier drafts and related pieces. Finally, I am grateful to the Shalom Hartman Institute of Jerusalem for much stimulation on these and related questions.

Shabbat	The Sabbath
Shofar	Ram's horn, blown during the month of Elul
Tallit	A prayer shawl
Yirah	Awe, also fear; often awe with an admixture of fear
yirat Ha'shem	Awe of God
yirat shamayim	Awe of heaven
y're Ha'shem	One who stands in awe of God
y're shamayim	One who stands in awe of heaven

4

Terra Firma

I. Naturalism

I have long felt that graduate education in philosophy, when successful, produces in its beneficiaries a strong antipathy, almost an
allergic reaction, to "ism" words. "Naturalism," nevertheless, is not
one that is easy to eschew. This is not because of anything like a
widely shared or especially intuitive doctrine associated with the
term. The numerous doctrines offered by way of characterization
often seem either suspicious because of their strength, or else plati-
tudinous, too easy and not sufficiently restrictive. The appeal of naturalism is rather a matter of a tendency of thought, a powerful one
despite its lack of easy definition.

"Naturalism" nowadays brings to mind one of several reductionist or eliminativist paradigms. To naturalize a concept, as we
say, is to reduce it to something physicalistically acceptable. Such
reductions respect the structure of ordinary talk; the original terms
remain, associated with new characterizations of the subject matter.
The eliminativist strategy—abolishing the customary modes of
speech—comes to the fore where such reductions are unattainable.

That naturalism has become so identified is unfortunate, for
such identification is entirely too restrictive. Aristotle, the father of
the view, wasn't much of a reductionist/eliminativist. This is not to
deny that contemporary reductionists and eliminativists share
something of the more general tendency. Their naturalism, however, is not the only one.

In the following sub-sections, I try to provide a feel for the sort of naturalism I have in mind. I do this by sketching with respect to several philosophic domains what are no more than points of departure for my preferred kind of naturalistic thinking. Then I turn, in the second half of this paper, to Wittgenstein, whose mature project was to bring any number of philosophically important notions down to earth. I see Wittgenstein as a fellow traveler.

A. Philosophy of Mind

If one thinks about the mind under the influence of modern philosophy, one is likely to see mind-body dualism as virtually written into our ordinary ways of thinking and talking. Many, finding this unacceptable, will be tempted to reinterpret the common idiom so as to show that our apparent talk of spirits goes over without remainder into talk of naturalistically respectable things. If this seems too ambitious, if our concepts seem reduction-resistant, it may be tempting to make do without them—in some ways an even more ambitious undertaking.

To do things in either of these ways is, I believe, to concede too much to the opponent. It is to concede that on the face of it, without reinterpretation, elimination, or such philosophical remedies, the spiritualist wins the day. What is needed, from my point of view, is a perspective on our ordinary talk and thought about mentality that reveals them to be considerably more innocent. This is, no doubt, Wittgenstein's idea, and an important part of his project. The following remarks from an old-fashioned (pre-Quine) American naturalist, F. J. E. Woodbridge, may furnish a useful starting point.

> The distinction [between the mental and the physical] is not the invention of philosophers. Each of us is led to make it when we express in words what we do. We think, perceive, remember, and imagine; we walk, sleep, digest and breathe. Our activities are many, and when we attempt to classify them, they fall naturally into two major classes which are distinct enough to be denoted by two names. Thinking, perceiving and remembering are so different from walking, digesting and breathing, that it strikes us as inappropriate to call them all by a common name without any qualifying adjective. The one set is mental, and the other, bodily or physical.
>
> The distinction is primarily between activities and not between objects. The history of language is one proof of this. It is clear that originally words which expressed the mental and the physical, expressed what objects do rather than what they are. . . . Man is a thinking being and a walking being; he is both mental and physical. He has a mind and

a body, not because one object properly called a body and another, a
mind, have conspired to produce him, but because he thinks and walks.
So the distinction gets transferred to objects.[1]

In the beginning then, there were not two substances, but a single
organism. A natural classification of the organism's functions distinguishes the bodily from the mental. This distinction begins at the
adjectival level, thinking being an activity of the organism that
belongs in the latter category, and breathing being an activity of the
same organism, an activity that belongs in the former category. Out
of such adjectival forms naturally evolve nominalizations by a kind
of linguistic concretion. One person is said to have a stronger mind
than another; another a stronger body. Such linguistic forms do not
commit us to new items in the inventory of the universe, human
bodies and minds as separate items.

A naturalistic approach to mind is of course not secured by the rejection of substance dualism. One might still proffer a non-naturalistic
account of mental events or activity, an account that sees mental events
as *sui generis* events that occur in the physical organism. My aim has
been to illustrate a tendency and to provide a point of departure.

B. Skepticism

We have been taught that the external world, other minds, past moments of time, all of these are problems, that their assumption
requires philosophic justification, a convincing response to the
skeptic. My naturalist, failing to have learned this lesson, begins in
the external world. Indeed, to think of the world as external, at least
in the way that we do, is already to concede too much to the power
of modern philosophy. We begin in the world, constituted (this is
our best shot at the moment) in the way that our colleagues in the
sciences suppose. This world contains, importantly for us, other
people whose "minds," for example, their intellectual and affective
capacities, are no less evident than our own. That these things are so
is not something that we come to philosophy to verify, that we think
of as up for grabs, awaiting the results of our work.

To deny that such things are up for grabs is not to suggest that
nothing is. People surely have looked and do look to philosophy for
help with their beliefs. But there are beliefs and there are beliefs.
What is required here is a sense of balance that, to slightly revise
Russell, is required even in the most abstract studies. That my name

---

[1] From *The Realm of Mind* (New York, 1926), pp. 2–4.

is "Howard Wettstein," that I am married to Barbara, that honesty and integrity are important to human life, that language is one of the things that makes humans distinctive, none of these are, or ever have been, on the negotiating table for me, not to speak of my belief that there have been past moments or a physical world.

The naturalistic outlook, as I understand it, thus makes it difficult for skepticism to get a foothold.[2] It is important—although perhaps it goes without saying—that this is no part of the motivation for the naturalism, as if the outlook were another move in the philosopher's arsenal for defeating skepticism.

The naturalist's starting point, out in the world, also provides important perspective, a distinctive vantage point, on skepticism. Whatever else skepticism is, it is a perennial intellectual preoccupation, and so philosophy might have something to say about its power. Providing perspective on skepticism is, of course, not an undertaking for a few paragraphs. Again, I attempt only a point of departure.

Distinctively human is the ability to represent to ourselves the ways things are, and not only the ways things are but also the ways they might have been, and still other ways that are thinkable, whether or not they are possible. Philosophers, occupied with such things, are somewhat in the position of Leibniz's God, peering at the worlds. It is perhaps not altogether surprising that they are sooner or later drawn to wonder about which of the worlds is truly their own. It is difficult to tell. To put the point close to the terms of the "First Meditation" Cartesian skeptic, the appearances are compatible with our living in very different worlds than we ordinarily suppose. While real worry about such things, worry in one's gut, is thankfully rare, concern about the justification and epistemic status of our ordinary beliefs is almost inevitable.

Dwelling among the worlds thus occasions a kind of vertigo, a confusion about our own abilities. If we can discern the worlds, perhaps we should be able to discern our real place. We ought to be able to look down from the heights and see ourselves below, as on a kind of magical flight over one's hometown. Or maybe such achievement is beyond our reach. Perhaps we can't intellectually defend our ordinary modes of thought.[3] But then it will seem that the skeptic has won, that we do not really know what we thought we knew.

---

[2] The view expressed here is very far from the naturalism associated with Hume, according to which there are philosophically convincing skeptical concerns, but such concerns are to be forgotten when one leaves one's study. The naturalistic outlook makes skepticism unattractive even in the study, or so I am arguing.

[3] Cf. Pears' "Wittgenstein's Naturalism," *The Monist* (1995), "The Mind in Wittgenstein's Later Philosophy," p. 3.

Alvin Plantinga once said, paraphrasing Hegel, that philosophy is "thinking about things." One would like to think that by focused and disciplined reflection, one might arrive at quite a different place than one began, knowing better, as Socrates says, what one means and what one loves. This is not to suggest, however, that by thinking hard one might be able, for example, to demonstrate the reality of the past without begging important questions.

C. Philosophy of Religion

When an undergraduate gets bit by the bug of philosophy, it is often for its distinctive concern with fundamentals: fundamental concepts, fundamental human values, and institutions. Yet large and fundamental areas have received woefully inadequate attention from my own analytic tradition during the past fifty years or so.[4] My favorite example is the philosophy of religion.[5] This is a fertile area for naturalistic exploration.

Here again, the dominant kind of naturalism, in this case eliminativist, gives away too much to the opponent. The naturalist typically concedes that the supernatural is at the heart of religion. But theism—belief in a supernatural deity—however large its historical and personal role, is a theoretical position if there ever was one. Perhaps the theist should be likened to a mathematician who has strong views, say Platonistic views, about mathematical entities. Such views, even if demonstrably correct, would be in an important sense external to the mathematical work, per se. As Larry Wright commented to me, it is usually assumed that in the domain of religion

---

[4]Such complaints are often heard from those who have no love for analytic philosophy or appreciation for what I see as its genuine and substantial accomplishments. To say that we have been too narrow in our vision is not to denigrate the accomplishments. In my undergraduate days, I studied a number of American philosophers, naturalists like Santayana and Woodbridge, who were genuinely visionary, but who lacked the analytic virtues so emphasized in our times. Nowadays, vision is almost a dirty word. As Hilary Putnam says, "The besetting sin of philosophers seems to be throwing the baby out with the bath water. From the beginning, each 'new wave' of philosophers has simply ignored the insight of the previous wave in the course of advancing its own." "Sense, Nonsense, and the Senses: An Inquiry into the Powers of the Human Mind," *Journal of Philosophy* 91, no. 9 (Sept. 1994): 445.

[5]In recent years there has been considerable attention paid to religion by analytic philosophers. Indeed some of the age-old battles between theists and atheists have never disappeared, and theists have become energized in recent years by the application of analytic techniques to the justification of theism. What has been absent, however, although present earlier in our century, is the general perception that it is in the domain of philosophy to explore the significance and power of religious ideas and institutions.

the interpretation drives the institution, but perhaps the institution is primary. Perhaps religious practice and the religious life are not essentially tied to the prevailing theistic interpretation.

Here, then, is an alternative picture.[6] Imagine a community for which a certain narrative—say the Bible along with a tradition of interpretation—plays a central role. The narrative provides something of a history of the community, and perhaps a history of the world. It is in terms of this narrative that the community's rituals and ethical norms are understood. The narrative binds the community; it is treasured, and passed along from parents to children.

To this point, there is agreement among community members. Beyond this point, however, when it comes to matters of rather high-level theory—specifically, the theoretical status of the narrative—there is much discussion and dissent. Some—the fundamentalists—take the theoretical status of the narrative to be like that of a weather report: it is precisely and literally true. Others—the orthodox practitioners—are with the fundamentalists on some fundamental matters, for example, on the existence of a supernatural creator. At the same time, they argue that there may be huge admixtures of mythology in the narrative. The story of creation, for example, is not one they take to be a serious historical record. Others—the naturalists—think of the narrative as allegorical and mythological at many key points. Its discussion of various historical events may or may not be correct; this is an open question. But its talk of God, a being with supernatural powers, powers of creation, resurrection, miracles, and so on, is clearly mythological. At the same time, even the naturalists maintain that these myths are "our myths," that they play an enormous and enormously rich role in the life of the community, and constitute a crucial ingredient in the tradition's distinctive understanding of human flourishing.

It is not, as I see it, a philosopher's naturalism that inclines him to see no special value in, and no special place for, myth. Of course, what place that is needs exploration. Indeed that we have not seen the need for such exploration is part of my complaint. Consider a related

[6]My remarks here are inspired by reflection upon my own religious tradition, Judaism, which is not to say that these remarks are uncontroversial even in that context; quite the contrary. Santayana's thinking about religion, perhaps inspired by his reflection on his own Catholic tradition, seems to me congenial. See especially, Chapter III, "Reason in Religion," in *The Life of Reason* (New York, 1955). Insofar as the emphasis is on community and ritualized forms, this picture is less straightforwardly applicable to many strains of Protestantism, but there may be reverberations there too. The question of the applicability of this sort of picture to the other great religions is even further beyond my competence.

topic: the role and value of ritual. Mencius, the Confucian virtue ethicist, maintained that a central category of virtue involves engagement with ritual. Some fundamental human things, certain forms of respect, for example, have no expression outside of ritual, according to Mencius. This is an exciting idea, suggestive with respect to our Western religious and even secular rituals.[7] That ritual, along with myth, are of no special interest to philosophy—nowadays a virtual dogma, and not only of empiricism—is not a dictate of naturalism.

The persistence of religion, not to speak of its power in human life, is often noted, and often given a deflationary explanation. Here as elsewhere with deflationary explanations, one may wonder whether there isn't something more positive and more important at work. Perhaps the power of religious institutions is a function of their touching something deep in what we are. Philosophy may have something to say on the matter.[8]

D. Philosophy of Language

Philosophical treatments of linguistic meaning and of—believe it or not—the soul sometimes bear a striking resemblance. Wittgenstein, in the *Philosophical Investigations*, speaks of meaning as "the soul of words,"[9] and in *The Blue Book* addresses what we might call the vitality of language. He criticizes Frege's idea that

> the propositions of mathematics, if they were just complexes of dashes, would be dead and utterly uninteresting, whereas they obviously have a kind of life. And the same, of course, could be said of any proposition: Without a sense, or without the thought, a proposition would be an utterly dead and trivial thing. And further it seems clear that no adding of inorganic signs can make the proposition live. And the conclusion which one draws from this is that what must be added to the dead signs in order to make a live proposition is something immaterial, with properties different from all mere signs.[10]

[7] A particularly powerful example of Mencius's point was recently powerfully described to me by David Shulman, the first government AIDS attorney. Shulman described participating in the production of the AIDS quilt. The activity and the product were expressions of a powerful sense of communal support and solidarity. This is a dramatic example, but once one starts to think of it, there are many everyday sort of examples.

[8] Needless to say, I am here only scratching the surface. What, for example, does one make of prayer, and of religious *belief*, on such a non-theistic view? I believe there is much to be said for this approach to religion, and I will try to make good on this elsewhere. See my "Awe and the Religious Life" A Naturalistic Approach," in this volume.

[9] *Philosophical Investigations*, § 530.

[10] *The Blue Book*, (Harper Torchbooks, 1965) p. 4.

Meanings, on the Fregean[11] approach with which Wittgenstein is unhappy, quicken the otherwise inert symbols, as souls are thought to vitalize bodies. Wittgenstein's express aim in *The Blue Book* is to bring the notion of meaning down to earth. Significance is not a function of the association of words with intrinsically alive entities, the meanings. The vitality of language is rather a function of what we do with the symbols, of our social practices.

> But if we had to name anything which is the life of the sign, we should have to say that it was its *use*.[12]

This is not the place to explore Wittgenstein's tantalizing, if highly perplexing, ideas on the subject. It is enough simply to note that Wittgenstein's direction here seems of a piece with a naturalistic approach to "soul," one that sees our spiritual dimension in terms of natural capacities of the organism.

In other writings,[13] I have explored what I see as a natural affinity between Wittgenstein's approach to meaning and the work of direct reference philosophers of language. A speaker's competence with a proper name is, for the latter approach, not a matter of the intellectual grasp of a meaning, as it was for Frege. Competence is rather a matter of the possession of a social instrument for making something a subject of discourse.

The really interesting and controversial heart of direct reference, as I want to develop it, is the denial of what I have called the cognitive fix requirement. This is the traditional idea that reference requires that the agent possess a strong cognitive relation to the referent. For Frege this meant that the agent needs to grasp a sense that has as reference the individual in question. For Russell, it was required that

[11] Frege's views have been vigorously criticized and defended throughout this century, defended sometimes on grounds that the critics are attacking views that Frege never held. What is most important, especially to the contemporary anti-Frege literature, however, is the correctness of these allegedly Fregean ideas, whether Frege's or not. Perhaps the designation "Fregean" (and related forms), in this paper and throughout this critical literature, should be read as naming an important constellation of views that many have found in Frege's writings. This "Fregean" outlook is important because it represents a natural take on the questions it addresses and is, in the best sense, unsophisticated. It represents, to be facetious, what Frege might have thought before he became sophisticated.

[12] Wittgenstein, *The Blue Book*, p. 4.

[13] See my book, *The Magic Prism: An Essay in the Philosophy of Language*, as well as a number of previously published papers, reprinted in *Has Semantics Rested On A Mistake?, and Other Essays* (Stanford University Press, 1991). See especially "Frege-Russell Semantics" (chapter 8), "Cognitive Significance Without Cognitive Content" (chapter 10), and "Turning the Tables on Frege" (chapter 11).

the agent stand to the referent in the extremely strong epistemic relation of direct acquaintance. Direct reference represents the denial of any such epistemic or cognitive requirement. One can speak about Aristotle because of the social power of his name, that is, because there is a socially available instrument for making him the subject of discourse. Direct reference thus shares something of Wittgenstein's naturalism about language.

II. Wittgenstein's Naturalism about Language

A. Language as a Refinement: In the Beginning Was the Deed
Wittgenstein's naturalism about language is highlighted in this passage from *Culture and Value*:

> The origin and the primitive form of the language-game is a reaction: only from this can more complicated forms develop. Language, I want to say, is a refinement and in the beginning was the deed. (p. 31).

That language begins as a refinement on the deed is perhaps uncontroversial. Who would deny that there was behavior prior to language, and that words evolve as a kind of refinement? Well, perhaps someone would find something objectionable here. But as a remark about origins, about pre-history, it does not really capture anything very distinctive, not to speak of distinctively naturalistic.

A suggestion of something more interesting emerges when we place the quotation in the context of Wittgenstein's work. The suggestion is that language, as a refinement, never quite forgets its roots, that its ancestry remains present in later forms. I want to explore two of Wittgenstein's examples, one immediately on the topic of conceptual precision, and one later in connection with Wittgenstein's ideas about pain vocabulary. In each case, what Wittgenstein does with the refinement idea makes for a stark contrast with traditional philosophical views about language, for which Wittgenstein often takes Frege to be the leading spokesman.

To begin with conceptual refinement, Wittgenstein, in *Philosophical Investigations* § 71, criticizes Frege's idea that concepts, like geometrical areas, require absolutely sharp boundaries. To place Frege's view in a larger context, Frege sees (what he calls) concepts, as well as (what he calls) senses (these are what we usually call concepts) as perfectly well-defined, changeless, eternally existing. Such abstract objects occupy a "third realm," a realm of things that are neither physical nor mental. Most important for our purposes are Frege's senses, the meanings, roughly, of linguistic expressions. Pieces of language are, as it were, the worldly (and so imperfect) incarnation of the well-defined, changeless, eternally existing senses, and Frege points out ways in which our language falls short of logical perfection.

Wittgenstein, like Frege, emphasizes the "worldliness," that is, the this-worldliness, of linguistic symbols. But for Wittgenstein, this emphasis is not by way of contrast with other-worldly perfection. The point is rather to underscore the connectedness of the symbols, and of the practices in which they are embedded, with the human goings-on from which the symbols and practices evolve.

In the beginning, we might say, were prelinguistic brutes, bumping into each other and grunting. How such grunting evolves into articulated speech is a difficult question, but that it does is clear. Indeed, over time, the grunting matures into something quite sophisticated. Don't think of this emerging conceptual distillation as reflecting the absolute refinement of other-worldly concepts. Articulation is a gradual and relative thing. Concepts are articulated as they need to be for purposes at hand. And purposes at hand, even in the most abstract studies, never require concepts with absolutely sharp boundaries. Language, even at its most rarefied, reflects its beginnings in the deed.

The global difference of orientation at issue here—Frege's worldliness vs. Wittgenstein's—leaves its traces throughout the philosophy of language and the philosophy of mind. One example, briefly noted in the last section, concerns linguistic competence. Frege saw competence as requiring the speaker's intellectual grasp of a (third realm) sense. On more naturalistic approaches, Wittgenstein's included, competence with language is characteristically understood in terms of *knowing how*, in terms of the speaker's getting the hang of the practice with the expression.

B. Two Grades of Worldly Involvement

I will return below to the theme of language as a refinement on the prelinguistic. I turn now to another aspect of Wittgenstein's naturalism about language. I begin with a brief discussion of an interpretation of Wittgenstein that distances him from my sort of naturalism.

Wittgenstein's emphasis on the use of language, on language as social practice, and perhaps especially his obscure remarks to the effect that meaning is just use, has encouraged some to suppose that significance can be understood in abstraction from what words are about, as if the real world of things under discussion had nothing to do with meaning. Whatever there is to meaning can be discerned by a study that is restricted to the actions, social interactions, and mental goings-on of speakers, in abstraction from the realm of things "out there" about which they might be supposed to be speaking. A cousin of this view, on the topic not of meaning but of reference, has it that Wittgenstein is an "anti-realist" about reference.

Such an "idealist" reading of Wittgenstein seems to me to misfire rather radically. To begin with *reference*, while Wittgenstein surely does remark critically on philosophers' use of the notion, he seems to me about as serious and naive concerning the application of words to the real world, about the fact that words pick out things, as are, say, contemporary direct reference advocates. Indeed, he writes, "it will often prove useful in philosophy to say to ourselves: naming something is like attaching a label to a thing."[14]

Let's turn from reference to the more general topic of significance. I began with the "idealist" reading of Wittgenstein in order to focus attention on the question of the contribution of the natural world to meaning. Wittgenstein, as I understand him, maintained that the natural world is deeply embedded in the meaning of our words. I need to do better, though, by way of saying what's at stake here. What is it for the world to be embedded in the significance of words? I begin with Frege's view, one that deemphasizes the contribution of the world to meaning, but not in the service of any kind of idealism.

For Frege, linguistic significance arises when a mind grasps a sense and associates it with a linguistic expression. What happened to the world of references in this picture? Where is its contribution to meaning? For Frege, any such contribution is indirect. Senses, of course, have references—at least when the universe cooperates. Stretching usage a bit, we might say that a sense means its reference.[15] So it's not that the world is irrelevant, that it fails to show up in the picture. But what makes an expression, for example "Gabriel," significant is not its relation to a particular piece of the world, in this case to my dog. Indeed the expression could have just the significance it has even if Gabe did not exist.

---

[14] *Philosophical Investigations*, § 15.

[15] If a sense means its reference, then the contribution of the world to the significance of an expression consists in the world's feeding directly into the significance of a posited intermediary. This seems related, or just the other side of the coin, to these ideas: thought about an object consists, for Frege, in the direct apprehension of an intermediary, and linguistic reference to an object consists in the expression of an intermediary.

Consider, in connection with Frege's setting the world at a distance from meaning, Frege's notion of a *thought*, what we nowadays call a *proposition*. Frege took thoughts to be (roughly) constellations of senses. Frege's approach, his idea that the constituents of propositions are purely conceptual, is perhaps the most intuitive way to construe propositions. To approach the subject this way is, however, to set the world of references at some distance not only from meaning, but from the contents of thought. The things we think about, real-world references, become outsiders to the contents of our thought.

One way to emphasize this alienation of the world of references from thought is to focus upon names that fail to refer and on thoughts expressed by sentences that contain such "empty" names. "Odysseus was set ashore at Ithaca while sound asleep," Frege tells us, formulates a complete thought, albeit one that lacks a truth-value, since "Odysseus" fails to refer. Let the whole world disappear. At least some thoughts would lose their truth-values; all would remain unexpressed. Still, the internal integrity of the thoughts would be unaffected.

Let's turn to direct reference for a view that gives considerably more weight to the world's contribution to significance. The direct reference idea—it's a bit like the story of Adam naming the creatures—is that the world presents us with items to which we may assign names, thought of as tags or labels. Proper names, on this view, "directly" designate the things to which they have been assigned. They designate their bearers, that is, without the mediation of ideas, senses, or concepts. A name is significant in that it stands for *this particular thing*. The significance of a name comes, so to speak, not from above, from the realm of senses, but from below, from the worldly realm of references. If one did not mind stealing cute turns of phrase, one might say that the direct reference approach represents a further grade of worldly involvement.[16] The world, as it were, gets into the meaning or significance of one's words.

What then becomes of propositions, which Frege understood as constellations of senses? Direct reference people who posit propositions give the notion a Russellian twist. For Russell, the proposition expressed by "John is happy" is constituted not by senses but by

---

[16]In addition to the primary theft from Quine, I've been borrowing this use of "worldly" from Joseph Almog.

references, that is, by John himself[17] and happiness, a universal. Such propositions, championed by David Kaplan who dubbed them "singular propositions,"[18] have been found by some to be unproblematic and by others to be completely unintelligible. (Such is the way of the life we have chosen.)

Whatever we do about singular propositions in the end,[19] the fundamental direct reference idea is that an assertion about John does not involve a conceptual representation of John, but rather John himself. Talk of "involvement" is fudgy, even if heuristically useful. So it would be better to put the point otherwise. We might say that on Frege's view assertion requires that the mind apprehend, that it be directed upon, a thought content, in this case the proposition *that John is happy.* A constituent of this proposition is the sense of "John," and the mind, in apprehending this proposition, apprehends the sense of "John."[20] The direct reference idea can now be put in this way: In thinking a thought about John, or in making such an assertion, the mind is directed not upon any such conceptual representation of John, but upon John himself. The world gets into the significance of one's words, even—given singular propositions—into the contents of one's thought.

One reflection of this greater degree of worldly involvement is the severe problem non-denoting names present for direct reference. If the significance of a name is purely a matter of its reference, then either "Odysseus" really fails to be significant or someone had better say something very smart, very fast. To editorialize just a bit: This is a fundamental problem for direct reference that should not be avoided or finessed. Given all the powerful considerations direct reference

---

[17]I here take Russell's lead and omit consideration of his doctrine about logically proper names (and the related idea that direct acquaintance is a necessary condition for name reference). Russell often gives examples of his view which abstract from these features, and contemporary singular propositions theorists, not taken with Russell's epistemic views, have largely ignored these matters.

[18]See Kaplan's classic monograph, "Demonstratives," in *Themes From Kaplan,* ed. J. Almog, J. Perry, and H. Wettstein (New York: Oxford University Press, 1989), pp. 481–566. The focus of direct reference advocates has been upon the subject position, and the contribution of a subject term to the proposition. So a commitment to singular propositions has come to mean a commitment to objects as constituents of propositions, but has not meant anything very clear about the predicate constituent of the proposition.

[19]My own view is that direct reference would do well to eschew propositions. See "Cognitive Significance without Cognitive Content," *supra* note 13.

[20]Perhaps grasping a thought does not entail grasping its constituents. The usual picture of Frege's conception, however, is that in grasping a proposition one grasps its constituent senses.

people have urged against Frege, and even given that one may (or, of course, one may not) feel that greater worldly involvement is a good thing, even so, one ought to hesitate over this one.[21]

So far, we have considered two grades of worldly involvement. Notice the inverse proportion: as the world's contribution to significance becomes greater, less is required of intellect. Frege's view is relatively undemanding of the world, relatively demanding of us. Both the introduction of a name and its subsequent use have a substantial cognitive prerequisite: the speaker must be in a position to conceptually single out the referent. Frege, you might say, presents a highly intellectualized picture of language.[22]

It is just this highly intellectualized conception that Wittgenstein criticizes time and again. And direct reference philosophers, joining with Wittgenstein, emphasize that the use of a name requires no such cognitive achievement. This is not to deny that mastering the practice of proper names represents a cognitive achievement, even a substantial one; Gabe, as smart as he is, cannot do it. But this is cognitive in a different sense, mastery of a highly sophisticated practice, *knowing how*.

Once the practice is in hand, moreover, the use of a particular name demands very little of intellect. A student wanders into a classroom where Aristotle is under discussion, hears the name, picks up a few facts about Aristotle (and perhaps some misinformation), and is off. The student, even though he may lack anything close to an accurate, uniquely identifying characterization of Aristotle is now able to say and think things about Aristotle. It's like magic.

When we turn to name introduction, as opposed to subsequent use, direct reference provides more role for intellect, the role of assigning names. This is important, and will contrast with the more extreme Wittgensteinian idea below. But assigning names is still a modest exercise of intellect relative to what Frege had in mind.

[21] I have addressed this problem in an unpublished talk, "That Name Means Nothing to Me." My contention is that insufficient attention has been given by direct reference to the radically un-Fregean social conception of language that, I argue, underlies the direct reference view. The notorious problems of "cognitive significance," including the problem of non-denoting names, look very different from the more social perspective.

[22] Russell's view, while it does not require the association, or even the possession, of an individuating concept, does require direct acquaintance, an exceedingly strong cognitive relation between speaker and referent.

C. Wittgenstein on Pain: A Third Grade of
Worldly Involvement

I want to explore the possibility of a deeper level of worldly involvement. Wittgenstein, as we will see, apportions even more responsibility to the world, even less to intellect.

> How do words *refer* to sensations?—There doesn't seem to be any problem here; don't we talk about sensations every day, and give them names? But how is the connexion between the name and the thing named set up? This question is the same as[23]: how does a human being learn the meaning of the names of sensations?—of the word "pain" for example. Here is one possibility: words are connected with the primitive, the natural, expressions of the sensation and used in their place. A child has hurt himself and he cries; and then adults talk to him and teach him exclamations and, later, sentences. They teach the child new pain-behaviour.
>
> "So are you saying that the word 'pain' really means crying?"—on the contrary: the verbal expression of pain replaces crying and does not describe it. (*Philosophical Investigations*, § 244).

I don't know if Wittgenstein is correct about pain language. Nor will I explore that question here. The mere possibility will keep us busy. Moreover, I don't know how far to extend his idea. I bet he did not intend his remarks to apply to our entire linguistic repertoire for talking about pain,[24] not to speak of other sensations. On the face of it, his idea does not seem to apply to third-person reports, to statements to the effect that someone else is in pain. My remark about your pain certainly doesn't seem like pain behavior on my part. Perhaps Wittgenstein's idea has merit only with regard to remarks like "it hurts," or "my foot hurts," perhaps to all first-person (present tense?) remarks that attribute pain. Or perhaps there is a way to extend it to even third-person cases,[25] or to other cases in addition to pain.

Wittgenstein's pain-behavior idea seems to touch a number of bases. First, it is suggestive about the functioning of at least some pain locutions. Second, it provides a model for how we learn pain

---

[23]The two questions Wittgenstein formulates seem very different. Andrew Hsu suggests that we read "This question is the same as. . . ." as something like "We might more profitably ask. . . ."

[24]The "about" in "talking about pain" is to be read noncommittally. Perhaps such "talking about" is mere non-symbolic pain behavior.

[25]See the passage in *Zettel*, §§ 540–542, mentioned by Pears, in which Wittgenstein may be suggesting that our natural reaction to the pain of others may ground our third-person ascriptions, so that such "ascriptions" may turn out to be their own kind of behavior surrogates.

vocabulary. Finally—thinking about the *Culture and Value* remark about language as a refinement on more primitive things—the pain-behavior idea is suggestive as to the birth of such vocabulary, how it may have entered our linguistic practice.

It is characteristic of Wittgenstein to focus our attention on the second and third of these, and this is very unlike what many of us do if left to our own devices. It seems to me salutary to consider such questions, perhaps especially fitting in the context of natural-istic exploration. Late twentieth-century discussions in the philos-ophy of mathematics have emphasized that there must be a fit between an account of things known, an account, for example, of the nature of the numbers, and an account of our coming to know such things. It would be an embarrassment if the things allegedly known turned out to be unknowable by creatures with our cogni-tive capacities. A parallel here is that a theory about the meaning or function of an expression has to square itself with how we learn language, and how expressions with such functions come to enter the practice.

This is of course not to suggest that one cannot profitably work on questions of function without exploring questions of language learning or of origin. But it is to recommend reflection on the learning process and the evolution of our practices. Such reflection may serve as a kind of corrective to high-flying ac-counts of linguistic function. More positively, plain facts or even speculations about language learning, and about origins, may be suggestive about the character of what we learn when we learn language. And a conception of linguistic function that coheres with a plausible story or stories from these other domains is that much stronger.

In my earlier discussion of Wittgenstein's language-as-refinement idea, I emphasized Wittgenstein's suggestion that elements of our practice never forget their roots, that ancestry remains present in later forms. This doesn't really predict anything in particular. But it does counsel that we keep an eye out. One example was the question of concepts without sharp boundaries, discussed above. Another comes to the fore here.

Some pain locutions, let's assume, really did begin as refine-ments on primitive pain behavior. To start small, groans evolve into something more like articulated words; "Ow!" is born. Let's take another step backward, beyond such linguistic or quasi-linguistic forms to groaning itself or wincing. We can distinguish two stages at this pre-linguistic level.

Stage one: One groans in immediate response to pain.

Stage two: One becomes attuned to the fact that, say, one's mother's care and attention are forthcoming when the groans are evident. So one learns to modulate one's groans for maximum advantage.[26]

Here, already, something of enormous significance begins to emerge, a birth of meaning. At stage one, the groans express pain, but not in the sense that they express pain at stage two, the modulation stage. Stage two groaning is behavior with a teleological aspect, aimed at eliciting response, even if none of this is formulable by the agent. Stage two groaning thus approaches linguistic expression. We might mark the distinction by saying that at the first stage, the pain expresses itself in the behavior, while at the second, the person expresses the pain.

To continue the fantasy, we can imagine that if it's in the interest of the creature to advertise his pains to others, then more articulate expressions eventually emerge. Perhaps "Ow!" emerges first, as an "expression" of pain in both senses just distinguished; it's the noise one learns to make as an immediate response when one hurts, and it's the noise one learns to make to let others in on one's hurts. Later, various refinements on, or substitutes for, "Ow!" emerge, for example, different noises for different kinds or intensities of pain. Still, the expressions remain primitive. They function, that is, only at stage two: the speaker makes these sounds to express his pain, but not, as we use pain expressions, to speak about his pains. Accordingly, his utterances do not count as assertions, as true or false (which is not to say that they cannot mislead, or even intentionally mislead).

The way is now prepared for a major new development in meaning's evolution. It now seems like a small step—one that could take no more than a few eons—to pain vocabulary as functioning in a referential fashion.[27] Here's how it might go: A painful experience or episode, once expressed by means of a stage two utterance, is in the public domain. Indeed, part of the speaker's motivation for utterance may have been to let others know. And it would certainly be nice if the others (and the speaker himself later on) had a way to get

---

[26]Cf. G. H. Mead's views on the evolution of language. See, e.g., "Mead on Mind, Self, and Society," in I. Scheffler's *Four Pragmatists* (London, 1974).

[27]Reference here is to be taken broadly. When we hear "reference," we often think of "singular reference." But "table," "evolution," "inertia" are all nouns, and in some sense referential devices. No account of the nature of pain is presupposed here; only that "pain" and other pain locutions are in the broad sense referential.

at the episode in thought and speech. All it takes is an ingenious wordsmith to extend a piece of pain vocabulary from its purely expressive function to a referential one. Indeed, we witness, and participate in, such linguistic developments with our own children. The term, "owie" is often used by parents as a noun, in reference to a child's pain expressed by "Ow!"

Talk of an ingenious wordsmith extending linguistic function makes it sound like a matter of conscious decision, the product of deliberation. And there may be moments of deliberation involved. But the development we are envisaging is no doubt gradual and less conscious than the wordsmith image suggests. We can imagine intermediate cases: before the epoch of straightforwardly referential pain talk, the primitive expressions may find their way into sentence frames. "There is pain in my leg," "my foot hurts," "I am in pain" may emerge, where the embedding sentence frames, for example, "there is x in y," have other uses, some of which are farther along the linguistic evolutionary ladder. What effect does the presence of the pain locution in such frames have on the functioning of the pain locution? Does it still function primitively, so that the resulting utterance fails to count as an assertion? Or does the presence of the frame determine that the speaker has unknowingly arrived at referential pain talk? About such intermediate cases, it is unclear what we are to say. Perhaps these questions, in such a context, admit of no determinate answers.

So "pain!" as an utterance of a primitive, pre-referential expression may yield to "pain" as a noun, as a referential device, as a device for attribution. You can think of attribution here as description, as long as you don't read description in the traditional fashion. To say that the term "pain" becomes available as a device for attribution is not to say that there becomes associated with it a characterization of pain, or even that it now designates a property shared by all instances of pain. It is rather to say that the term becomes our device for collecting the rough assemblage of hurts originally expressed by its use. Given our crucial ability to extend usage in ways that seem to us and our fellows entirely natural, the term becomes available for pain ascription generally.

The foregoing story about origins is suggestive about language learning as well as about actual function. As for the latter, we need to go slow. Let's grant such a story about origins, and even that something of the primitive function is preserved, so that first-person pain utterances are expressions—perhaps in both senses—of pain. Still, it does not follow that first-person utterances are not really ascriptions, that they are *mere* expressions of pain, mere "avowals," that they fail to possess truth-values.

Pure expression, mere "avowal," may have been the correct characterization of the practice at the primitive stage, but we are no longer there. We now have a general term in the public domain that we use to characterize others' experiences. Is there something that prevents us from characterizing our own? Why insist that our first-person utterances are *mere* anythings? Such insistence seems unmotivated, and in any case conflicts with so much that we ordinarily say and think about people, for example, that they can lie about their own pain, or tell the truth. If Wittgenstein is correct about the core idea, perhaps the lesson should be that speech that constitutes "expression" can also represent, or purport to represent, the way things are.

In exploring Wittgenstein's ideas about pain ascription, we have been exploring another way in which language constitutes a refinement on the prelinguistic. I introduced Wittgenstein's pain-behavior remarks with the promise that there was here another kind of naturalistic theme, a third grade of worldly involvement. I turn to that promise.

If there is indeed another level of worldly involvement in meaning, and if primitive pain locutions are the ones that exhibit the phenomenon, then it would seem to be important that they are genuine bearers of linguistic meaning. Is this so? Should we count the primitive, pre-referential pain locutions as meaningful linguistic expressions? Clearly such locutions do some work; they have a function. The question is one of continuity: How similar in function are the primitive expressions to paradigm linguistic expressions? I find the continuities impressive. The primitive expressions, after all, are repeatable expressions that have a discernible function in communication. When we turn to the somewhat later development considered above in which the still primitive pain vocabulary is embedded in sentence frames, the case gets stronger for linguistic significance. In such examples, the pain locutions begin to function in more deeply systematic ways, combining with other expressions in a variety of constructions. Since it is unclear, even indeterminate, whether in this intermediate case the pain locutions have a referential function, one might take it to be unclear, or indeterminate, whether they have linguistic meaning. But referential function as a criterion of linguistic significance is surely too strong. It would rule out clearly meaningful words like our "no." I will provisionally assume that the primitive pain vocabulary bears linguistic significance, and return below to this assumption.

So far we have discussed two models for how expressions come to bear meaning. In ascending order of worldly involvement, and descending order of the contribution of intellect: Frege's, that an agent associates an expression with an intellectually apprehended sense, and the direct reference idea that an agent assigns an expression to something provided by nature. The model we are now considering seems very different. Like direct reference, the significance of the primitive "pain" pertains to association, in a very general sense, with the worldly realm; certainly no senses are involved. But "assignment" of words to aspects of the worldly realm is the wrong idea. Here's how it works. Early on, the agent learns to control himself, not to writhe in pain in ways that may hurt others, not to scream offensively. At some point vocables emerge as even more acceptable expressions of pain. After some training, the agent learns to make these noises rather than engage in cruder forms of pain behavior. (This is stage one.) When he begins to make these noises in order to elicit a response—that is, when he begins to utter what we are assuming to be meaningful vocables—he is making use of locutions whose associations with the world have already been fixed at an earlier stage, at a stage at which the vocables failed to bear linguistic meaning.

With respect to world/intellect inverse proportion, Wittgenstein's primitive pain expressions provide a limiting case. Notice how little the mind has to do: no associating words with concepts, and not even assigning words to things. The primitive symbol is born with meaning; it comes to us interpreted.[28] This represents a new and third grade of worldly involvement in meaning, a new idea.

Let's return to my provisional assumption that the primitive expressions bear linguistic significance. If someone has strong intuitions that this is not so—perhaps on the grounds that until the arrival of the referential function there is no real language and/or no real linguistic meaning—I will not argue. Still, we now see continuities where we saw discrete forms. Even if the primitive "pain" does not possess specifically linguistic meaning, "Pain!" is surely a significant noise. The primitive "pain" is a precursor to our word "pain," and what we might call the communicative significance of the former is a precursor to genuinely linguistic significance. Even if

---

[28]Cf. Pears: "We do not face the intellectual task of identifying a sensation as painful, because nature has done most of the work for us. All that we have to do is to substitute the word 'pain' for the natural reaction, and the contribution required from our intellects is minimal."

there is no third grade of worldly involvement in linguistic meaning, there is such a grade of worldly involvement in pre-linguistic significance.

There is more that is new. Wittgenstein is no fan of intermediate entities as explanatory posits, but he sees great importance in "finding and inventing *intermediate cases*." (*Philosophical Investigations*, § 122). What Wittgenstein has done in the pain case is, as I see it, to find or invent a crucial intermediate case, and I have tried to assist in such efforts above. Indeed, on any view that sees great significance in the fact that language is a refinement on the pre-linguistic, the transition from the pre-linguistic to the linguistic will be crucial. Do we have any sense of how such a transition might go? Wittgenstein's discussion provides insight on this question.

Grice distinguishes natural from non-natural meaning, meaning^n from meaning^{nn}. That smoke means fire exemplifies the former; that "smoke" stands for smoke, the latter. Natural meaning is the original; non-natural meaning, of which linguistic meaning is one kind, presumably evolves from the more primitive natural meaning. Wittgenstein's intermediate case—pre-referential "pain"—can help us understand this development.

Notice that Wittgenstein's primitive "pain" furnishes an example of Grice's natural meaning. The stage one utterance, "Pain!," no less than a groan or grimace, is correlated with pain, and can serve as an indication that pain is being experienced. So "Pain!" means^n pain. That stage one "Pain!" means^n pain figures in its coming to be used by a pained person to communicate his pain—we are now at stage two. The stage two utterance, with its non-natural meaning—I have allowed that this may be only "communicative" significance—evolves from stage one pain-expression, and gives rise, given human ingenuity, to later stages, to stages at which the expressions are paradigms of linguistic significance. Wittgenstein's intermediate case provides a picture of one way in which non-natural meaning can arise out of natural meaning.

The sort of naturalism that I advocate, one that rejects reductionist and eliminativist strategies and that extends as far as religion, has not had much play in recent times. My aim in this paper has been first to create a feel for such an approach, and then to explore several themes in Wittgenstein's later work that seem to me congenial.

While it is well known that Wittgenstein emphasizes the deeply social character of language and meaning, the naturalistic character of Wittgenstein's conception is less widely acknowledged. My focus here has been the contrast between Wittgenstein's view that emphasizes the natural basis for language and the continuities between later forms and the prelinguistic, and one that sees language as the embodiment of the eternal structure of thought, as Tyler Burge once put it.[29]

[29]The present paper derives from remarks I offered on David Pears' "Wittgenstein's Naturalism" at the UCSD conference on Wittgenstein organized by Avrum Stroll and was originally published in *The Monist* (1995, Vol. 78). I am grateful for many illuminating discussions on these matters with Larry Wright, and for comments upon earlier drafts to Arthur Collins, Eros Corazza, Andrew Eschleman, John Fischer, Carl Hoefer, Paul Hoffman, Andrew Hsu, and Genoveva Marti.

5

Theological Impressionism

Religions are systems of thought. So we tend to suppose.[1] What certainly qualify as systems of thought are the products of philosophical theology. But there is some tension, at least in the context of Judaism, between such constellations of theological doctrine and the primary religious works—the Hebrew Bible[2] as understood through, and supplemented by, the Rabbis of the Talmud.[3]

This tension is a product of the genesis of philosophical theology, the application of Greek philosophical thought to a very different tradition, one that emerged from a very different world. The primary religious works speak of God impressionistically. Their mode of description is as remote from definition as poetry is from mathematics. Their imagery is strikingly anthropomorphic.

Medieval religious philosophy, by contrast, disparages anthropomorphic description.[4] While not quite an abstract entity, God is described, even defined, in abstract terms. The flavor of this is perhaps

[1] I owe this way of formulating the tendency to Joel Gereboff, who is also skeptical about the supposition.

[2] When I speak in this essay of the Bible, I mean to refer to the Hebrew Bible. This is not quite the Old Testament of the Christian Bible, both in terms of the order of the books—the prophets come immediately after the Pentateuch in the Hebrew Bible—and, in some versions, the addition in the Old Testament of certain books not in the Hebrew canon, e.g., Maccabees.

[3] Roughly, first to fifth century of the Common Era.

[4] The role of anthropomorphism in the contrast between the two traditions constitutes a central focus of *Idolatry*, M. Halbertal and A. Margalit (Cambridge, MA and London, 1996).

best conveyed by an example from the Christian philosophic tradition, St. Anselm's characterization of God as "the most perfect being."
This is no mere honorific supplement to the anthropomorphic characterizations. It is a definition, one that subsumes specific divine
perfections.

My aim here is to explore this tension with an eye to the fate
or ultimate status of the doctrinal output of the philosophers. I
will argue that theological doctrine[5] is not a natural tool for
thinking about biblical/rabbinic Judaism. The "system of thought"
model applies to biblical/rabbinic Judaism only with the application of force.

As a preliminary, let me distinguish two aspects of Talmudic
discussion: *Halacha*, the legal component, and *Aggada*, the non-
legal. The legal discussions of the Talmud are often interrupted with
remarks on ethical or spiritual matters, homiletic comments, exegetical discussions, stories about the lives of the Rabbis as well as of
ordinary folk, parables, and the like. These *aggadic* passages are less
authoritative than the legal discussions. This is not to make little of
them, or to diminish their significance for the religious life.

As a related preliminary, let me distinguish my anti-doctrine
approach from another with which it might be confused. It is sometimes said that in Judaism all that matters is practice, *Halacha*, conformity with the law. It is clear that Judaism is not possessed of an
official theology. Indeed, the variety of ways of thinking about God
in Jewish tradition is striking. Begin with the highly anthropomorphic picture of the Bible and *Aggada*.[6] Move to the medieval rationalist conception, Neo-Platonist and/or Aristotelian. God is, as it
were, an unmoved mover; God's transcendence gets top billing,
and—to oversimplify—his immanence in the world somehow takes
care of itself. Now turn to the Kabbalah, the mystical tradition, with
its quite distinctive—sometimes super-immanent—modes of
characterization.[7]

It does not follow, however, from the lack of a canonical theology
that conformity with traditional practice is enough, all that matters.
Practice is central, and not only in that there is a more or less canonical

---

[5]I will use "doctrine" to refer to the output of philosophical theology. While I
want to deny the appropriateness of doctrine, I certainly do not deny the appropriateness of religious belief or religious tenets. More on the distinction later.

[6]Not that the Rabbis always speak in quite the same ways as the Bible. See Halbertal and Margalit, *supra* note 4, at p. 31ff.

[7]Perhaps it would be better to say that the Kabbalists provide a more transcendent characterization of people and of the world.

practice.[8] How one thinks about theological things, or even whether one thinks much about such things, is clearly less important than how one lives in the world. Still, questions of relative importance aside, it would seem to be a mere shadow of Jewish religious life merely to observe the practices, with no attendant mode of religious thought and feeling. I am skeptical about theological doctrine, but this is not to say that practice, *Halacha*, is all that matters.

To vivify the contrast between theological doctrine and religious imagery, I begin with the classical problem of evil, a platform that prominently displays theological doctrine.

I. Anthropomorphism and the Problem of Evil

The argument from evil, so-called, purports to refute traditional theism. The fact of unjust suffering—some of it palpably so, grotesquely unfair—is, it is argued, logically incompatible with the traditional conception of God, specifically with God's moral perfection, omniscience, and omnipotence.

The argument relies upon what it takes to be the Judeo-Christian-Islamic conception of God. The conception to which the argument appeals is, so to speak, the received conception, within Judaism and without, certainly since medieval times. But the Bible and Rabbis, as noted, speak in quite a different idiom.

The project of distinguishing Rabbinic from medieval conceptions, however, is no trivial matter. Medieval modes of theological thinking are entrenched, by now second nature to us. Indeed, that there is any distance between the Biblical conception and definitions like Anselm's will come as a surprise to many. Furthermore, it is difficult to approach the Talmud except under the tutelage of our medieval teachers. It is especially difficult for *Halacha*, less so for *Aggada*. But even the latter is a substantial undertaking.

A. J. Heschel, an important American Jewish scholar and thinker, comments that much of his career was devoted to elucidating distinctively Jewish—as opposed to medieval Greek-inspired—modes of religious thought. "It is not an easy enterprise," Heschel notes.[9]

---

[8]There are relatively minor differences in practice that derive from different historic Jewish communities, for example, Sephardic as opposed to Ashkenazic, as well as differences that reflect different local customs or the different rulings of different Rabbis on questions of law.

[9]A.J. Heschel, *Moral Grandeur and Spiritual Audacity*, ed. S. Heschel (Farrar, Straus, and Giroux, 1997).

The Hellenization of Jewish theology actually goes back to Philo [first century BCE] . . . [and] the impact of Philo on theology was radical. To oversimplify the matter, this approach would have Plato and Moses, for example, say the same thing, only Plato would say it in Greek. . . . This view has had a great impact on much of Jewish medieval philosophy. They talk about God in the language of the Greeks.

One might say, mimicking Heschel's hyperbole, that Maimonides puts Aristotle in place of Philo's Plato and sees Moses as an Aristotelian.

Perhaps we should not suppose any failure on the part of the medievals to discern the distance between biblical-rabbinic and Greek-inspired modes of theological thought. Rather for the medievals, this was the only way to make sense of the God of the tradition; the only way to square revealed and philosophic truth. Rabbinic tradition is speaking of this God, even if the Rabbis would not quite have seen it this way.

If this was the medieval tendency, Heschel's criticism may seem less damaging. One who wants to make philosophical sense of biblical/rabbinic remarks about God will inevitably do so in terms of one's own idiom and conceptual repertoire. It might seem, then, that the medievals only did what we all do, what is inevitable.

However, the interpreter of tradition needs to be alert to the possibility of gross imposition. As Heschel sees it, Philo's innovation violates something at the heart of the tradition. And it is not only a question of imposition. After such innovation, the tradition may take on new burdens, problems and puzzles that are artifacts of the new ideas. The classical problem of evil, I will argue, is an example.

The introduction of Greek modes of philosophical thought encouraged the minimization or outright rejection of biblical and rabbinic anthropomorphism. The God of the Hebrew Bible is, among other things, loving, nurturing/merciful,[10] just, even angry. The Bible speaks of relations between people and God in the language of personal relationships. What grounds obligation to God, for example, is nothing very abstract. It is rather the community's historic and personal relation to God, a relationship that begins with the Exodus.[11]

---

[10]The Hebrew word *rachamim*, often translated "mercy," might better be seen as conveying nurture or something with both dimensions. Mercy, for me at least, connotes grace, and this seems not to capture the feel of *rachamim*. The Hebrew word may be etymologically related to the word for womb, *rechem*.

[11]I am indebted to Halbertal and Margalit for this point about the basis of obligation being personal. See *supra* note 4, at p. 31.

The *aggadic* imagery humanizes God even more. Just as we pray, God prays. And not only does he pray, but his prayers reflect, as it were, his worries—that in his treatment of his creatures his desire for strict justice will not overwhelm his nurturing, merciful side. Even more astounding, God prays wearing *t'fillin*, phylacteries, as do his people. Our *t'fillin* contain several Biblical passages, including the famous *Sh'ma*, "Hear, O Israel, *Adonai* is our God, *Adonai* is one [or is unified, or whole, or unique]." God's *t'fillin* contain a parallel passage (roughly), "Who is like my people, Israel, a unique people?" God, we are told, weeps for his children, exiled from their homeland, their (and God's) Temple destroyed.

To take such imagery seriously is not to take it all literally. To talk of God's *t'fillin*, or of God weeping, is not to suggest that God has a body, an idea that does violence to mainstream Rabbinic understanding. But it is to think of God as the bearer of attitudes, thoughts, even feelings and vulnerabilities. The imagery of God's *t'fillin* suggests that God's stance toward his people is characterized by awe and love, the concomitants of our own recital of the *Sh'ma*, at least when we are sufficiently focused and prepared. But love involves vulnerability to the fortunes—even to the will—of one's beloved. Awe involves a certain humility.

Such robustly anthropomorphic characterizations of God play an apparently indispensable role in the religious life. That God loves and cares are, for the religious practitioner, no throwaways. To attempt to relegate anthropomorphism to the status of a mere surface-level phenomenon is to engage in an uphill battle. The burden of proof, given the character of religious life, surely seems on the other side. On the face of it, the distance between biblical/rabbinic and medieval thinking is enormous.

Robust anthropomorphism presents insuperable difficulties for the medievals. A God whose love involves vulnerabilities is a God with limitations. We seem no longer to be speaking of than which none greater can be conceived.

Biblical/rabbinic anthropomorphism, then, seems to violate God's perfection. But it is the medievals' supremely perfect God that is pertinent to argument from evil. This suggests the problem of evil—at least as classically formulated—may indeed be an artifact of medieval innovation.

One may reinforce the point by reference to the perfections specifically relevant to the problem of evil. Heschel suggests that omnipotence—perfection in the realm of power—is not a biblical/rabbinic idea. He speculates that perhaps Islam, with its emphasis on the contrast

between human subservience and the almighty God, bequeathed omnipotence to medieval religious philosophy. Whether or not he is correct about the history—his remark may be no more than his own
Aggada-style comment—Heschel's reading of the biblical/rabbinic literature, his understanding of the Rabbis' stance on the question of
power, yields a God whose awesome power is nevertheless limited.[12]

God's moral perfection is another good candidate for a second
look. It is not obvious that the absolute moral perfection so important to the medievals corresponds or even coheres well with biblical/
rabbinic tradition. It is at least an interesting question whether the
God of the Bible and the Rabbis exhibits such ethical impeccability.
Abraham, after all, argues with God that God's impending destruction of Sodom would be unjust; it would victimize the innocent along
with the guilty.[13] And then there is the rabbinic depiction of God's
own prayer, that His desire for strict justice stays within its proper
limits, that it stays in balance with His compassion. This sounds
very much like a loving God who, aware of His limitations, is concerned that He, as it were, gets it right. And although the Rabbis do
not emphasize the matter—as do the Kabbalists later—the God of the
Hebrew Bible is a very complex deity, arguably one with a dark side.

To put the classical problem of evil to the side is not to deny that
there are real issues in the neighborhood. The biblical/rabbinic literature does emphasize, after all, God's justice. What do we make of
this? Furthermore, if there really is something to the idea of God's
dark side, how does this cohere with His justice, indeed with God's
being an object of worship? I hope to return to these very real problems of evil in future work. My topic here is the contrast between
biblical/rabbinic and doctrinal ways of approaching religion.

II. Poetic Imagery and Religious Belief

A. Poetic Imagery

Let's consider a somewhat lengthier list of anthropomorphic images
of God in biblical/rabbinic literature: loving and nurturing, even if
demanding, parent; benevolent judge/ruler who does not forget acts

---

[12]See Abraham Joshua Heschel, "Jewish Theology," pp. 154–63, especially p. 159
in *Moral Grandeur and Spiritual Audacity*, ed. Susannah Heschel (New York, 1996).
Heschel notes on page 160 that he has "many serious reservations" about the Maimonidean theological system.

[13]There are ways of reading such biblical passages according to which they do
not suggest any divine limitation. Still, God's ethical impeccability is at least an interesting question in connection with such passages.

of loving kindness and generously and lovingly passes on the rewards to one's progeny; righteous judge who has access to our deepest secrets and who rewards and punishes accordingly; king of the universe, to be treated with lordly deference; bridegroom; husband; woman in labor; angry, regretful, even vengeful, remembering the sins of the parents and visiting them upon even distant generations. When one scans this panoply of images, doctrine seems far away. Many of the images fail to yield anything like a characterization of God that could figure in doctrine. Among the images, moreover, are striking dissonances, hardly a doctrine-friendly phenomenon.

Clearly, conceptual refinement and coherence is not a high priority in the Bible and *Aggada*. One has the sense that one is dealing with something more like poetry; sometimes poetry per se, as in Psalms, other times poetic, image-laden prose.

The virtues of this poetry, any poetry, do not include the discursive articulation characteristic of philosophy. The sorts of things one seeks from poetry are brilliance and depth of perception, suggestiveness; these inextricably bound with beauty of formulation. A collection of poetry on the subject of, say, love might include pieces reflecting different attitudes, moods, experiences. The poet seeks to illuminate the phenomena, sometimes casting them in a positive light, sometimes in a negative light. Many of the images, perhaps even the most beautiful and suggestive ones, do not yield easily to anything like a philosophically adequate idea.[14] Nor would the images presumably constitute a coherent set. Imagine the folly of trying to derive any sort of theory of love from such poetry.

Doctrine—the theory of God, as it were—is equally remote from biblical/rabbinic characterizations of God. The point holds not only for Psalms and the like; one of the fundamental ideas of Genesis, that humans were created in God's image, provides an example from Biblical prose. The idea of reflecting divinity is potent, pregnant with meaning. But it is imagery, not doctrine. Its very magnificence—literary and religious—seems to place it at some distance from doctrine.

---

[14]Such imagery often simply is not subject to explication in propositional terms without remainder, as it were. For one thing, many poetic images are propositionally indeterminate; were one to work at explicating or articulating the imagery long enough, one might see several ways it might be explicated, none of which is dictated or even suggested by the original. This is a bit like what Carnap thought about the explication of terms of ordinary language. But analogies with Carnap's views aside, the point here is that imagery is what it is; it does not yield to propositional formulation.

B. The Language of Poetry

The central concept in the philosophy of language is arguably that of meaning or significance. What one takes meaning to be, to consist in, may well depend upon what form of discourse is in view. Starting from mathematics—and mathematical language was Frege's first love, or perhaps second after mathematical thought—or starting from scientific language as does Quine, or starting from poetry, or literature more generally, may yield very different ways of thinking about meaning. Analytic philosophy of language has come a long way in the past decades. But its practitioners have not explored—nor been interested in exploring—the question of whether or how its work might be extended to literary contexts.

The study of poetic language would require, no doubt, some re-tooling. Our hard-won insights about meaning and reference may turn out to be relevant; it would seem unlikely for them to be alto-gether irrelevant. What is needed, though, is a fresh look followed by sustained attention. Here I can only make brief comments, barely a start.

One should not suppose that literary or poetic "imagery," any more than other forms of discourse, is necessarily connected with visual or mental images. Perhaps literary imagery is more likely than is say, a weather report, to stimulate one to form an image in one's mind. But that is not essential. We do not refer to these figures of speech as *imagery* because they induce mental images. How to char-acterize literary imagery—why exactly we call it "imagery"—is more difficult, something I won't explore here. But simple examples of metaphor, one form of such imagery, make it clear that mental imaging is not essential. "Sea of troubles," mentioned below, will do.

Here is the *American Heritage Dictionary*'s definition of meta-phor: A figure of speech in which a word or phrase that ordinarily designates one thing is used to designate another, thus making an implicit comparison, as in "a sea of troubles." When we explain metaphor to our students—say in connection with some philosoph-ical metaphor—metaphorical language, we suggest, is second best. We revert to it when we are not in a position to provide literal de-scription, when we can't do better than mere analogies, implicit comparisons. What we don't mention—because we are not really thinking about poetry and literary language—is that in literary con-texts, metaphor is often used for its own sake; it is not second best.

Why is metaphorical language sometimes preferable? It goes to the heart of literary imagery—here we go beyond metaphor—that the words resonate. One might speak about this phenomenon in

terms of levels or layers of meaning. But "resonance" better conveys
the lingering intimations, the echoes, the movement of the mind.[15]
In poetry or poetic prose, a single word or phrase may have multiple
resonances. Sometimes one predominates, comes to the fore; others
linger in the background. Other times one finds oneself moving
between them, sometimes repeatedly. Resonances have many deter-
minants: the occurrence of the expression in famous literary contexts; or other contexts, or other ways, in which the words are
customarily used; or other words that sound alike or that come from
the same root—these are a sample.

Where does meaning, significance, come in? We should not try to
say what the meaning of a word in poetry consists in—a bad idea even
in, as it were, straight philosophy of language. Instead, let's say that an
expression's significance has everything to do with the networks of
resonance in which it is embedded. A host of just such miscellaneous
considerations, for example, figures in the significance of "God," as
well as of its many Hebrew correlates (or approximate correlates).

C. Mere Poetry?

Have I distanced the biblical/rabbinic literature too far from theological doctrine? If imagery is at the heart of biblical/rabbinic characterization of God, then what becomes of religious belief, of the
tenets of religion?

Heschel writes, "In Biblical language the religious man is not
called 'believer' as he is for example in Islam (*mu'min*), but *yare
hashem* [one who stands in awe of the Lord]."[16] In the present context this is extremely interesting; it suggests that in thinking about
religion we make too much of the doxastic dimension and too little
of the affective. What I take from this is not that the concept of religious belief has no purchase in Judaism. Or that the religious life
does not require appropriate beliefs. Rather belief is not at the heart
of the matter; one gets a misleading picture of Jewish religiosity if
one's focus is a set of beliefs. There is an analogy with the question

[15]The superiority of "resonance" over "levels of meaning" was suggested to me
by Rachel Adler.
[16]*God in Search of Man* (New York and Philadelphia, 1959), p. 77. See also Richard Friedman, in *The Disappearance of God* (Boston, 1995):

> Indeed there is no word for "to believe" in biblical Hebrew. The word that is
> frequently translated as "to believe" means, in the original, something more like
> "to trust"; that is, it means that one can rely on this God to do what He has said
> He will do (e.g., Exodus 14:31). It does not mean "to believe" in the sense of
> belief that God exists.

of linguistic meaning in poetry. It's not that a linguistic expression in poetry does not mean what it ordinarily does, say, in a newspaper article. But that dimension of its meaning is often not at the heart of its function in poetry.

What then do I make of religious belief, given my emphasis on poetic imagery? My answer is that likening biblical/rabbinic remarks to poetry certainly does not imply or even suggest that these remarks involve no beliefs, no real commitments; that they are, as one might say, "just poetry." For such commitment-neutrality is surely not true of poetry itself.

Poetry may assume, for example, straightforward factual information about the world, that there are people, that they behave in certain ways, and so on. Second and more interestingly, poetry may be committal even where there is no way to formulate the relevant belief in straightforward, literal language. If we wish to formulate such belief, we do one of two things. We can approximate, extracting a piece of the picture, one that is propositionally manageable, and attributing that piece. Alternatively, we can mimic the poet, attributing belief using the very imagery she used—or related imagery. This may be a philosophical no-no; it will strike some as bizarre to suppose that such a thing counts as belief. Here as elsewhere, as Wittgenstein urged, philosophy would do well to look at actual practice rather than think about what it must be like.

Before exploring this belief-reporting practice, let's turn back to the biblical/rabbinic literature. Here many things are assumed about the world, many beliefs can be distilled from the imagery. All the old standards, as it were: belief in God, in God creating the world, creating people in his image, freeing his people from Egyptian bondage, revealing himself to Moses and giving the Torah on Mt. Sinai, and the like.

How should we think about these beliefs? Are they like the straightforward propositional claims that we can often distill from poetry or are they of the second variety mentioned, claims that remain at the level of imagery? When we report someone as having such and such religious belief, to what extent are we discursively articulating propositional content; to what extent are we ourselves using religious imagery?

I am not sure that the question can be answered across the board. Where the believer uses imagery, the reporter, using the same or closely related expressions, utilizes the imagery to characterize the belief. But even if one takes much of biblical/rabbinic talk of God's doings and ways to be impressionistic, is it all imagery? What of the term "God" itself, or more appropriately in the present context, the various Hebrew expressions for the deity? This leads to very difficult questions concerning those expressions. Do we really have a proper name for the deity? Do we have descriptions that apply uniquely? It is interesting—but of course only suggestive—that when Moses asks God his name, what he is given is something to think about. I am almost inclined to say that in speaking of the divine, intimation is the rule. Perhaps attribution of religious belief remains at the level of imagery. Religious belief, one might then say, lives at the level of imagery. It goes without saying that the matter bears serious attention.

How then am I thinking about belief? What sort of belief is this that has no propositional content? In fact, on grounds that are completely independent of the current discussion, I think that the usual sort of thinking about belief—the propositional content model—is misconceived.[17] Indeed, that the propositional content model is not consonant with my emphasis on religious imagery is fine with me. This is not the place to motivate my contrary conception. But we can at least see how it works out for the case of religious belief.

Let's distinguish two different ways of appreciating biblical/rabbinic statements about God, for example, that people reflect God's image (call it p, just to maintain respectability). One may appreciate p and its attendant imagery from the outside, as it were. Call this the Bible-as-literature approach. Alternatively, one may make p one's own, see the world through it, declare it, for example, in prayer. The question is whether one signs on, as it were; whether the poetic resonances reflect one's own take on the world.

If one wholeheartedly endorses p, then we may use p to characterize the person's commitments, to keep track of him with respect to how he approaches the world. He is, we might say, one of the p-endorsers. In so saying, we not only use p to keep track of him with respect to how he approaches the world, we use p to classify him with respect to others. It's like putting p at the top of the page and then listing p's endorsers.

This is what we do when we ascribe belief in p, when we say that he believes that p. Let p be as imagerial as you like, let it be an obvious non-conveyer of propositional content. If such imagery plays a fundamental role in one's approach to the world, then we can use p—its imagery intact—to characterize one.

---

[17] I spell out my conception of belief and belief ascription in "Bringing Belief Down to Earth," chapter 8 and 9 of my book, *The Magic Prism: An Essay in the Philosophy of Language* (New York: Oxford University Press, 2004).

To "read off" a belief from the imagery is thus to abstract a piece of the imagery, to kidnap it in a way, to absorb it into a different genre. It is to use the image in a new way. To ascribe such a belief to someone is like saying "This image plays a fundamental role for her."

Involved here is a sliding scale, from those parts of the imagery that are more serious and fundamental from those that are less so.[18] Consider the imagery of God's right arm. It is as if one kidnaps the imagery of God's right arm and then learns that one cannot make straightforward use of it; it fails to go quietly into the belief ascription genre. This is so because it is an image we are happy to let go. At least we are after we learn from it. Religious Jews believe that God created the world, but not that he has a right arm. The latter is not part of the imagery with which they approach the world. It is not a constituent of the story that serves as a backdrop to their lives. So, as our belief reporting practices go, it is inappropriate to use this imagery to keep track of their religious whereabouts. This is not to say that the image has no power for them.

III. Interlude: Is There Doctrine in Halacha?

Is it thinkable that even in the realm of *Halacha* the notion of doctrine has no application? This seems very unlikely. After all, the idea I have been advancing with respect to biblical/rabbinic characterizations of God, that conceptual refinement and coherence is not a high priority, is surely not true of *Halacha*. Talmudic study is notoriously wonderful training in analytical and conceptual skills important to philosophy. That this is so reflects the conceptual rigor implicit in the Talmudic texts, the emphasis on

---

[18]Philosopher Willard Van Orman Quine's picture of language comes to mind here: a circle enclosing a web of sentences, some nodes on the perimeter, as it were, some at or near the center, some intermediate. Quine's interest in this image concerned his idea that no sentences are analytic—in principle not subject to revision. Instead, the most secure sentences—truths of logic and so-called definitional truths—live at the center, while others, increasingly subject to the real possibility of revision, lie farther away from the center. My interest in the picture is quite different. Those images at the center suggest core religious beliefs; those at the periphery are highly suggestive, but are much more open to interpretation. But nothing is fixed; no sharp divisions are part of the picture. Perhaps there is a further analogy with Quine: for him, the sentences at the periphery enjoy a distinctive privilege. They are the ones that make the most direct contact with empirical reality. Not that I have explored the relevant examples in detail, but I am wondering whether the images at the periphery are some of the most exquisite and suggestive, for example the mystical images of the divine chariot.

fine distinctions, on clarity. If the notion of doctrine has a home anywhere in Jewish thought, it certainly has a home in the realm of *Halacha*. But does it?

The tradition speaks of the sea of the Talmud; and when one includes the commentaries, one might well speak in oceanic terms. As one who has not ventured out far from shore, and in no more than a rowboat, I am not in a position to answer the question. But ideas are what our field is all about, and the anti-doctrine idea—even in the domain of *Halacha*—is at least interesting, perhaps even exciting. Or so I will suggest.

When I was an undergraduate, being introduced to the joys of Talmudic study, the question arose about how *Halacha* is applied when social structures change and with the advent of new technologies. The Rabbis of the Talmud did not know about electricity, for example, and so couldn't have prohibited its manipulation on the Sabbath. The explanation I received is that at the heart of *Halacha* are principles, and what happens over time is the application of these principles to new sorts of examples.

Leave aside the question of whether this is too simple, the sort of oversimplification one might supply to beginners. There is a certain picture here, even if it needs qualification and refinement. It is that underlying the particular prescriptions and proscriptions is a set of high-level principles, a system of axioms, as it were, from which the Rabbis draw inferences about actual cases, new situations, and the like.

Rabbi Soloveitchik, in *Halakhic Man*,[19] likens *Halacha* to mathematics, and speaks of it as a set of *a priori* concepts through which "halakhic man looks at the world."

> The foundation of foundations and the pillar of halakhic thought is not the practical ruling but the determination of the theoretical halakhah. . . . [P]ractical decisions . . . do not stand at the center of [the] concerns of [many great Talmudists]. . . . The theoretical Halakhah, not the practical decision, the ideal creation, not the empirical one, represent the longing of the halakhic man.

The resonances of both Plato and Kant are apparent here, and while the remark does not decisively endorse the high-level principle conception, it strongly suggests it. But consider the following from Nachmanides's commentary on Deuteronomy 6:18, "Do what is right (or 'upright') and good in the sight of the Lord."

---

[19] Philadelphia: Jewish Publication Society of America, 1983. See pages 23–24.

[I]t is impossible to mention in the Torah all aspects of man's conduct with his neighbors and friends, and all his various transactions, and the ordinances of all societies and countries. But . . . [God] mentioned many of them—such as, Thou shalt not go up and down as a talebearer; Thou shalt not take vengeance, nor bear any grudge; neither shalt thou stand idly by the blood of thy neighbor; thou shalt not curse the deaf . . . and the like—[Therefore, since He could not mention all, God] reverted to state in a general way that, in all matters, one should do what is good and right. . . .

Nachmanides makes a similar comment on the famous passage in Leviticus 19:2, "Be holy, for I, Adonai your God, am holy." He sees this passage as the same sort of general statement that goes beyond the particulars previously mentioned.

Nachmanides says that it is that it is impossible to enumerate any complete set of prescriptions and proscriptions. What we are given explicitly by God is rather an extensive set of examples. And then a "general statement." Together, these constitute enough to create a sense of what is required, a sense of what are natural extensions of the examples provided and also presumably of the limits, what would not be a natural extension of the examples.

The idea that the explicit commandments are only examples seems radical and quite exciting. But what is most crucial here is the character of what God states "in a general way," the character of this statement that goes beyond the explicitly mentioned examples. For these general statements are by no means high-level principles, discursive articulations of inclusive formulas, statements from which one can infer all the particular laws. They are more like the imagery that has been my focus in discussing *Aggada*. Indeed, they are just that sort of imagery. It is not, after all, as if a substantive account of "the good and the upright" or of "the holy" is provided.[20] The imagery of "the good and the upright" in its context, and of "the holy" in its context are sufficient, according to Nachmanides, to generate a sense of how to proceed, of what counts as a natural extension of the examples and what does not.

---

[20]That holiness, for example, is imagerial does not imply that we are totally dumbstruck, that we have nothing to say about it. Holiness, for example, suggests separation from the ordinary, a separation that reflects reverence. But this is certainly not a formula for the application of the term. Indeed, it seems to me important to explore what more we can say about holiness, and like imagery. Our thinking, however, will be directed largely by the explicit examples the Bible provides. As I mention at the end of this section, the explicit examples guide the interpretation of the imagery.

One way to conceive Talmudic legal debate and analysis—the arguing over and comparing cases, citing precedents, and so on—locates the real action at the level of underlying (or overarching) high-level legal principles. But there is an alternative. One might suppose instead that the real action is at the level of cases. Talmudic debate concerns natural and unnatural extensions, the sort of thing for which one can develop a feel in the absence of any grasp of high-level principles. This second alternative recognizes, of course, that in the course of debate, there will be appeals to principles—legal, interpretive and so on. But the question is in the end, whether there is something like a system of doctrine—high-level inclusive formulae—that underlies the legal system.

There is an analogy here to the vexed question of our mastery of general terms in language. Is our command of general terms—like "intelligence" or even "game," Wittgenstein's favorite example—a consequence of our grasping general concepts, or equivalently, grasping general definitions? Or is the concept-talk a kind of mythology? Perhaps general principles are irrelevant; mastery is a matter of the learner's developing a feel for what are natural ways to extend the terminology from cases of known application.

Whether Nachmanides rejects the inclusive-theoretical-principle model for *Halacha* I do not know. But he does furnish an alternative model: The Torah provides examples and guides us in how they are to be extended. It is possible that he himself thinks quite differently about the character of *Halacha* at the deepest level. That is, although the Torah does not teach us the high-level principles explicitly—indeed it supplies only examples plus imagery—one can and should go on to formulate the relevant inclusive principles. But the thought that he might have rejected the very idea of inclusive principles is to me an exciting one.

Understood in this more radical way, Nachmanides would be playing Wittgenstein to Rabbi Soloveitchik's Plato. As Wittgenstein saw things, Plato is responsible for the original philosophic sin: the idea that what matters is not at the level of the particular example, but at the level of the higher, inclusive principle.

We have been considering the idea that the Torah teaches the law by examples supplemented by imagery. What is more certain is that the explicit prescriptions and proscriptions supplement the imagery, and in an essential way. For imagery, taken in isolation, is amorphous. Upright might get confused with overly rigorous. Intoxication with holiness might issue in a range of patterns of action, some at odds with how the tradition understands *kedushah*, holiness. So the proscriptions and prescriptions give content to the imagery. They guide its interpretation. This phenomenon seems quite general, applying to all the sorts of imagery I have discussed throughout this essay. That people reflect God's image, for example, could lead in multiple directions, and it is the ethical commandments that guide its understanding.

IV. Theology

A. Philosophical Ambition

The medievals, blessed with a more-or-less stable first philosophy, lived philosophically charmed lives. There is some parallel in our attitude to, say, physics. We are not sure of the details of our physics, not confident that we have final answers, but pretty sure we are in the ballpark, playing by the right rules, very confident of some general outlines. Perhaps the medievals were even more confident about philosophy. They were, after all, looking backward toward the Philosophers, while we are looking forward to a somewhat uncertain future, humbled by the history of past scientific upheavals.

Possession of philosophic truth grounded in a stable first philosophy makes many things possible: philosophy providing foundations for religious belief, philosophy clarifying the content of revealed religion, philosophy determining the nature of God, or perhaps determining that God's nature is demonstrably, as it were, beyond us. Doctrine, the propositional articulation of the religious fundamentals, is at home in such a setting.

A doctrine approach need not deny what I have been arguing about the impressionism of biblical/rabbinic characterization of God. One might argue—as Maimonides indeed suggests—that it is only because of philosophically available truths about God that we are in any position to discriminate among the images, to know which to take seriously and which not. The ordinary person has no independent access to God, so how can he discern Biblical talk of God's unity and God's creation of the world from the merely figurative attribution of bodily properties to God? Absent our access to philosophical truth and we would be religiously deprived.

This seems an extreme view, one that gives more independent weight to philosophy than many of the medievals, and probably more than Maimonides himself in other moods, or literary modes. But it nicely dramatizes the contrast with our own philosophic environment. The medieval conception (or cluster of them) of how religion and philosophy might join forces seems to many of

us inapplicable nowadays. The crucial philosophic truth comple-
ment seems missing in action. It is not only that the traditional
proofs of God's existence are in disrepute. Nor is it merely the lack
of a received view—or even a widely accepted consensus—in philosophy, substantively or methodologically. For many of us, philosophy simply cannot be brought to bear on religion the way that
the medievals supposed.

One might assume that this makes it natural for us to think
with the Rabbis, who also carry on without a first philosophy. However, the tradition, as we have it, has acquired much medieval philosophy, much doctrine, at least semi-officially. This of course was
Heschel's gripe. If we follow his lead, trying to recover what he
called Jewish as opposed to Greek ways of thinking about Judaism,
we are indeed led straight back to biblical/rabbinic mode of religious
expression.

To reject medieval philosophic ambition is not to suggest that
philosophic training is irrelevant to the understanding of religious
thought, Jewish or other. In philosophy we are trained to think carefully, analytically, to be sensitive to conceptual distinctions, to
extend our thinking, as it were, both vertically, persistently pressing
beneath the surface, and horizontally, taking a comprehensive view
of the domain. There is no reason why such virtues would be irrelevant to the understanding of religion and religious ideas. But this is
a far cry from the sort of access to philosophic truth that fuels the
medieval project.

B. Theorizing about God

Woody Allen quips that many of the things our parents taught us
were good for us are not so: milk, sun, red meat, college.[21] I would
add doctrine to the list. If one tries to think with the Rabbis, it no
longer seems a natural category. The Rabbis do not seem much interested in it. They do not seem driven by the quest for theorizing
about God that Hellenistic culture bequeathed to Jewish tradition.
With all their notorious questioning, with all the focus on clarity
and fine distinctions in the *Halachic* realm, they fail to evince much
interest in rigorous treatment of the theological. The nature of the
being that lies behind the imagery is not a question that apparently
kept them up at night.

---

[21]The line occurs in *Annie Hall*. His later *Sleeper* involves a variation on the
theme. It turns out that all the things we now think are bad for us—the ones our
parents recommended—turn out to be good after all. What we need is a movie—even
a *Star Trek* episode—in which doctrine turns out to be just the right idea.

Why is this? Why is theory not worthy of pursuit in this most important of realms? Even if one gives up on deriving the relevant theory from a first philosophy, or from philosophy at all, one might still attempt to come to intellectual terms with the theological. One might begin with the poetry and imagery of the Bible and *Aggada*. One might bring to bear insights gained from experience along with the analytical and dialectical skills exhibited by the Rabbis of the Talmud, virtues that seem closely connected with the virtues of philosophy, on the more modest conception mentioned at the end of the last section. Perhaps *Halachic* knowledge is also relevant. One cannot rule out the idea that knowing what God wants of us—the character of the religious life—is relevant. Reflection is reflexive; if people indeed mirror divinity, perhaps one can learn something about divinity by attending to its religiously developed human representation.

Even this sort of theorizing, however, seems not to have been on the rabbinic agenda. Why not? I do not know the answer to this question, but I do want to explore several sorts of considerations that may play a role.

1. What's It Your Business?

One idea, an obvious one, is suggested by reflection of what one might call Jewish sensibility. In *Hannah and Her Sisters*, Woody Allen's character is trying to explain his impending conversion to Catholicism to his parents. "If there is a God," he asks, "why was there a Holocaust?" His mother, rather hysterical, has locked herself in the bathroom. Her response to his query takes the form of an order to her husband: "Saul, you tell him!" Saul's answer is instructive, "Explain the Holocaust; I can't even figure out how a can opener works." The sense that God's ways are imponderable runs deep in us. The possibility that by careful reflection we might come to an understanding of God's nature seems even more remote.

One might arrive at this last idea on the basis of serious theological inquiry; such a conclusion seems to be the upshot of Maimonides's thought about negative attribution. But the sense that runs so deep in Jewish culture is much less refined. It is the sense that the universe is a pretty crazy place, filled with wonders and with all manner of irony: the pleasures and comforts of family, community, and God and his world, and the agonies imposed by those same agencies. The sense is not so theoretically grounded as it is in collective and individual experience. And one wonders whether this wasn't so for the Rabbis as well.

2. *God's Gift to Us*

There is a second, related, sort of consideration that may shed light
on the Rabbis' lack of interest in theology—in the sense of the theory
of God. I have in mind a certain picture of what God has and has not
given us, and of what we are to do with what we have been given.

What we have not been given is a theory of God. Nor does the
Torah encourage us to suppose that we might attain to any such
thing. The person closest to such things, after all, was Moses, and he
never got a good look, even a straightforward statement of God's
name.

What we have been given is a complicated business—there are
many ways to come at it, and any particular way will be only partial.
But somewhere near the heart of it is set of directions for how to live
as Jews; indeed, how to live a life of holiness, both communally and
individually.

This is not to say that there is in the offing anything like a theoretical treatment of holiness. The Rabbis, with holiness as with
the theory of God, seem more tied to the earth. Their interest is not
in a science of the subject, as it were. As a first approximation, we
might say that their interest is in developing a manual, a set of instructions for a life of holiness. They were engineers, as it were, not
physicists.

But even this is anachronistic, for a manual suggests a systematic arrangement, something like the Codes, the medieval codifications of *Halacha*. The Rabbis' interest, more accurately, is in a range
that includes understanding, clarifying, sometimes refining the
practices, both ritual and ethical. And we should not leave out their
devotion to guarding the law, constructing fences around it, enact-
ing further law that serves to maintain adequate distance from the
original laws' violation. For convenience, I will ignore the anachro-
nism, and continue to speak of the manual.

At the heart of the manual is *Halacha*. One should not forget,
however, the crucial role of its helpmate, the historical/dramatic
materials of the Bible, supplemented by the *Aggada*. Without these,
no set of do's and don'ts would suffice. Indeed, thinking of the practices as do's and don'ts is misleading, reductionistic. Both ritual and
ethical practices, themselves, like poetry, resonate with meanings.
Some of these meanings reflect the imagery, some the historic narrative, some the relation to other ritual and ethical practices. When
we think of the giants of the tradition, models of the heights of spiritual development, their achievement was no simple matter of dis-
charge of positive and negative duties. Their achievement reflects

the way they approached those *mitzvot* (commandments), or even better, their approach—*mitzvot* in hand—to the universe and to life, their conception of how one is to carry on, with its behavioral, cognitive and affective components. So the non-*Halachic* materials constitute a crucial part of, or supplement to, the manual. And not to be neglected is role of exemplars, both the giants of the tradition and, closer to home, parents and teachers who model the form of life.

This, then, is what we have and have not been given; and what we are to do with what we have been given. One of the central practices is the study of the tradition, the most advanced form of which is the study of the Talmud. One learns a great deal about the practices by way of Talmudic study, but the value of the study is not thereby exhausted. Indeed, one studies tractates that, since the destruction of the Temple, have no practical application. So Talmud is a theoretical study. But there is theory and there is theory. In section III above, I raised the question of whether there is an overarching, high-level theory implicit in *Halacha*. The idea that I found intriguing is of a piece with the idea that in these other realms—the theory of God, the theory of holiness—the Rabbis were not theoretical minded. Might it be that the taste for theory in all of these domains is part and parcel of the Hellenistic legacy?

3. Poetic Inconsistency

Let's return to our question: Why not start from the imagery and try to figure out what's going on with the leading figure? One of the aims of such theorizing would be to make sense of the tremendous multiplicity of roles that God plays in the imagery. What is this all about? What sort of being underlies these images and why are they fitting images for this being?

I begin with two examples that share some features with our situation. In both of these examples we begin with ideas that stand in conflict with one another. Think of this as analogous to the panoply of biblical/rabbinic characterizations of God, some of which are strikingly discordant with others. And in both examples something short of theoretical resolution is what seems natural and satisfying. Indeed, theoretical resolution seems out of place. These examples are mere analogies, but they will help illuminate one way of thinking about the theoretical reticence of the Rabbis.

There is a Hasidic adage that a person should carry in his pocket two pieces of paper with dissonant messages: "I am but dust and ashes," and "The world was created for me." I have often thought that the really difficult trick is to get both on the same piece of paper; to live a life that is not so compartmentalized, that integrates the superficially incompatible messages.

Maurice Friedman suggested to me that it would be better to leave them on separate sheets, maybe even in different pockets. The imagery of a single piece of paper suggested to Friedman what he took to be a bad idea: that the philosophic job is to render these insights coherent, to articulate an inclusive principle. What one needs is rather a kind of practical skill, the ability to negotiate experience respecting both truths—that is, both images, each of which illuminates human experience.

My second example concerns the universalistic and particularistic tendencies in Jewish religious thought. There are places in which the biblical/rabbinic literature reads as if what really matters is the human community. It is people, all people, who mirror divinity. Other times the virtually exclusive emphasis seems to be on our own community, the Jewish people. These are disparate ideas, and it is religiously crucial that we achieve a sense of balance, that we find coherence between them. Placing disproportionate weight on either represents a great loss. Overemphasizing the universalistic threatens the loss of the richness of the tradition; overemphasizing the particularistic threatens all manner of ugliness. Again, however, the sort of coherence we are after is not necessarily theoretical coherence in the form of an inclusive principle. More important is the ability to negotiate experience, appealing to one idea or the other when fitting, allowing each to call a halt when we are nearing excessive attention to the other.[22]

Neither example is supposed to demonstrate the impossibility of producing a kind of super-principle, one that delineates the experiences in which one or the other of the opposing ideas is applicable. But—and this is more clear with regard to the universalism-particularism example—we don't even know the shape, so to speak, of such a principle. Do we, or ought we, have any confidence that the cases fall under some illuminating formula? Think about the cases in which one's universalistic scruples might usefully be brought into play. Ought we to be confident that all share some common feature or features, other than, of course, being cases in which particularism is getting undue weight? Even if one identified a plausible candidate principle, isn't it likely that it would have to be

---

[22] The matter seems related to the Aristotelian outlook on ethics that gives pride of place to practical skill over articulated principle.

gerrymandered repeatedly to meet the needs of novel cases? While there remains the possibility of an inclusive principle, there is reason to be skeptical.[23]

Both examples exhibit two features that are salient for us. First, there are conflicting ideas, each of which possesses a kind of truth or validity. Second, the tension is resolved not by discovering a higher order principle, but by the acquisition of a practical ability or skill, a kind of "knowing how." The agent develops a sense of balance, the ability to call upon the idea appropriate to the situation at hand.

How does the first feature apply to the sundry characterizations of God? Think of the diverse, sometimes conflicting, images of God as profiles, as views from a perspective. Each profile is crucial for the religious life. Each has validity. Each illuminates in its own way. There are situations in which the image of God as nurturing parent is salient. In other situations other imagery may be salient, perhaps God as an impartial judge, or as a friend, or as creator of heaven and earth, or as one you have wronged, or as the parent of one you have wronged.

There are still other situations in which two or more profiles of God are somehow salient. Some of these may be very pleasant; as if one were taking in several varieties of beauty at once, or through several sensory modalities. Some of these situations, though, may be troubling, confusing. Such situations, as Halbertal and Margalit point out in their excellent discussion in *Idolatry*,[24] are analogous to one who works for his father-in-law, who also happens to be his teacher, landlord, and plays unnamed other roles in his life. One can readily imagine situations that become quite complicated and confusing. One doesn't quite know where one stands.

Let's turn to the second highlighted feature: the resolution of the tension between the ideas takes place on the plane of action rather than theory; it involves a practical ability or skill. Theoretical resolution in the form of a comprehensive principle seems unnecessary. This is of course the critical issue in the present context. For theoretical resolution—at least a leading candidate for such a resolution—would involve an account of the entity that lies behind the profiles, an account of how these could possibly be perspectives on the same being.

[23] This of course brings to mind Wittgenstein's discussion of family resemblance. As with Wittgenstein's examples, there may well be some more or less trivial common features that constitute necessary conditions. All games are human activities, but that is beside the point.

[24] See chapter 1.

How does this apply to the biblical/rabbinic imagery? The story here is more complicated than in the two examples. The religious life involves a combination of practical abilities or skills that are grounded in understanding, intuitive if not articulate. The religious life also involves habits, behavioral and affective. All of this requires education, training, and practice. As is our way with such things, some are more given to it, more gifted at it, some will take to it more easily than others, others may come along more slowly, but may attain greater heights in the end.

One stage in religious development is understanding the many different human relationships in terms of which these profiles of God are formulated: developing a sense of what it is to relate to another as child to parent, as subject to monarch, as defendant to judge, as creature to creator, as lover, as friend, and so on.[25] Developing a sense of these with their directions reversed is also of great utility: parent to child, monarch to subject, and so on. The more vivid one's grasp, the more deeply one sees into these relationships, the farther along one is in this stage of the training. Some of this understanding requires the accumulation—sometimes years—of experience. This education is a lifelong affair.

The next step—not that these need to be separated in time—is the application of this growing understanding to the relationships between people and God. One needs to think about and practice seeing oneself in relation to God as child to parent, with the variety of complications that entails; and to think about it from both sides of the relationship. And as lover to lover, friend to friend, judged to judge, and all the rest.

The payoff of one's work—the propriety and caring for others, the comfort and solace, the elevation and dignity that are the concomitants of developed religious character—depends upon one's ability to negotiate the world feeling and acting in ways appropriate to just such relationships. One needs to feel and act as if one has a Godly parent, a Godly lover or friend, a Godly judge who sees all, a creator of inexorable laws of nature that proceed as if we did not exist,[26] even—I suspect—an angry, even vengeful Godly ruler—this last being more complicated and controversial.

---

[25] Cf. Halbertal and Margalit: "Our understanding of . . . God in the Bible depends on our ability to enter into the heart of these images with all their connotations of prevalent interpersonal relationships." (page 9)

[26] Perhaps this is part of what is involved in God's *midat ha'din*, often translated, as I did earlier in this paper, as God's attribute of strict justice, but more literally translated as his attribute of law. It may be the notion of "moral law" that facilitates the transition from the literal translation to the more usual.

Of course, one doesn't feel and act in these ways all the time, or all at the same time. Part of the skill—what takes training, practice, and experience—is to call upon, or be called upon by, the appropriate image at the appropriate time, sometimes a single image, sometimes multiple ones. The latter can be confusing, disconcerting, as Halbertal and Margalit point out, and it can be wonderful, sometimes both. At the death of a parent, for example, many of these images may strike: God as creator of inexorable laws of nature; God as friend and comforter; (and since belonging and community becomes so important at such times) God as focal point—glue, as it were—of Jewish community, a community that extends horizontally—the present community—and vertically—the community over time; and perhaps others.

Jewish ritualized prayer—something that also takes training and practice if it is to be more than mechanical (and even if it is merely mechanical)—provides another example of the sometimes confusing but wonderful multiplicity. In prayer, when it works, many of the magnificent images are summoned. One is provided with the opportunity of experiencing these relationships and of reflecting upon them, seeing more deeply into them, seeing new aspects all the time.

That there are multiple images, that they seem discordant—properties that make theory seem very far away—are thus rationalized. We do not do so by finding a theoretical account of God that puts the images in their right place. Rather, the miscellany, the mixed multitude of robustly anthropomorphic ideas and images, facilitate the religious life.

In my discussion of religious belief (section II. C), I argued that we can make sense of that notion even within my anti-doctrine conception. At the same time, I evinced uneasiness with the notion of religious belief in the context of Judaism. The notion fails to get at the heart of the Jewish religious orientation. I want to connect that discussion with the present one, with the idea that the discordant images of God enrich religious life. Unfortunately my remarks here will be very sketchy; I will return to the issue elsewhere.

As I explained, my approach to religious belief, the imagery that plays a fundamental role for the believer finds its way into the report of the person's belief. Belief lives at the level of imagery. But the transition from the imagery as it functions for the religious person to the imagery as it functions in the report of her belief is a very significant one. For the original context is one of poetry, or image-laden prose. And in that context, consistency of imagery is hardly a virtue. Indeed, the very multiplicity and variety facilitate the religious life. But once the imagery has found its way into the context of belief, into a report of someone's belief, inconsistency becomes a substantial liability. This reflects the utility of belief talk, what it does for us.

The belief idiom is a fundamental tool for locating people cognitively, for tracking their cognitive whereabouts, their take on how things stand. For that very reason, it is quite sensitive to matters of consistency. To see this, don't think of beliefs about religious matters, but about the weather, or about history, or elementary particles. When, however, we speak of belief with respect to a domain in which imagery plays such a fundamental role, the idiom has limitations. Along with talk of belief comes the suggestion that it is not a good thing to have conflicting ones. And that simply is not true of the sort of domain in question.

Should we think of Judaism as a system of thought? What we have been given, thinks the religious Jew, are directions for living a life of holiness—as individuals but as ones whose flourishing demands community. The essential constituent of such a life is a system of communal and individual practice, both ritual and ethical, informed by a narrative history interwoven with religious imagery. The imagery, in all its variety and inconsistency, along with the historical narrative provide many dimensions of meaning to the practices. And the practices in turn give definition to the otherwise abstract and elusive imagery. The constellation of practices, historical narrative, and imagery issue in a distinctive kind of life with its own substantial virtues and rewards. It seems reductive and misleading to represent this as a system of doctrine, a set of well-formed beliefs, a system of thought.[27]

I am skeptical about theological doctrine, but this is not to say that practice, *Halacha*, is all that matters.

[27]I am indebted to Eleonore Stump for helpful comments on this paper and even more for her encouragement; also to Joel Gereboff and Paul Hoffman for helpful discussions, and especially to the Shalom Hartman Institute in Jerusalem for much stimulation on the sorts of questions I discuss here.

6

Against Theology[1]

That Athens and Jerusalem represent dramatically different ways in the world is hardly a new idea. But there are implications that remain to be explored. Twentieth century thinkers like A. J. Heschel and Max Kadushin inspire my project. Their voices, though, have been dimmed by current theological orthodoxy—I don't mean denominational Orthodoxy but rather the standard modes of theological thought bequeathed by the medievals. Developments in philosophy—like the work of Wittgenstein—suggest that the time may be ripe for another pass through the terrain.

Philosophy, born in Greece, is one of the supreme achievements of that culture, a reflection of its distinctive greatness. The Hebrew Bible is a parallel reflection, another supreme achievement, but of a very different culture. Eventually, considerably later than Biblical times, the two cultures met; their subsequent marriage issued in another of the world's cultural wonders, medieval theological philosophy, or philosophical theology.

In conventional terms, the match was a great success; its offspring has had an illustrious history. The way we—theists, agnostics, and atheists—think about religious things is a tribute to the philosophical theology of the medievals. And yet. . . .

[1] Versions of this paper were presented at Brandeis University, Hendrix College, London School of Jewish Studies, and at a conference on Biblical Theology at the University of Maryland in 2006. I'm grateful to David Berger, Brian Copenhaver, Eli Hirsch, Menachem Kellner, Chip Manekin, Josef Stern, and Eleonore Stump for comments on earlier drafts.

The situation has analogies to that of the philosophical tradition itself, when it came upon modern times. So much of the way we—and our post-Cartesian forbears—pursue philosophy is a tribute to Descartes, often honored as the father of Modern Philosophy. And yet some, me included, contend that the Cartesian revolution in philosophy imposed significant costs and in some ways represented a step backward.[2] The liabilities include some of the most well known features of Descartes' thought, like his famous distinction between mind and body—the realm of spirit vs. that of the mechanical. Something funny, one might say, happened in the early 1600's in philosophy that for better and worse changed its subsequent course.

My contention is that something similarly funny happened in early medieval times when the Jewish religious tradition[3] entered into a long-term flirtation with the philosophical tradition. When I say that something funny happened, I don't mean that it was all bad, and I certainly don't mean that we have nothing to learn from the new course. We have much to learn. Still, the substantial change was not without cost, or so I'll be arguing. My central concern in this paper is not the cost. It is rather the idea that we are dealing here with a major transition, a new paradigm in Kuhn's vocabulary.[4]

Previously, mainstream Jewish tradition, having resisted the incursion of philosophic modes of reflection, was more or less philosophically innocent. The Greek-inspired style of thinking would show up here and there—in the relatively early work of Philo, for example. But it never really caught on until considerably later; by the time the Jews found themselves in the world of *Sepharad*, the Muslim world in which philosophy played a dominant

---

[2]See for example, Richard Rorty, *Philosophy and the Mirror of Nature*, Princeton University Press, 1981.

[3]My exclusive concern in this paper is Jewish tradition, Rabbinic Judaism. If my approach has merit, there likely will be wider applications. But here I'll be satisfied to navigate local waters, deep as they are.

[4]Kuhn's approach to the history of science is important here. Kuhn sensitized historians of science to the existence of radical differences, discontinuities, between scientific epochs, for example that of Newton and that of Einstein. Previous to Kuhn there was a tendency to see Einstein's work, for example, as simply building on Newton's. Kuhn argued convincingly that the differences needed new emphasis and that it was more correct to see Einstein as a revolutionary, overthrowing the Newtonian approach rather than supplementing it. Einstein's view was indeed not only radically different than what came before, it was in some ways incommensurable with it. *Incommensurability* cries out for clarification, but the idea is certainly highly suggestive, equally so in connection with my topic in this paper.

role in intellectual culture, the philosophical mode had become central, even if still controversial.[5]

A philosophical interpretation of the earlier Jewish religious ways was, however, quite an ambitious undertaking. It was to convert an outlook not fundamentally philosophic into a philosophy. And that was to take a way of thinking and feeling native to one culture and reformulate it in very different cultural terms.

That the philosophic interpretation could be seen (broadly, certainly not universally) as revealing the real meaning of the tradition was a tribute to the stature of its main architects, most importantly Maimonides, whose honorific place in the tradition hardly depends upon his philosophic activity: the *Mishnah Torah*, Maimonides's *halachik magnum opus*, independently renders him a premier figure in post-Talmud times. His *Guide for the Perplexed* became at once *the* Jewish philosophical work both for those inside and outside the tradition as well as a source of great discomfort for those traditionalists who remained suspicious of the incursions of philosophic thought.

In this paper I highlight the enormity of the medieval transformation.[6] My larger aim, in the book from which this paper derives, is twofold. First, I wish to explore the theological implications of the earlier religious ways. Pre-medieval theological reflection has a distinctive character, continuous with literature and the arts more than with philosophy as practiced by the medievals. What, I will be asking in the sequel, is it to take seriously that early theological reflection was not in this way philosophical? How might this change the way we think about religion and religious things?

A second larger aim pursued briefly here and at more length in the sequel is to explore the role of philosophy in illuminating religious phenomena. Philosophy is a matter of thinking hard about fundamentals. But as Wittgenstein taught, philosophy often tends to a kind of imperialism, recreating in its own image the domains it investigates. A striking example is the philosophical idea that learning one's first

[5]This is not to say that philosophy first caught on in Jewish tradition in Andalusia/Sefarad. Saddiah Gaon, in ninth century Babylonia, was already there. But with later medieval times, philosophy comes to be intellectually central in an important part of the Jewish world.

[6]That some sort of major transformation occurred is not news. Below I quote Halbertal and Margalit's fine work, *Idolatry* (Harvard University Press, 1992), from which I have learned, and certainly Shapiro's *The Limits of Orthodox Theology* is relevant here. An important contribution is Menachem Kellner's *Must a Jew Believe Anything?* See footnote 25 below for a brief discussion of my differences with Kellner.

language involves something like theory formation. Thus an activity that is quite primitive (and of course also involves breathtaking sophistication) becomes a theoretical business, somehow a matter of intellect. Religion also is less about the head than we have learned to suppose.[7] My point is not to deny philosophy a significant role in the understanding of theological matters. The trick is to illuminate religious phenomena without imperialistic reconception.

I begin my story with the philosophically innocent approaches of the Bible and the oral tradition, the latter codified in the *Talmud* (and other Talmudic era works). I will then turn, for the contrast, to the thought of Maimonides.

I. Literary Theology

A. Biblical Literature

It is a commonplace that the Bible is a work of literary magnificence. Magnificence granted and aside, I want to focus on its literary character. The Bible, in its talk of God and theological matters, generally treats these as a poet might, or a writer of literary prose. The contrast is with philosophy.

Philosophy, though, is a many things to many people. Philosophers, beginning no later than Plato, have been great literary craftsmen. But there is an approach, beginning no later than Aristotle, notable in the middle ages as well as in the analytic philosophy of our times, where the literary gives way to the logical and analytical, even scholastic.[8] For those of us brought up in the latter kind of philosophy, there is a tendency to think of it simply as "philosophy."[9]

Indulging this tendency, let us explore the contrast with a literary treatment of theological matters by asking what would one expect from a philosophical treatment.

- To begin with, one might expect definitions—at least clarification—of key terms, for example 'God': is "God" a proper name? Is it

---

[7] This is not to deny that there are aspects that are uncontroversially heady, for example, the *halakhic*, or legal side, of Talmudic study, clearly taken by the tradition to constitute a kind of intellectual worship of God.

[8] To see something importantly common to those who emphasize the logical and anylytical is not to see that they look at things in quite the same way. One modern variant sees a philosopher simply as an intellectual worker in a certain domain; an ancient variant sees a commitment to a certain way of life as definitive.

[9] This is not always honorific, as in Wittgenstein's deep ambivalence about what he calls philosophy. In what follows, it is this genre of philosophy—the logical, analytical—of which I speak.

simply a tag or pointer to its putative referent, or is the term associated with a descriptive concept like "Creator of the universe"? And so for the other names of God.[10],[11]

- One might also expect to hear from the theory of knowledge. Is it possible, for example, to *know* that there is a God? Are there proofs? If not, what makes "God exists" acceptable, intellectually respectable? And even if this can be handled, how does one establish the superiority of one religion over another? Another arena of epistemological inquiry concerns eschatology. What can we know, and how can we know, about the afterlife, about messianic times, and the like?

- Then there are notorious theological puzzles, the problem of evil for example: Given God's perfections, specifically his goodness, knowledge, and power, how can there be any evil at all in the world, not to speak of the unspeakable horrors visited upon so many whether righteous, religious, or not?

- Another sort of theological puzzle—although not often formulated as a puzzle—is the matter of how we manage to speak of God. The philosophical tradition beginning with the medievals has taken such talk to be problematic. For Maimonides, for example, one cannot speak significantly of God using concepts whose primary application is to us and our world. That is, anthropomorphic vocabulary cannot signify in its usual way, with its usual meanings. So philosophy needs to address the possibility of meaningful discourse about God.

I could go on, but the general idea should be clear. The Bible steers clear of such issues. Theological matters are addressed of course, but in the manner of poetry or literary prose.

Having said a bit about the philosophical let me say something about the literary, the Bible's literary mode. In addition to large bodies

[10] My aim in this bulleted list is to engender a sense of difference between theological genres. In this first item I speak of a contemporary issue (in this case, to philosophers of language). The other items express concerns of the medievals as well.

[11] I couch the issue here in terms of the English word, 'God'. But of course it pertains in the first instance to the relevant Hebrew expressions, some of which seem more or less descriptive—e.g. *Elohim*, often translated as "God," and some of which seem quite clearly to be names, e.g. the Tetragrammaton, often (badly) transliterated as "Jahweh" and often translated as "The Lord." The situation with translation, especially of the Tetragrammaton, is delightfully confusing. The Hebrew word is a proper name but it is not intelligibly vocalized (voweled, as it were). Traditionally it's pronounced as if it were quite another word, the formal "Lord." So the situation is this: We have a real proper name, read as if it were quite another sort of word. Imagine the havoc this wreaks.

of explicit poetry—Psalms, for example, and poetic sections of other works, for example the Book of Job—the Bible abounds with imagery, poetic prose. Think of the characterization of people as reflecting God's image, a turn of phrase that eludes literal rendering.

We often speak of the biblical *narrative*, and narrative is another aspect of the Bible's literary character. The Bible's characteristic mode of "theology" is story telling, the stories overlaid with poetic language. Never does one find the sort of conceptually refined doctrinal propositions characteristic of a philosophical approach.

When the divine protagonist comes into view, we are not told much about His *properties*. Think about the divine perfections, the highly abstract *omni*-properties (omnipotence, omniscience, and the like), so dominant in medieval and post-medieval theology. One has to work very hard—too hard—to find even hints of these in the Biblical text.

Instead of properties, perfections, and the like the Bible speaks of God's *roles*—father, king, friend, lover, judge, creator, and the like.[12] Roles, as opposed to properties; this should give one pause. And even when there is mention of God's properties, they are not philosophically central *omni* properties but ethical ones, anthropomorphically characterized—slow to anger, quick to forgive, and the like.

To further emphasize the literary side of all of this—and the distance from philosophical theorizing—it's important that God's multiple roles don't cohere all that well.[12] God is, or plays the role of, parent, ruler, friend, lover, judge, and so on. This is fine in the right sort of literary context.[13] Love poetry, for example, is not diminished by sundry characterizations of one's love. Indeed highly varied depictions often facilitate literary richness, as does the inevitable imagistic language.

If the Bible's portrayal of God, His thoughts, feelings, plans, His role in history, and the like is to count as theology—and why not call it theology?—it is of a very different sort than what, under the influence of the medievals, usually goes by that name. When I suggest in the title of this paper that I am "against theology," I mean of course theology of the medieval sort.

[12]As Halbertal and Margalit emphasize in *Idolatry*.

[13]It is also theologically important. Our experience of God, and derivatively our ways of thinking about God, reflect not a consistent, single-track sort of experience but rather an experience of, as it were, someone who fills these quite different roles. There is a certain inchoate quality both to religious experience and conception.

Attention to the concept of *religious belief* may help to sharpen the distinction between theological modes. When we think about religion and religious commitment, the idea of *belief* is never far from view. It's striking, though, that *religious belief* is not a topic that gets any discussion in the Hebrew Bible. The Bible does speak of trusting in God, of fidelity to God, of fearing (or standing in awe)[14] of God, of believing *in* God (which concerns trust rather than belief in a thesis, doctrine, or proposition), of knowing God (where the Hebrew verb *la'da'at* suggests intimacy). But of belief that God exists we hear nothing.[15] Indeed, try to say of someone in Biblical Hebrew that she is or is not a "believer" in our sense.[16] It's not hard to see how the available biblical language might be stretched to this end. But we should not forget that it would be an extension of the linguistic apparatus.

Still, something like our concept of belief seems implicated in the Bible.[17] After all, the Bible puts forth various truths about God, history, the future.[18] And while it does not speak of believing these things, it certainly seems to take the putative facts for granted. Accordingly one who adheres to the Bible, one who takes it to be *his Bible*, would presumably take these things to be true, that is, to believe them.

Even if, as we would put it, material about what one ought to think (about God, history, etc.) is all over the Bible, it remains important that the Bible, with all its instructions and commandments,

[14]The Hebrew *yirah* means both fear and awe. In many of the relevant Biblical concepts, though, it would seem that awe dominates, even if the relevant sort of awe involves fear.

[15]The only exception that comes to mind is Psalm 14—The fool saith in his heart, "There is no God." Even putting aside how exceptional this language is, in context this too seems not about theoretical atheism but about those who ignore, turn their back upon, God.

[16]A. J. Heschel, in *God In Search of Man*, emphasizes that there is no natural way in Biblical Hebrew to characterize one as a believer, as opposed say to a *y're shamayim*, one who stands in awe of heaven.

[17]Perhaps it would be better to say that we can apply our concept of belief to the Bible in the way I go on to indicate.

[18]The extent of this is easy to exaggerate. For one thing, the text does not tell us which of its narratives depict historical events and which are, as it were, parables. And such things are sometimes controversial within the tradition, e.g. the story of Job, the story of the flood. Second, perhaps due to our tendency to see implicit theory in the text, there is a tendency to smooth out differences between Biblical texts. Thus the ways of thinking about God's providence in Deuteronomy and, say, in Job make claims about the Biblical view of providence quite risky. Nor in many of these cases does the Rabbinic understanding in the Talmud rescue the situation.

does not command us to have the right thoughts.[19] When God is upset with mankind—in early Genesis for example—or later, say in Exodus with the Israelites, or still later in the prophets with the people Israel, his gripe is not about their doctrinal irregularities but about how they live, about their betrayal of His trust, and the like.

Moreover, and of utmost importance for my project of distinguishing Biblical from medieval theology, there is belief and there is belief. Eloquently put by Max Kadushin in his classic work, *The Rabbinic Mind*, the Bible's theological concepts and implicit beliefs remain *uncrystallized*. That is to say they are formulated by way of literary tropes, perfectly appropriate in context, but resistant to anything like definition. Biblical theology is poetically infused, not propositionally articulated.

While the Bible's poetic character distinguishes it from much ordinary talk, its lack of strictly defined terms does not. Ordinary concepts, as Wittgenstein emphasizes, typically lack precise definition; this is one source of their great utility, their smooth and flexible functioning in actual (including intellectual) practice. One can always choose to impose strict definitions on what was a coherent (in practical terms) if theoretically ill-defined practice. But this is not, says Wittgenstein, a matter of discovering what the real definitions are; there are none. It's rather a matter of imposing a more precise set of rules on the use of the term than were present before. Needless to say, there are all sorts of considerations that might motivate us to do this, that might recommend one definition over others. Still, the new definition is new; it's not built into the original practice with the terms, even implicitly.

The analogy of boundaries may be of use here. Imagine that two parties live separated by several miles of forest and that such has been the case for many generations. Never has the question arisen of where the property of one ends and where the other's begins. In some sense there is no fact of the matter; perhaps both families descend from original settlers and the question never arose. Now a feud arises and the question is raised, where exactly is the boundary? What has happened is this: certain practical considerations have emerged that make it important that there be a boundary. And the

---

[19] Not according to the medievals. Maimonides maintains, for example, that the first of the so-called ten commandments ("commandment" is not a Biblical designation; "sayings" is closer), which appears to be a kind of introduction, a preamble, Maimonides interprets as a commandment to believe in God. Similarly the second commandment (about not putting any other gods before God) appears to be quite personal. Maimonides interprets it as command to believe in God's unity. See Chap. Xxx of the *Guide*.

choice of boundaries may not be altogether arbitrary; there may be reasons that motivate a choice or that exclude certain choices. But still, there is no pre-existent fact of the matter.

Viewed in this light, one important thrust of the medieval theological tradition—trying to find conceptually refined formulations for the Bible's literary-theological tropes—is arguably not a mission of pure discovery. Doubly so: first, the poetic character of Biblical theology renders at least problematic the quest for the "straight" theological, i.e. propositional, material lurking behind the imagery. And Wittgenstein adds another layer: never mind the poetry; ordinary vocabulary suffers from a lack of (or flourishes without) definition. Perhaps the Bible's literary theological ideas were fine as they stood and the medieval philosopher is imposing boundaries, as it were.

I will highlight the contrast between Biblical and philosophical theology by saying—a bit provocatively—that the Bible lacks theological doctrine. Of course, this depends upon what one counts as doctrine. My own predilection is to use this term for the sort of relatively clear, non-imagistic propositional articulation of theological truths (or candidates for theological truth), the sort of thing we do not find in the Bible. Here's an example: "The universe was created *ex nihilo* by a God who himself exists in a realm that is not part of the natural world."[20] As I use the term 'doctrine' then, the Bible's theological remarks are typically if not virtually always non-doctrinal, formulated in figurative—often anthropomorphic—language, for example, "people reflect God's image."

Of course, the term 'doctrine' is often used more widely than I'm suggesting, subsuming even highly imagistic theological sentences. Although I'll often use terms like 'doctrine' in my preferred manner, this really is just a matter of expressive convenience and nothing hinges upon it. If someone prefers the broader usage, I can put my points in longer winded ways.[21]

B. The Oral Tradition

The Bible's literary way with theological matters might leave one unprepared for Talmudic passages in which theological belief has become an official topic; for example, the famous passage in Tractate Sanhedrin, Chapter 10, in which the World-to-Come is denied

---

[20] Notice, even such refinement would hardly count as non-anthropomorphic. As Maimonides points out, our use of terms, even ones like "create" and "exists," have their home in talk about our world. And thus it's not clear what's going on in using them in connection to God.

[21] For more on the notion of doctrine, see my paper "Theological Impressionism" this volume.

to those who fail to accept certain theological claims.[22] Is the Talmud here going philosophical as it were, or at least taking a step towards medieval philosophical theology?

I will return below to the passage just mentioned with its emphasis on belief. But notwithstanding such occasional passages, it is clear that in general the Talmud is not going philosophical; quite the contrary. Consider anthropomorphism. That the Bible portrays God in anthropomorphic imagery is a source of (almost) embarrassment to the medieval theological mind. Maimonides in *The Guide for the Perplexed* works (arguably too) hard to show that such language goes only skin deep. But the Talmud seems to revel in anthropomorphic characterization of God.[23] One might call it hyper-anthropomorphism. I'll illustrate it in the following excursion concerning *Eichah Rabbah*, the Rabbinic *Midrash* on the Book of Lamentations. [24]

I'll turn to *Eichah Rabbah* in a moment; but first an example of Biblical (relatively tame) anthropomorphism: early in Genesis, at the time of the Flood, God is angry at our antics, even regretful that he initiated the human experiment. This is of course unabashedly anthropomorphic, but the context of early Genesis imposes limits. For the God of early Genesis is despite the anthropomorphism wholly other, the awesome and remote Creator of the universe in whose hands was its annihilation.

The contrasting Talmudic-era text that is my focus here has God at considerably less distance. It has been said that the Biblical narrative is the history of God's learning that He cannot do it alone, that His plan crucially requires partnership with His human reflections. By the time of the *Midrash* on Lamentations, and in the perception of its authors, the lesson is well learned. Not only can He not do it alone, the project is not going well. And God's reaction reveals a new level of affective engagement and self-awareness. Indeed, God has become affectively almost one of us. He suffers, weeps, He mourns. "Woe is Me!" He cries in Proem 24, "What have I done?"

Sometimes the *Midrash* sees God in maternal terms—or, more accurately, God, as the *Midrash* has it, sees Him/Herself in such terms (Proem 22):

---

[22] See Kadushin, Chapter 7 for other examples and an illuminating discussion.

[23] This is to some extent true of the prophetic literature as well. Thus what is new in Rabbinic works is a matter of degree and sustained emphasis.

[24] My discussion of *Eichah Rabbah* is adapted from my paper, "Coming to Terms with Exile" this volume. See that paper for more detail. I am indebted here as I am in that paper to Alan Mintz's *Hurban: Responses to Catastrophe in Hebrew Literature*, (Syracuse, N.Y., 1996).

"Just as when you take away its young a sparrow is left solitary," so spake the Holy One, blessed be He, "I burnt my house, destroyed My city, exiled My children among the nations of the world, and I sit solitary."

Sometimes the imagery is paternal: God is compared with a king who, enraged at his two sons (perhaps symbolically, the people Israel just before the destruction of each of the two Temples), thrashes them and drives them away. The king afterward exclaims, "The fault is with me, since I must have brought them up badly" (Proem 2). In Proem 24 God laments:

> Woe to the King who succeeds in His youth and fails in His old age.
> . . . .
>
> The Holy one, blessed be He, said to Jeremiah, "I am now like a man who had an only son, for whom he prepared a marriage canopy, but he dies under it. Feelest thou no anguish for Me and My children? Go summon Abraham, Isaac, and Jacob, and Moses from their sepulchres, for they know how to weep."

Not only does God mourn. He, it would seem, needs instruction in mourning from us.[25]

One aspect of this humanizing of the divine, interestingly parallel to (roughly simultaneous) Christian developments,[26] is a new emphasis on divine vulnerability. God is, as it were, exposed to the elements to a degree scarcely predictable by what we knew of Him.

Closely related is what we might call divine approachability and emotional responsiveness. God, in Genesis, is available to the patriarchs, and to some extent to the matriarchs. The *Midrash* on Lamentations (in the continuation of Proem 24) imagines the three patriarchs—Abraham, Isaac, and Jacob—and Moses pleading with God for mercy towards Israel. God, however, is unaffected; he cannot or will not comply. Eventually, he does promise to restore Israel to its place, but the promise is made not to the patriarchs or Moses. It is only mother Rachel who can move Him. Rachel tells God that she knew of her father's plan concerning the marriage to Jacob, his plan to substitute Leah for her. Rachel attempted to foil the plan, but when that failed

> I relented, suppressed my desire, and had pity upon my sister that she should not be exposed to shame . . . I delivered over to my sister all the signs which I had arranged with Jacob so that he should think

---

[25] As Mintz emphasizes. See p. 60.

[26] Of course, in the Christian context new meaning is given to what I'm calling the humanizing of the divine.

that she was Rachel. More than that, I went beneath the bed upon which he lay with my sister; and when he spoke to her she remained silent and I made all the replies in order that he should not recognize my sister's voice. I did her a kindness, was not jealous of her, and did not expose her to shame. And if I, a creature of flesh and blood, formed of dust and ashes, was not envious of my rival and did not expose her to shame and contempt, why should You, a King who lives eternally and is merciful, be jealous of idolatry in which there is not reality, and exile my children and let them be slain by the sword . . .

Forthwith, the mercy of the Holy One, blessed be He, was stirred, and He said, "For your sake, Rachel, I will restore Israel to its place."

It is interesting that Rachel does not argue, as did Abraham in Genesis 18:23-33, on the grounds of what divine justice requires. Nor does she appeal on the basis of her own merit, as do (earlier in Proem 24) the patriarchs, Abraham, Isaac, and Jacob. Hers is a more personal appeal, predicated on issues of character, God's character.

These developments are underscored and pushed to still another level with the Talmudic idea that after the Second Temple's destruction, God Himself leads only an exilic existence; that the divine presence resides, as it were, in *galut*. This is no doubt in part a matter of empathy. To say that God's presence is in *galut* is to say that He is with us, He feels for us. But it is equally an expression of divine dislocation and a constricted existence. Here we approach discontinuity with what we know of God from the Bible, certainly from the Pentateuch, a kind of anthropomorphic quantum leap.[27]

I've been focused on the Rabbinic response to Lamentations in *Midrash Rabbah*. But Rabbinic hyper-anthropomorphism is by no means limited to contexts of mourning. The Talmud speaks in various places about God hurting when we hurt, about God praying that His attribute of mercy/nurture overcomes his demand for strict justice. It speaks of God's wearing *t'fillin* when He prays. The point, I hope, is made. Talmudic theologizing is hardly an intermediate phase, *en route*, as it were, to medieval philosophical theology.

Hyper-anthropomorphism dramatizes the literary character of Talmudic theology. But here's another way to see what I have in

[27]One might argue that there is no quantum leap here, but that the powerful imagery of divine exile is a mere rhetorically supercharged variation on what we have already seen, God in a state of mourning, weeping bitterly, feeling lost, even at times hopeless. But one has the sense that this is not simply a matter of divine affect; something more "objective" is at stake here. God's project for humanity, His partnership with Israel for *tikkun olam*, the repair and redemption of the world, has been thwarted. The universe is thus dislocated, thrown off course. Israel's political, social, and national catastrophe is thus transformed into a metaphysical cataclysm, a real cosmic jolt. The universe is shaken to its foundations.

mind. The Talmud is renowned for its highly analytical legal (*halakhic*) discussions. But interspersed are passages a very different genre, *aggada*, a literary treatment of theological and ethical issues, narratives, parables, and the like. The almost seamless movement between these radically different styles presumably reflects the *Talmud's* recording of free-flowing discussions in the academies.

The shift from *halakha* to *aggada* can seem stark, from the most acute analysis to the most powerful religious imagery. It can also be bewildering: How can it be the the sages do not use their highly developed conceptual acumen to analytically dissect the *aggada?* Why are these lovers of definition and distinction not tempted to inquire about what lies behind all the impressionistic imagery? Who exactly is the Protagonist? What are his properties? Instead of raising these and other fundamental questions, they tell more stories.

This—and here is my suggestion—makes sense on the following assumption: perhaps there is something particularly appropriate or natural about what I'm calling the literary mode in theological—as opposed to legal—discourse. Perhaps the apparently good questions that are so natural to the philosophical bent of mind are, or anyway seemed to the Rabbis, less appropriate, even irrelevant.

Why should that be so? My suggestion for the present—a more complete discussion is the burden of the book to which this paper is an introduction—is as follows. The Rabbis see themselves as articulating a way of life. What I am calling their literary theology is provides a situating environment for the *mitzvot*. The *aggadic* material specifically provides the edification, comfort, and meaning that together with the practices constitute the religious life. Their aims are thus dramatically different than those of later theologians. The questions and modes of approaching those questions that are natural to the philosopher are not theirs.

I now return to the topic with which I began this section—a possible problem for my conception—the occasional Talmudic emphasis on belief. My picture is as follows: The Bible provides narratives like the splitting of the Red Sea, the revelation on Mt. Sinai, even suggestions about the eschatological future (later in the prophets). The Rabbis remind us of these things, occasionally even add to them, and insist that they be believed. Still, this leaves intact the uncrystallized character of the theological concepts. The imagery, the poetically infused narratives, and the like, remain philosophically undeveloped. A philosopher would find them puzzling; and the puzzles remain unaddressed in the Talmud. So while the Rabbis not only endorse Biblical theology and produce some new theological ideas and emphases and indeed explicitly require certain beliefs, this is not to make the Rabbis into philosophers or anything of the like. Their way in theology remains literary and contrasts dramatically with the later philosophical approach.

Still, we should not suppose that Rabbinic culture was hermetically sealed against the influence of Greece. Perhaps the attention to belief—albeit philosophically undeveloped belief—does represent some philosophical influence. But there is, I'm inclined to think, another and at least in some times and places a more powerful causal factor. I mean the phenomenon of heresy, or rather the social and political conditions that prompt the identification of heresies.[28]

The idea is that when religious authority or the religious identity of the community is internally or externally threatened, one sort of defensive reaction is to draw boundaries; to say, "this is what it takes to be one of us." And so it becomes important to say what otherwise might have remained unsaid. The heresy, after all, might consist in a strange reading of the theological imagery or narrative.

In an era of political, social, and religious tranquility, the need for doctrinal articulation may not be felt. The images, stories, and the rest do their work of supplementing and enriching religious practice; one is not pressed to sharpen up the ideas, to articulate further the conditions of membership. Even radical, unorthodox, interpretations of the narrative or of the commandments may be tolerated. Alternatively, such outré interpretations may be strongly criticized without the suggestion that their propounders are somehow outside the fold.

But in troubled times, things are different. In the middle ages, for example, the exiled Jews are a minority, living in communities that threaten them sometimes physically, sometimes culturally, and certainly theologically. This should issue in the prediction, or postdiction, that more or less sharp lines will be drawn. Who is in and who is out will be important questions.[29] Similarly in earlier, Talmudic times, we see at least the seed of doctrine and the beginnings of the emphasis on belief. For the Rabbis are worried about the Sadducees, the Karaites, the emerging Christians and so on. This tendency remains restrained for the Rabbis; they are worried about Greek culture and its philosophy, and so we don't see movement towards philosophically refined doctrinal explication. The medievals, by contrast, live in a

---

[28] Too late for inclusion in my discussion here, I have come across Daniel Boyarin's *Border Lines*, an extremely valuable discussion of the role of heresy and related matters.

[29] At the same time, even in medieval times (but arguably less so in our own) one finds the phenomenon of radical critique of unorthodox ideas without hint of personal exclusion. See for example, Nachmanides's commentary on Genesis 18:20 where he roundly criticizes Abraham Ibn Ezra for the latter's idea that God knows only the world in general terms, a radical idea then as now.

time and culture in which philosophical theology is the reigning intellectual norm.

The competing religious orientations of medieval times, I'm suggesting, is a factor in the period's doctrinal orgy.[30] Needless to say, this is only part of the story. Clearly the work of the medieval giants is not driven by the need to exclude heretics; philosophical ideas have their own power; nevertheless the times have their influence.[31]

What I am suggesting militates towards reversing the usual understanding that exclusion of heretics is grounded in their denial of previously well-known and well-articulated doctrine. A related thought concerning Judaism in our times is this: the Reform movement, in posing what was perceived as a grave threat to the tradition, prompts Orthodoxy, a new movement of those committed to the traditional ways, to a renewed and intense focus on theological doctrine and the sharpening of theological boundaries.[32]

---

[30] See T. M. Rudavsky, "The Impact of Scholasticism upon Jewish Philosophy in the Fourteenth and Fifteenth Centuries," in *The Cambridge Companion to Medieval Jewish Philosophy*, ed. D. H. Frank and O. Leaman (Cambridge, 2003), p. 347:

> The subject of dogma and belief is revisited with even greater urgency in the fifteenth century. In large part this is due to the intense Christian persecutions experienced by Iberian Jews between 1391 and 1418. Jewish intellectual leaders were drawn into the debate not only to define who is a Jew, and who merits immortality, but also to articulate the doctrinal content of Judaism in contradistinction to Christianity. Jews were forced to respond to a Christian challenge rooted in creedal concerns, thus bringing to the fore questions concerning the nature of belief.

[31] As Pierre Keller suggested, the importance of excluding heresy may be a factor in the centrality of doctrine in early Christianity.

[32] Having completed my discussion of literary theology, I can now say more about my differences with Kellner's *Must a Jew Believe Anything?* Kellner appears to go farther than I do in denying Rabbinic theological belief. Along the lines suggested by one of Kellner's critics, David Berger, I'm not at all sure that the theological sounding passage in the Mishnah in *Sanhedrin* 10:1 does not mean what it says about denying the world to come to certain heretics. (Which is not to say that I find it appealing to make God into, as it were, a one-issue candidate. But the interpretation of the Mishnah is another matter.) Moreover, as I argue above, while it's surely significant that required beliefs are never spoken of in the Bible and barely spoken of in Talmudic-era literature (*Sanhedrin* 10 is an exception), still it's clear that there are things one is supposed to think. At the same time, I argue that these key "beliefs" are in Kadushin's word uncrystallized. It is not only that they are not articulated in a philosophically adequate way by the Rabbis; they are likely not articulable in such terms, at least not without imposition. Accordingly, Rabbinic "dogmas" can be required and yet still fail to count as philosophical doctrine. Kellner asks in the "Afterward" to the new edition of his book, "Had the authors of the Mishnah really held [that the Torah is "from heaven"—*Sanhedrin 10-1*] to be a dogma of Judaism, does it not seem odd that not one of them, or their amoraic successors, or the *ge'onim* who followed them took the trouble the define the term ["heaven"] with any specificity." It is just this question that I have tried to resolve here. Beliefs they had, but they were not philosophers and never saw those beliefs as standing in need of the sort of conceptual clarification characteristic of philosophy.

II. Philosophical Theology

The literary style of theology—naïve from the vantage point of later philosophy—makes immediate contact with religious life. The narratives, parables, and the like provide the edification, comfort, and meaning that together with religious practice constitute the hallmark of that life. When one turns to the philosophical writings of *the* medieval Jewish philosopher—a philosopher's philosopher I will suggest—Maimonides,[33] one finds a very different and esoteric style of theology, one that is suggestive of a dramatically different religious sensibility.[34] In thinking one's way from one theological style to the other and from one religious sensibility to the other, one finds oneself engaged in a virtual gestalt switch.

Not that such is the common perception. If the contrast is as dramatic as I suggest, how is this missed? First, Maimonides's ideas are developed differently—in some aspects dramatically so—in his philosophical and halakhic texts.[35] It becomes tempting to harmonize the radical philosophic ideas with the more traditional characterizations of practice, a temptation that has a long history. And who is to say exactly how to balance these elements? What is clear is that that over time, certainly in the communal perception of the overall picture, the more radical elements have been reined in. This seems at least in part a function of the fact that the (largely) legal (*Mishnah Torah*) characterizations are exceptionally lucid, written in

---

[33]Maimonides's views are in some ways typical of Jewish medieval theology, in other ways not so. Some of the philosophic ideas and tendencies already mentioned as characteristic of medieval theology are Maimonidean, some not so. Nevertheless, for good reason he is often seen as the central player in medieval Jewish philosophy.

[34]I am grateful here to a remark by David Hartman to the effect that Maimonides's approach reflects a different "religious sensibility" than that of the *Midrash*. I think that the concept of religious sensibility—incorporating both cognitive and affective dimensions—is an important one for further reflection. It is (importantly) not the same idea as religious philosophy or anything of the like.

[35]Josef Stern in conversation pointed out that that this distinction between the philosophic and legal works is hardly an absolute one; there are, for example, important philosophic developments in *Mishnah Torah*. No doubt this is correct. Indeed high-level theoretical legal texts often have implications for, and sometimes explicit discussions of, pertinent philosophic issues; all the more so if the legal thinker lives, as it were, in philosophic issues. Similarly for halakhically relevant remarks in the *Guide*. Nevertheless, in some plain sense one is a philosophic work, the other a legal one. And as I say, there are significant ideas that get very different developments in the two works.

Stern prefers another way of distinguishing the two texts, a way that I find helpful but not inconsistent with what I just said. The *Mishnah Torah*, he says, aims at articulating a way of life for the community; the *Guide*, on the other hand, is written for the exceptional individual, a manual to supplement the *Mishnah Torah*'s instructions and to give new and different perspective on the religious life.

a beautiful, plain Hebrew, while the *Guide,* originally in Arabic, is relatively tortured stylistically. Indeed, perhaps the radical philosophic material was meant to be so reined in. Certainly, as Maimonides notes, it was never meant to be publicized to the community.

In what follows I will highlight aspects of Maimonides's philosophic thought that are particularly relevant to the distinction in styles of theology in which I'm interested. Even if in the end one rejects my thesis of ancient to medieval paradigm change, the exercise of seeing these in gestalt terms may be useful; this since we are so accustomed to the assimilation of the older and medieval views.

Sound bites are for politicians, not philosophers. Yet occasionally there is a turn of phrase that encapsulates something crucial about a philosophic outlook, Descartes dictum, for example, that the mind is better known than the body. Consider in this light Maimonides's idea that the intellect constitutes the bridge between man and God.

To give intellect such pride of place seems striking—even astounding—in the context of Jewish religious life. More consonant with that life is the recognition that in trying to understand God we are, to put it lightly, out of our depth. The Bible suggestively relates that Moses, God's intimate, was allowed to see only God's back.[36] Jewish religious life proceeds in the absence of theoretically adequate theological ideas.

Not that Maimonides, in the end, allows us much in the way of conceptual contact. Indeed, on his view our thinking about God has (more than) severe limitations. First, since God's unity does not allow even for the possession of properties—this quite a difficult idea—our attribution to Him of *any* property must be mistaken. Indeed, God's essence, a property-less unity, is unknowable.[37]

Second, even were we to admit property talk about God, the property terms that we use in connection with God—goodness, unity, power, even existence—cannot mean anything like what they usually mean in the human/this-worldly context. Consider ascriptions of goodness to God. Maimonides insists that if one were careful in one's talk about God, one would not say or wish to say that God is good in something like our sense, just much better than we are or could be. That's not it at all. Such a conception of goodness is much too derivative from our own application of ethical vocabulary to people. God

---

[36] *Exodus* 33:23.

[37] These ideas are very difficult given our (probably Aristotle-inspired) intuitive thinking about property-possession. But in the Neo-Platonic tradition—one of the important influences in medieval theological thought—it's commonplace to suppose that unity of The One defies any division, even intellectual division.

and His goodness are altogether other. Indeed, in connection to God we don't get so far as to attach (positive) concepts to our property terms. But this seems to leave talk of God's goodness without cognitive content.

Not quite. There is a kind of content, but not the usual kind. I allude here to Maimonides's famous doctrine of negative attribution. The intuitive idea is that there may be circumstances in which we don't know much about a thing, but in which we can circumscribe the thing by saying what it is not. To use property terms in connection to God, according to Maimonides, can at most be to circumscribe God's nature in that way, by saying what He is not.

It is often supposed, at least in more or less popular discussions, that the *via negativa* restores some measure of cognitive content to talk of God's properties. I'm not sure that this is even Maimonides's view; I'm not sure that it isn't. In any case, the content of discourse about God remains extremely thin. Indeed given how meager it is, it becomes very difficult to wrap one's mind around Maimonides's idea that the intellect constitutes the human-divine meeting ground. If intellect is indeed the meeting ground what sort of religious life might this support?

Let's reconsider the intellect-as-meeting-ground idea. Perhaps I have been too fixed on intellect as a faculty for the intellectual apprehension of God. An alternative is suggested by the famous remark of Einstein—no doubt reflecting the spirit of Spinoza as well as Maimonides—that his interest was in sharing God's thoughts, all the rest being mere commentary. On Maimonides's view the student of physics has special access to God's thoughts about the natural world.

Metaphysics, moreover, is for Maimonides the only tool for thinking effectively about God and God's nature, at least negatively. One can, for example, see that there is no other route to God than intellect, and that all thought about God is (at best) negative. Does this really constitute a bridge to the divine? While it is more like a bridge that ends in mid-air, Maimonides presumably would be quick to add that it takes one as close as one can get to unknowable divine. And as with physics, but concerning the subject matter of God himself, the student of metaphysics shares God's thoughts.

Perhaps, to supplement these last reflections, we ought to focus not on the product, the result, of theological inquiry so much as the process. In Book 3, Section 51 of the *Guide*,[38] Maimonides waxes poetic about "the intellectual worship of God." He writes, almost in the exhortative style of a work of *mussar*,

[38] Translation is from the Pines Edition, University of Chicago Press, 1963.

When you are alone by yourself, when you are awake on your couch, be careful to meditate in such precious moments on nothing but the intellectual worship of God, viz. to approach Him and to minister before Him in the true manner which I have described to you—not in hollow emotions. This I consider as the highest perfection wise men can attain . . .

One is reminded here of the tradition's way of seeing deep involvement in Talmudic study as edifying, almost cleansing. One engages in such study not only, not even mostly, for practical knowledge of *halakha*. Indeed, such practical knowledge requires a very different kind of study.[39] Rather the process itself, albeit a sort of heady, unemotional business, constitutes a refined form of religious worship. With some irony Maimonides, Talmudic giant *per excellence*, elevates philosophic inquiry above Talmudic inquiry.[40] The philosopher on his couch approaches as close to God as is humanly possible and ministers to Him in the true manner, with his mind and not with what Maimonides calls hollow emotions.[41],[42]

Another corollary of the Maimonidean elevation of intellect is the role given to philosophy. Just imagine announcing in one of the *amoraic* academies—or indeed nowadays in a *yeshiva*—that philosophy is the *sine qua non* for understanding the Bible. Yet this is Maimonides's thesis. Only philosophy equips us to know which of the

---

[39] Although unquestionably, study of the theoretical underpinnings can enhance practice and add dimensions of meaning.

[40] At the beginning of Book 3, Chapter 51, Maimonides presents a highly suggestive parable of the palace in which various categories of people are thought of as occupying various stages of proximity to the Ruler in his palace. Talmudists are thought of as having "come up to the habitation and walked around it," but having never even entered the antechamber, the latter requiring that one explore the fundamental principles of religion. Sarah Pessin suggested to me that for Maimonides the philosopher's study *becomes*—replaces—the traditional study hall, the *beit ha'midrash*, as the primary locus of the intellectual worship of God.

[41] However especially in *Mishah Torah* he sometimes speaks in a very different religious voice. In *Mishnah Torah*, "Hilchot T'shuvah," Chapter 10, he sings the praises of a passionate, boundless love of God, one he compares to a man's lovesickness for a woman—the latter being apparently less passionate in his view than what one might feel for God. It is striking that Maimonides takes as a kind of model for our love of God such passionate, first-moments-of-love episodes, rather than the sustained love of a long-term relationship. If one is thinking about the love between God and Israel—their extended relationship--one would presumably emphasize the latter. It's also worth noting Maimonides's individualistic emphasis in his Chapter 10 discussion of love, a topic to which I return below.

[42] I've been struggling with Maimonides's conception of the intellect as meeting ground. Additional to the considerations I mentioned, his view may reflect his very different philosophical framework from our own, specifically Aristotelian ideas about Active Intellect and the like, material beyond the scope of this paper.

things the Bible says about God are literally true, which are metaphorical, and the like. It is only on the basis of philosophy that we
know that, for example, the Bible's talk of God's right arm must be
figurative. We know this because divine corporeality is incompatible with established philosophic truth.

The demonstrations of philosophy are, moreover, final; they
need no sanction from religion. Indeed, if—contrary to fact according to Maimonides—the Aristotelian attempts succeeded in demon-
strating the eternity of the world, we would be forced to read the
Genesis creation story in a figurative way.[43]

Maimonides position that philosophy is essential to the proper
reading of the Bible and in effect the final arbiter of the facts is quite
extreme even among medieval philosophers. He is, one might say, a
philosopher's philosopher. But this makes him a perfect example for
my purposes, perfect in representing the philosophical tendency in a
particularly pure form.

The idea that the intellectual realm is the meeting place of man
and God has not become commonplace, the accepted wisdom. But
along with that idea came something that did become commonplace,
something that seems to us to go without saying: the centrality of belief
and doctrine.[44] We speak of religious people as believers; of irreligious
as non-believers.[45] And this despite the oddness of this characterization
given the way the Bible and the Rabbis address the religious stance.

[43] The implications of this are radical. I spoke above about the fact that there are
beliefs that are crucial to the tradition, even if in Kadushin's expression they remain
uncrystallized. Maimonides's remark about the failed Aristotelian attempt to demonstrate eternity of matter in effect tells us that if one of these *prima facie* crucial
religious beliefs conflicts with the dictates of the highest standards of human
knowledge—philosophy, science, etc.—then one should reinterpret the traditional
idea. Maimonides here anticipates a not uncommon liberal religious idea from that
there cannot be a conflict between science/philosophy and religion for the former is
authoritative in the realm of the factual.

[44] Strictly speaking, Maimonides in the *Guide* is concerned with knowledge of
God rather than belief. Not only that but he in effect denies that we can have knowledge of God. Still, it is the elevation of the epistemic dimension by him and other
medieval philosophers that is responsible for the tendency in question.

[45] This tendency to put belief at the center is restrained in the context of Judaism, as
opposed say to certain strains in Christianity, by the tremendous role of practice. It's
difficult to even imagine one who wholeheartedly believes but does not at least mini-
mally observe the practices. Nevertheless, the idiom of "believer" is one that has caught
on, and this testifies to the centrality of belief. If one claims to be Orthodox but does not
adhere to the Maimonidean thirteen principles of faith, one's claim will in many, most,
circles be thought to be tenuous at best. But see Marc B. Shapiro, *The Limits of Orthodox
Theology: Maimonides Thirteen Principles Reappraised* (Littman Library of Jewish Civilization, 2003), for a scholarly argument that these principles are, every one of them,
controversial from a traditional point of view, that is, in traditional Jewish sources.

The Maimonidean elevation of belief to a pivotal position is occasionally evident even in the *halakhic* realm. Consider religious conversion. When one wants to convert to Judaism, one is told what he is, as it were, getting into. Maimonides's elaboration gives pride of place in the conversion process to articulating for the convert the "fundamentals of the faith, i.e. the unity of God. . . ."[46] The Talmudic discussion mentions no such thing![47] For the Rabbis of the Talmud it was a matter of the person's sincere commitment to the Jewish people and the difficult life of Jewish religious observance.

Let's turn to the implications for religious practice. When Maimonides reflects (still in Book 3, Chapter 51) on the point of religious ritual, he gives it relatively short shrift. One of its central purposes is to separate people from the everyday worldly encounters that divert a person from deep thought about God. The practices—his examples are reading the *Torah*, prayer, performing the other commandments—constitute training to be involved with God's commandments rather than with, say, your checkbook, this towards the ultimate end of freedom from worldly things so important for philosophic contemplation. And it's the latter that constitutes the real religious encounter. Prayer then—like the other practices—is of instrumental value, not the religious moment, as it were.

It would be one thing to complain that much of ordinary religious practice is insufficiently focused, and Maimonides also comments upon that in Chapter 51. But our limited success aside, prayer, for us and the Rabbis of the Talmud, is all about communication with God. This is no stretching exercise, as it were, in the service of detached philosophic contemplation. It is an important religious moment, one of the central ones. And when it works, when we are able to focus, to succeed in overcoming distraction, prayer can represent a religious intimacy that stands at great distance from detached contemplation.[48] Not that there is only one way that prayer works, or indeed one sort of religious moment. Perhaps there are times that prayer succeeds just because one is contemplative, even

[46] In *Mishnah Torah, Hilchot Issurei Bi'ah*, Chapter 14, tr. Rabbi Eilyahu Touger, Moznaim Publishing Company, New York, 2002.

[47] *Babylonian Talmud, Tractate Yevamot* 47a.

[48] There are Talmudic stories of Rabbi Akiva's praying, beginning the *amidah*—a standing prayer during which one does not move one's feet—in one location and somehow ending up across the room. Or think of our sometimes profound sense of God's presence at the end of the *N'eilah* prayer at the end of a 25 hour fast on *Yom Kippur*.

One thing that makes all of this quite confusing is the thought that surely Maimonides not only knew stories like that of Rabbi Akiva, but he must have, one supposes, himself known the intimacy of prayer.

detached. Nevertheless, all of this remains a far cry from the religious sensibility of Chapter 51.

Another thing that's striking about this side of Maimonides's thought is its stark individualism. The Maimonidean philosophic/religious moment is a solitary one. Of course there are genuinely solitary religious experiences. But it seems hasty to suppose, in the context of Jewish religious life, that the essential moment is either solitary or communal. Surely there is a place for each. Think about the encounter at Sinai, which has aspects of both the individual and the communal. And in the *amidah*, the heart of every prayer service, one speaks in the midst of a sometimes very personal encounter not of "I," but of "we."

Let me turn to the conception of the religious giant,[49] of religious greatness. When we think of people who exhibit such greatness, they may or may not be philosophers. They are typically Talmudic masters whose intellectual mastery is integrated with, and perhaps partly responsible for a kind of heightened ethical and spiritual sense. To put it as Heschel might have, such a person lives with one eye on God, in a kind of intimacy with God. While awe and love towards God are for us sometime affairs, the *gadol* lives in God's presence.

Maimonides, again by stark contrast, sees religious greatness in terms of philosophic profundity. I don't mean that he would grant such greatness to a philosophically profound scoundrel, if on his view this were possible. But there cannot be religious greatness—dwelling with the King in the inner courtyard—in the absence of philosophic profundity. The prophets, according to Maimonides, were philosophers, from Abraham on.

III. Conclusion

Since medieval times—and this is a tribute to the power of medieval theological philosophy—it has seemed natural to suppose that religion and philosophy are natural bedfellows. Indeed, the word "theology"—not unlike "doctrine"—rings with the marriage of religion and philosophy. Still, "theology," as I've noted, can have a more neutral resonance, as it does when we consider pre-medieval Jewish theological reflection.

---

[49]The word "giant" seems not quite apt here. But it translates a wonderful expression in Hebrew. We speak of a *gadol*, of a *gadol b'dor*—a giant (or great person), a giant (great person) of a particular generation. One could use the word "leader," but even if a giant is almost necessarily a leader, the term *gadol* means "giant," not leader.

My larger project is to shift focus back to the literary expression of theological themes. Indeed the arts more generally deserve attention here, as a glance at the history of western religion suggests. The role of music, for example, in the ancient Temple service, or in the Christian liturgical tradition. Or in the liturgical practice of certain sects of Hasidism, as well as in much contemporary synagogue practice that derives from Hasidism. Or the role of art in Christianity. Or the role of dance and bodily movement in certain traditional rituals (prostration, for example) or again in Hasidic dance.

But medieval philosophical theology is formidable. And this is so even where the philosophical approach has failed to win the hearts and minds of religious practitioners. In the context of contemporary traditional Jewish religious life, other approaches dominate: various strains and forms of mysticism—*kabbalah*, including the powerful *Chassidic* tradition—as well as *mussar*, a 19th century ethical revival. These have considerably more influence on actual religious life and thought than medieval inspired Jewish philosophy. And yet the power of the latter somehow remains.

Example: *anthropomorphism*. Notwithstanding the inestimable power of anthropomorphic ways of thinking of God in actual religious life—as loving, caring, and so on—still one constantly hears the comment that of course as Maimonides taught, such anthropomorphic characterizations are literally incorrect.[50] Second example: *God's perfections*. Ask almost anyone—theist, agnostic, or atheist—about her concept of God and typically you will receive the same (medieval-inspired) answer: God as a constellation of perfections, omnipotent, omniscient, perfectly good, etc.

These examples of the power of medieval theological thought are striking in part because neither one is in any obvious way true of the tradition in its pre-medieval incarnation. To begin with anthropomorphism, one does find among the Rabbis considerable discomfort with anthropomorphism. But as Kadushin points out this is not the

---

[50]When we characterize God in terms of such imagery, so the comment will often continue, we adopt the Torah's practice of "speaking in the common language," *lashon b'nei adam* (literally, the language or vocabulary of people, "human talk," as it were). This is a medieval analog to Bishop Berkeley's remark (on another topic) that the philosopher should speak with the vulgar, but think with the learned. The thought that in all these contexts the Bible and the Rabbis are speaking "with the vulgar" is itself a medieval idea, as Halbertal and Margalit point out in Chapter 2, "Idolatry and Representation" of *Idolatry*. While we do find in the Talmud the idea that the Torah "speaks in the common language, *lashon b'nei adam*," the Talmudic context is, as Halbertal and Margalit emphasize, very different and has nothing to do with anthropomorphism.

medieval philosophers' theoretical discomfort with the very idea of anthropomorphic characterization of God. The Rabbis' hesitation has, one might say, religious rather than philosophical/theoretical motivation. God, in the rabbinic experience and imagination, is both like us (thus anthropomorphic talk) and wholly other. One has two sorts of intuitions and is not prepared to deny either, on pain of falsifying the experience. The problem for the Rabbis is that anthropomorphic talk, crucial as it is, brings us to the edge of presumption, of reducing God to our terms. And this is something about which the Rabbis are especially sensitive. A second and related reason for Rabbinic anxiety about such talk concerns the religious intuition that when we speak of God we are in deep water, over our heads. In some quite strong sense, we don't know what we are talking about. Anthropomorphic talk, true as it is to our experience, threatens on this front as well.

The second example I gave of the power of medieval thought, the persistence of the idea that God is a constellation of perfections, requires much more discussion than I can give it here. Certainly the perfections picture, even if it awaits medieval times to become the received view, has early antecedents. Still, it is very striking how much of Bible is, in its plain meaning, at odds with the perfections picture. There are countless Biblical texts, passages in which God fails to know something, in which he changes his mind, regrets what he has done, suffers from rage, frustration, and the like. Think of the Garden of Eden and God's question to Adam, "Where are you?" Or God's taking moral instruction from Abraham in Chapter 17 of Genesis. Of course, we know how to read those passages to preserve the medieval perfections picture; we have indeed learned our lessons quite well. But the plain meaning of the Biblical text is so often otherwise.

Not that the Bible always talks in ways that are at odds with the perfections picture: the Bible sings God's praises as, for example, flawless. But this is poetry, a profound expression of love, awe, gratitude, and the like, hardly a theoretical pronouncement. No more than in love poetry in which the poet declares that his lover is flawless. Clearly, according to the Biblical text God is amazingly—supremely if you like—powerful, similarly outstanding in His knowledge, character, and the rest. But this is hardly to endorse the philosophers' conception of absolute perfection. To be supreme in power is not necessarily to be theoretically unlimited in power; similarly for knowledge, character and the rest.

I have emphasized the lingering power of medieval philosophical theology. Indeed one sees its influence not only in popular religious thinking, but even in *Hasidism* and *mussar* that can hardly be accused of rationalism. We are dealing here, or so I want to suggest, with a phenomenon highlighted by Alasdair MacIntyre in his seminal work, *After Virtue*. MacIntyre advances his idea in connection with ethics but I believe it to have widespread application. Our ethical thinking, he points out, is influenced by the diverse ethical approaches of our ancestors, representing many different epochs and cultures. Greek philosophy and the culture from which it emerged emphasized the social dimension of the ethical life and the virtues. A very different and more individualistic direction was pursued by Kant, who gave less play to character and virtue and more to the individual's moral duty. Later utilitarianism emphasized not the intrinsically obligatory character of an act, a la Kant, but the desirability of its consequences. And so on. Our own ethical thought, maintains MacIntyre, is often is a kind of admixture of considerations, each having its home in some one of these approaches. An important consequence is that our thinking shows signs of incoherence bred of its sundry antecedents.

MacIntyre's remarks are suggestive with regard to many areas of philosophy, indeed many arenas of reflective life.[51] In the present context the idea is that medieval Jewish philosophy figures as a key ingredient—admixed with others—in a not necessarily coherent overall approach. Observe our religious lives, the things we find religiously moving, comforting, and the like, the sorts of things we turn to in dark or happy times, and one finds the religious world of the Bible, *midrash, aggadah*. The God that is, as it were, relevant is the anthropomorphic God who feels for us, who is with us in troubled and wonderful times, with whom we share our sorrows and joys and wishes. But then ask us about our conception of God and one hears the echoes of medieval philosophy.

Perhaps it will seem as if my aim in this paper has been anti-philosophical, a plea for a return to pre-philosophical theological innocence. Compare: Wittgenstein himself is often accused of being anti-philosophical. But Wittgenstein, in his critique of philosophical theorizing, evinces great respect for the illumination that philosophic reflection can provide. The problem is that philosophy is just so hard to get right; in an all-too-human way philosophers fall into characteristic traps.[52] They tend, for example, to recreate the subject

---

[51]In my book *The Magic Prism*, I saw the MacIntyre phenomenon at work in philosophers' treatments of Frege's famous puzzle concerning the informativeness of identity statements.

[52]I hear Larry Wright's voice here.

matter under scrutiny in their own image, to over-intellectualize the object of study. "Don't think; look" is one of Wittgenstein's characteristic exhortations. Don't think about what our practices must be like if they are to make sense (by one's philosophical lights). Instead observe; for it is actual practice that is our intellectual quarry. And this is so whether one is exploring the character of linguistic practice, or the character of religious practice and religious life.

My gripe has not been that philosophers have subjected Jewish religious life—its practices and the integrated structure of meanings—to philosophic scrutiny. Perhaps one could lodge such a complaint. One could begin as I did with the dramatic differences between Israelite and Athenian cultures. My own complaint was different. It concerned a certain indelicacy in thinking about one culture from the point of view of the other, an indelicacy that issued in a denial of the relevant differences. Maimonides's view that the prophets and even the Patriarchs were philosophers is more than a perfect example.

It would be one thing to self-consciously explore/explicate the "uncrystallized" theological ideas that are so integral to Jewish religious life, bringing to bear one's favored philosophical outlook. One could appeal to aid from the neo-Kantians, or Wittgenstein, or Levinas, or for that matter Aristotle. One would then need to face a crucial question: how much and in what ways one's favored way of thinking maps on to that of the Rabbis. It's quite another to claim, as is the thrust of much medieval philosophical theology, that Biblical and Rabbinic theological ideas are captured, virtually without remainder, by some favored philosophical explication. If one sympathetic to the medieval project were to forego this latter claim, there would remain the other problem to which I've directed attention: the Maimonidean philosophical theology substantially alters the religious sensibility of Biblical/Rabbinic tradition.

Here I am of two minds. On one side is the methodological idea that philosophy would do better to give up its imperialism. On my preferred picture it is the tradition itself and not philosophic criticism that dictates the character of religious life, of the religious moment. To substantially alter the traditional religious sensibility is to thus violate what might well be considered to be a condition of adequacy for a non-imperialistic philosophic account.

On the other side is the thought that drawing lines between us and them, particularly when the them are giants of Talmudic scholarship (and of course full participants in the practices of the community), needs to be tempered by a welcoming of differences and new ideas. It is plausible that one of the factors in the survival of the tradition is the extreme flexibility at the interpretive level, this against the background of shared practice.[53] Not that this flexibility always comes easily, as with the case of the difficult beginnings of early *Hasidism*. In this spirit it is better to welcome our interpretive opponents, Maimonidean or other, as sharing an interpretive *Beit HaMidrash*.[54]

[53] It is not bare practice that we share but some sort of basic understanding. What I have in mind is the sense in which right-thinking Americans agree that "all men are created equal," without any agreement about what this comes to. Similarly, it is not only bare practice that different interpretive approaches to Jewish tradition share, it is also basic (and uncrystallized) thoughts about God and Torah.

[54] Thanks to Avi Ravitsky for pointing out the "with us or against us" exclusivity of an earlier draft.

7

The Significance of Religious Experience

His kind of faith is a gift.
It's like an ear for music or the talent to draw.

—Woody Allen, *Crimes and Misdemeanors*

I. Introduction: Proofs, Old and New

Occasionally one meets or reads about people who were, as we say, born at the wrong time or place. Their gifts, tendencies, and ways, awkward in the context of their lives, would have seemed natural at some other time or place. The classical proofs for the existence of God suffer a different fate. Born at precisely the right time and place, they now seem out of context, no longer compelling in the way they must have been. At least they seem that way to many of us.

The natural habitat of the proofs was the medieval philosophical world, an intellectual culture in which philosophical justification of the religious fundamentals was just what was needed.[1] If

[1] The motivation for the production of the proofs seems mixed. For some, e.g., in the tenth century, Saadia Gaon, *The Book of Beliefs and Opinions*, trans. Samuel Rosenblatt (New Haven: Yale University Press, 1948), Introduction, pp. 6–9—part of the motivation seems to have been to assist those in doubt and to defeat heresies. The proofs were also thought (by various medieval philosophers and theologians) to help purify the opinions of the masses by providing insight and understanding, to supply intellectual foundations for opinions that were otherwise held on faith or on the basis of revelation, to provide the sort of foundations that intellectual virtue requires of a reputable theology.

one moves back some centuries to ancient Israel and its Jewish and arguably early Christian aftermath, rational justification of religion is not on the horizon. To defend belief in God's existence would have seemed bizarre, like defending belief in the existence of the weather.

Indeed, strange as this seems to our ears, belief itself is never mentioned in the Hebrew Bible. There is talk of believing *in* God, i.e., trusting, relying upon God. But no talk of believing doctrines, believing that something is the case;[2] no commandment—no explicit one at least—to believe anything.[3] However by the early middle ages in Jewish religious culture—earlier in Christianity— beliefs, thoughts, and the like become very much the center of attention, and there is a felt need to justify religious belief.[4]

The medieval attitude to belief's centrality has become the norm. We identify the belief that God exists as a *sine qua non* of religious commitment. The Hebrew Bible's interest is rather in one's overall stance, the essential components of which are affective and behavioral, most importantly awe/fear and love of God as realized in lived experience.

But while belief has become central, the proofs of the medievals—the classic philosophic defenses of that belief—have lost their punch. The considerations to which they appeal—like the order and beauty of the universe—have by no means lost their suggestiveness,

---

[2]It does not follow that the ascription of belief—utilizing *our* notion—to the ancients is illegitimate. But the matter is delicate. I return to it in section VI.

[3]Medieval interpretations are another thing. Maimonides, for example, hears a commandment to believe in the first of the Ten Commandments (more literally and correctly, the ten statements or pronouncements): "I am the Lord, your God, who. . . ." Similarly, with respect to the prohibition to worship other gods; for Maimonides this concerns certain false beliefs. Cf. Halbertal and Margalit, *Idolatry* (Harvard University Press, 1998). The Bible's preferred approach is in terms of illicit intimacy, adultery as it were. For an almost overdramatized biblical example, see the Book of Hosea.

[4]Robert Bellah, in *Beyond Belief* (University of California Press, 1991), chapter 13, "Religion and Belief: The Historical Background of 'Non-Belief'," argues—and I have thought this for some time—that the emphasis on *belief that*, as opposed to *belief in*, is a function of the influence of Greek philosophical thought. I argue for this in "Against Theology," chapter 6 of this volume.

My focus in "Against Theology" is the Hebrew Bible, but Bellah speaks more generally: even in the New Testament, the dominant notion of belief is *belief in*. At the conclusion of the present paper, I quote Buber in *Two Types of Faith* (Macmillan Publishing Company, 1951), according to whom *belief in* is indeed the dominant notion until the Gospel of John.

their relevance to and significance for religious thought and feeling. But proof is another thing.[5]

My aim here is to reflect on a relatively new style of proof—a distant relative of the classical arguments—current throughout the twentieth century and in recent decades even more vital, the argument from individual religious experience. Here too, or so I will argue, we should distinguish the proof's cogency from the religious significance of the considerations to which the proof appeals, my topic at the conclusion of this paper.

The focus on individual religious experience brings to mind the Protestant religious orientation. Not that individual religious experience is a mere afterthought in the other monotheisms. Indeed the proof's advocates appeal to religious experiences in a variety of traditions. Likewise, advocates of the argument include philosophers as diverse as William Alston and Richard Swinburne on the Protestant side, Gary Gutting, a Catholic, and Jewish thinker Jerome Gellman.[6] For the most part, however, contemporary discussions of proofs of God's existence in the Catholic, Jewish, or Muslim traditions—as I say, they are hardly the central topic nowadays—are of the classical arguments.

My aim here is to explore the fundamental ideas of the argument, this as opposed to the numerous sophisticated variations that have emerged. I begin with William James, early in the twentieth century. Whatever the specifics of his religious views, James emerges from the American Protestant world and gives such proofs a great deal of respect. It is good to begin with James moreover since he has a gift for raising fundamental questions in an intuitive, technically unencumbered way. In this way, he is like later philosophers P. F. Strawson and Harry Frankfurt; penetrating minds whose insights give rise to rather technical literatures.

---

[5]It has been suggested that perhaps the proofs were an intellectualized (and historically conditioned) mode of expressing religious affect. For example, one could see the argument from design as the intellectualized expression of awe toward God concerning the order of the universe. It is plausible that those who propounded the proofs were in part expressing such things, but one does not want to minimize the intellectual content of the proofs.

[6]William Alston, *Perceiving God* (Cornell University Press, 1991); Gary Gutting, *Religious Belief and Religious Skepticism* (University of Notre Dame Press, 1983); Jerome Gellman, *Experience of God and the Rationality of Theistic Belief* (Cornell University Press, 1997) and *Mystical Experience of God, a Philosophical Enquiry* (Ashgate Publishers, 2001); Richard Swinburne, *The Existence of God* (Oxford University Press, 2004).

II. Gifts to the Spirit

James characterizes experiences that purport to be of God—he includes them in the category of mystical experiences—as "gifts to our spirit." "No account of the universe in its totality can be final which leaves these . . . forms of consciousness quite disregarded."

Such experiences for James bespeak quite literally another form of consciousness. It is an open question, he supposes, as to whether such forms reveal worlds, as it were, that are ordinarily beyond our reach. It is difficult to know what to do with James's seemingly extravagant notion of forms of consciousness. This raises issues of the paranormal; James was a founder of the American Society for Psychical Research in 1885.

Whatever one thinks about the paranormal, James's remarks about "gifts to the spirit" are themselves gifts. Here, James evinces an appreciation of religion that is nowadays lost to many. John Dewey, a similarly sympathetic critic of religion,[7] writes:

> A writer says: "I broke down from overwork and soon came to the verge of nervous prostration. One morning after a long and sleepless night . . . I resolved to stop drawing upon myself so continuously and begin drawing upon God. I determined to set apart a quiet time every day in which I could relate my life to its ultimate source, regain the consciousness that in god I live, move and have my being. That was thirty years ago. Since then I have had literally not one hour of darkness or despair."
>
> This [life story constitutes] an impressive record. I do not doubt its authenticity nor that of the experience related. It illustrates a religious aspect of experience. But it illustrates also the use of that quality to carry a superimposed load of a particular religion. For having been brought up in the Christian religion, its subject interprets it in the terms of the personal God characteristic of that religion.[8]

Dewey's expression, "a religious aspect of experience" is no throwaway; he emphasizes the reality and significance of such aspects. In this passage he suggests and in the sequel he greatly expands upon the power of religion and its potential for influencing positively the course of life. At the same time he much more clearly and forcefully than James rejects the supernaturalist metaphysics associated with traditional religion. Nevertheless I

---

[7] As opposed to a flurry of recent books by Daniel Dennett, Christopher Hitchins, and Richard Dawkins that are critical of religion in a more wholesale fashion.

[8] *A Common Faith* (Yale University Press, 1934), pp. 11–12.

suspect that James's phrase "gifts to the spirit" would sit well for Dewey.[9]

Speaking for myself, I very much like James's characterization. This is in part because I think with Dewey that such peak moments, and religious life more generally, can have a beneficial influence, including one's psychological balance, ability to negotiate life's challenges, the significance one accords to one's life, and the dignity one assigns to others.[10] But there is another and perhaps deeper reason, albeit one that I find difficult to express.

What makes "gifts to the spirit" so difficult to explicate is "spirit." I could explain James's idea if I could explain the concept of the spirit, and related idea of the spiritual. There is significantly more to these ideas than the largely psychological dimension that Dewey emphasizes—the various beneficial effects mentioned above as well as "the unification of the self" of which Dewey speaks.

The quotation from *Crimes and Misdemeanors* at the head of this paper suggests that an affinity for things of the spirit is grounded in a natural gift, a human capacity, analogous to, in the aesthetic domain, having an ear for music or the talent to draw. I will begin with the latter and return to religion shortly. As we will see, there is more to mine here than a mere analogy. The aesthetic dimension has its own ties to matters of the spirit.

One obstacle to establishing the link I am after is that "aesthetic" is often heard in a reductive way; ascriptions of beauty, for example, are sometimes thought of, dismissed as, merely subjective. This is a function, I believe, of thinking too abstractly about this sphere. Consider by contrast actual aesthetic gifts, like musical talent or even having an ear for music. These abilities are far along the continuum from subjective toward objective, which is not to suggest that this distinction is either sharp or clear. Surely musical talent, an ear for music, and the like are no less aspects of the world than other abilities—including those in the domain of athletics—to perform, to discern and appreciate, etc. The "tone deaf" idiom suggests that one, otherwise sound in auditory capacities, can systematically miss something important.

---

[9] And, perhaps surprisingly, even for Nietzsche, who, in *Human, All Too Human* (Prometheus Books, 2009), p. 40, refers to religion as among "the blossoms of the world." This does not mean, he adds, that this blossom is close to the root of the world, that through religion one can better understand the nature of things.

[10] This is not to deny the awfulness unleashed in human history by the religions. Religion represents and unleashes powerful forces, potentially and actually in many directions.

One who is musically advanced may hear the same performance as the rest of us but may alone penetrate to profound levels of appreciation. Similarly, one advanced in the appreciation of the visual arts may bring something very different to, and take something very different from, a painting, or indeed a natural scene, for example a landscape with its play of light, shadow, color, and the like.

Profound aesthetic experiences, no less than the religious experiences of which James wrote, deserve to be thought of as gifts to the spirit. They may engender a sense of awe and mystery, and of the sublime; they may provoke a feeling of being privileged and so of gratitude. The experience may be at once elevating and humbling. These represent important points of contact with religious moments.

The points of contact are not limited to such reactions. Artistic and religious virtuosity both involve, even begin with, natural aptitude, as noted in the quotation from *Crimes and Misdemeanors.* Some are more given to these things than others. And in both domains, hard work, genuine focus—at times single-minded—is essential if one is to approach one's potential. We are less apt to think this way about the religious domain than the artistic. But a religious giant, a Mozart of the spirit, is a rare find; she is (certainly typically) one who has labored strenuously in pursuit of excellence.[11] And just as one who is tone-deaf can appreciate the musically gifted as responding to something of substance, one who is less able than another in matters of the spirit can recognize the latter's accomplishment. Needless to say, being tone-deaf is a rare condition in either domain. Ordinarily people occupy an intermediate position within a wide spectrum of which being tone-deaf is at one extreme.

I have been emphasizing the analogies between the two domains, and the quasi-religious character of profound aesthetic experience. Now consider one who has undergone considerable development in both domains. A religious orientation—bringing God into the

---

[11] Occasionally one finds an individual whose natural gifts seem to emerge virtually whole (although I suspect this is often apocryphal or at least exaggerated). Perhaps Mozart himself; perhaps some of the religious giants. And John McEnroe practiced his tennis serve very little, or so I seem to remember. Nevertheless, typically, almost essentially, one's initial gifts await focused development. It is particularly inspiring to read of strenuous labor in the pursuit of excellence. See Bill Russell's autobiographical *Second Wind* (Random House, 1979) for an account of extreme devotion in just such service. Russell's book articulates the spiritual heights that such devotion makes possible, perhaps surprisingly in the context of sports. See especially pages 155–58.

picture—may heighten and deepen one's reactions to beauty. Explaining this is another matter, and not a trivial one. There may be no single story. God may play the role of an object of gratefulness, someone as it were on whom one bestows one's gratitude. Sometimes the felt presence of God links experiences that would otherwise feel discrete; one comes to see an array in place of discrete dots. The points in the array seem to accrue added significance; aesthetic experience can thus partake of something analogous to what is sometimes called intertextuality.[12] Sometimes it may be God's role as a partner and, as it were, friend with whom to share the wonder. There are no doubt other dimensions, and the experience of several of these at once adds considerable power. One shares the wonders with their source, takes pleasure in their array.

Consideration of the aesthetic domain may be illuminating. Still, in much religious experience the aesthetic dimension is marginal or not present. All sorts of things can stimulate religious reflection and feeling: another's death, or the prospect of death—one's own or that of others, various sorts of horrors or extreme ugliness, witnessing simple acts of particularly touching human kindness, childbirth, the intellectual and/or moral growth of one's child or simply of another person, to name a few. It seems too much of a stretch to assimilate the religious reactions that may be prompted to reactions in the aesthetic domain.

And finally, there are James's favorite examples of gifts of the spirit, quasi-perceptual experiences of God's presence. There is no reason to assimilate these—certainly not all of them—to the aesthetic. They represent a spiritual achievement, the sense of being in God's presence. Of course, many experiences can provoke a sense of the divine presence, for example, some of the aesthetic ones discussed above. But the quasi-perceptual experiences are quite another thing, face to face with God, as James puts it.[13]

To approach religious sensibility with James is to bring to center stage the experiential side of the religious orientation. But what of religious belief? James, while he writes that religion is fundamentally a phenomenon of the gut rather than of the head, argues forcefully

---

[12] A religious orientation may help to create this sense of significant array. This is not to say, however, that such a sense is not available otherwise.

[13] The Bible suggests that only Moses spoke with God "face to face." At the same time, when Moses asks to see God's face, his request is unceremoniously denied; it is not possible, he is told, for a human being. But there are moments at which one feels that one has come close.

that the experiential aspect has important implications for the doxastic side of religion.

III. What, If Anything, Do Religious Experiences Prove?

James and many of the more recent advocates of the argument from religious experience treat such experiences on the model of perception; James calls them, "face to face presentations." They are, he says, "absolutely authoritative."

> Our own more "rational" beliefs are based on evidence exactly similar in nature to that which mystics quote for theirs. Our senses, namely, have assured us of certain states of fact; but mystical experiences are as direct perceptions of fact for those who have them as any sensations ever were for us.[14]

This powerful "warrant for truth" does not however extend to those who have not themselves had such experiences. Testimony about religious experiences, according to James, is vitiated by what would seem to be a very powerful consideration, the great variety of such reports of experiences, testifying as it were to many different gods, non-gods, various metaphysical realities, and the like.[15] Here James sounds a bit like Hume who famously denies that claims to miraculous experiences have epistemic value for those who merely hear testimony about them. By contrast, some more recent advocates maintain that such "perceptual" experiences constitute objective evidence, evidence for all of us, not only for participants.

By way of reaction to James's "absolutely authoritative" claim, it seems important that the experiences in question are not phenomenally like ordinary sense perception. Consider one of James's examples.

> God is more real to me than any thought of thing or person. I feel his presence positively, and the more as I live in closer harmony with his laws as written in my body and mind. I feel him in the sunshine and rain; and awe mingled with a delicious restfulness most nearly describes my feelings. I talk to him as to a companion in prayer and praise, and our communion is delightful. He answers me again and again, often in

---

[14] *Varieties of Religious Experience*, Lecture XVII, p. 382, in *William James: Writings 1902–1910*.

[15] On the face of it, or so it seems to me, James's point has great power. This matter has received considerable attention in the literature, some defending, some criticizing, James's contention concerning the epistemic significance of such varied, often competing, pieces of testimony.

words so clearly spoken that it seems my outer ear must have carried the tone, but generally in strong mental impressions. Usually a text of scripture, unfolding some new view of him and his love for me, and care for my safety. I could give hundreds of instances, in school matters, social problems, financial difficulties, etc. That he is mine and I am his never leaves me, it is an abiding joy. Without it life would be a blank, a desert, a shoreless, trackless waste. (p. 81).

For the most part the people James quotes are not claiming literally to see or hear God. Their sense is that they are experiencing God—in some way that is difficult for us (and them) to define. The experiences are to be sure various, ranging from ones that involve a deeply felt sense of God's presence, God's love, etc. to quasi-sensual "almost seeings, almost hearings," and the like. In the quotation just given, there is only one reference to actual hearing, and it may well be that the writer is speaking of an as-if hearing. The closer to claims of actual perceptual experience, the more likely we are to take them to be a bit crazy. Interestingly, St. Teresa of Avila, the sixteenth-century mystic, suggests, according to Rowan Williams,[16] that as a rule of thumb "the closer such perception is to . . . actually supposing the object of vision to be present to the senses . . . the less likely it is to be genuinely of God."

The differences with ordinary perception are not limited to the phenomenal aspects. The religious experiences in question are for most of the subjects once (or at most several) in a lifetime experiences. There are those mystics who more regularly enjoy such privileges but it would be surprising in the extreme if they could call them up at will. Ordinary, everyday perception, by contrast, is reliably repeatable. One can return to a room and typically see exactly what one expects to see.

In addition to the matter of repeatability, there is the question of whether what one perceives—and indeed one's perceiving it—is available to other normal perceivers. The question is not only whether others can have similar experiences, but also whether what one takes in on a particular occasion is open to others' perception. In the example above, the person talks with God and receives answers—in the special "as-if perception" mode. Whatever else one thinks about the give and take, no one takes the interaction to be available to others.

These differences do not themselves imply that anything short of veridical perception is occurring. But they do strain the analogy

---

[16]Williams is the Archbishop of Canterbury. The quote is from his *Teresa of Avila* (Continuum International Publishing Group, 2000), p. 147ff.

with ordinary sense perception. While it is less than clear that James's is exactly an argument from analogy, it is worth keeping our eyes upon these differences.

Perhaps more important, though, is James's Hume-like point about testimony, what we might call "the many-gods problem." Indeed it is difficult to understand why James supposes that the agent's "warrant for truth" survives the agent's own knowledge of the many-gods problem. After all, if one were having a notoriously unreliable sort of sense perception one would do well, despite the appearances, to question what one seems to be seeing. In the case of religious experience, the Jamesian agent would not trust another's testimony. Why then should she not apply this lesson to her own case?

Finally, and perhaps most important of all, these religious experiences do not involve sensory apparatus. This seems to me—but evidently not to James and his followers—perhaps the most important point of all, one that puts the other points mentioned into proper perspective. I will linger a bit on it.

The accumulated experience of humankind gives much weight to the senses as yielding more or less reliable information about the environment. However this is to be rationalized, understood, theorized, all but the most strident skeptic is on board here. Indeed the rough outline of how this all works is well known. One does not need contemporary neuroscience; Locke had something like the basic idea.

So sense perception has for us a privileged epistemic status. But this has everything to do with the idea that our senses are trained on aspects of the environment. There are other experiences that are in a wider sense "perceptual," experiences like the religious ones we are considering, but also mental images, hallucinations, dreams. These are phenomenally more like perception than like, for example, conceptual thinking. But they do not therefore somehow automatically inherit the epistemic credentials of sense perception.

James's contrary contention, apparently, is roughly that any sufficiently vivid (if that is the right word) presentation has as much claim as any other to being veridical, the disclosure of an independent reality. But why should vividness, *pace* Hume, or the sense that one is making genuine perceptual contact, bridge the gap between actual perception of the environment and these other sorts of "perceptual" experiences?

It is as if, under the influence of the Cartesian tradition, one were working from the inside. Sufficiently vivid perceptual states are on a par unless one can find grounds to distinguish them. And from such a perspective, working one's way from inside to outside—finding such grounds—is the major undertaking. But this is not the only way to approach these matters. It is plausible that as human beings in perceptual touch with our surroundings, we are already outside. We begin, as Quine says, with ordinary things.[17] But such perception of the environment is a very different business than perceptual experience of the wider variety, including quasi-perceptual religious experience.

Accordingly, a reflective person, privileged to have an intense religious moment of the sort in question, might bracket the epistemology of the experience. It means ever so much, she might well say, but it proves little. My own certainly fit this pattern. They were at once powerfully significant—even if relatively tame—and epistemically inert. The question of what the experience verified never so much as arose.

Here I am not alone. Rowan Williams writes:

> [For Teresa] the mysticism is demystified, and mystical experience *as such* is accorded no particular authority. Its authority . . . has to be displayed in the shape of the vocation of which it is part. [Still, . . .] there is good reason for intensified phenomenological interest in the varieties of preternatural or paranormal occurrence in prayer, especially when (as in Teresa's case) these are to some extent organized as an ascending series. Teresa herself is fascinated by her experiences. . . . (Williams, p. 148).
>
> Teresa and her contemporaries would have found this [the idea of trying to validate doctrine] in light of such mystical experiences surprising. For all Teresa's interest in the visionary and paranormal, she is not disposed to use it as evidence for the way the universe is. "Do mystical states establish the truth [of religious claims]?," asks William James in the course of a discussion of Teresa. Teresa herself would never have imagined that "mystical states" could do such a job. . . [or that they] had any part whatever to play in doctrinal discussion. So far from "mystical states" being a sort of paradigm of certainty, they have authority only within a frame of reference which is believed in on quite other grounds, and are therefore properly to be tested according to their consistency with this. (Williams, p. 149).

St. Teresa, then, brackets her experiences in epistemological terms. This does not, in her view, however, militate against their

---

[17]What Quine means by this phrase—it is the title of the first section of *Word and Object*—is another matter. Without prejudice, I like the phrase.

being religiously significant. Indeed, she seems to measure spiritual progress, at least of one significant variety, by something like the intensity and perhaps the frequency of the experiences.

Such epistemological neutrality does not entail metaphysical neutrality. I am sure that St. Teresa believed she was making contact with God that in mystical experience. Unlike a Jamesian, however, she did not presume that one could, from reflecting on the perceptual character of the experience, rationally conclude that it really was contact with God.

Imagine now another grade of removal from the Jamesian picture. One undergoes a powerful religious experience but is less than sure about, even skeptical about, any sort of real contact with the supernatural. "I know," he might say, "that this experience reflects my deep religious involvement, but whether I've actually achieved contact with God is hard to say." Another example is provided by the advocate of a perfect being theology and some associated anti-anthropomorphism. Divinity, on such a view, might be taken to be beyond our perceptual (or even conceptual) reach. But such a theological position historically has not led to giving up prayer.[18] And such a person might indeed be subject to various sorts of religious experiences. Whatever these experiences are, she might reflect, they are powerful, elevating, and humbling; their intensity and regularity a measure of one's spiritual situation. In short, one who departs from metaphysical/epistemological claims about the experiences might still adopt St. Teresa's Jamesian attitude about their religious value.

IV. Interlude: Epistemic Legalism

James's treatment of these phenomena—and even more so later advocates of the argument from religious experience—exhibits what I will call "epistemic legalism." What I have in mind here is analogous to what Bernard Williams and others have called "scientism," roughly the misapplication to philosophy of modes of explanation that have their home in scientific theorizing.

In Charles Griswold's recent book, *Forgiveness*,[19] he speaks frequently of *warranted* and *unwarranted* resentment, of the *obligation*

---

[18] How to work out the theory is another question. But certainly some philosophers, from medieval times to the present, have held extreme anti-anthropomorphic views about God without abandoning traditional religious practice.

[19] Cambridge University Press, 2008.

to forgive, to forswear *unjustified* resentment, of the question of who has *standing* to forgive. In remarks on Griswold's book in a 2008 Pacific APA symposium,[20] I called attention to what seemed to me like an invasion of legal terminology/conceptualization into the ethical domain. The legalism, or so I argued, does not do justice to our experience of forgiving and being forgiven.

Of course the whole matter is controversial; for deontologists the legalistic terminology is apt. But that it is apt does not go without saying, and it is worth noting that it does not. Here too, in discussions of the epistemology of religion by James and his followers, notions like justification, warrant, and obligation are central. Since we are in the domain of epistemology, perhaps you will think that all this indeed goes without saying, that these are inevitably the pivotal notions. But perhaps not.

I spent my college years increasingly engaged with and committed to Orthodox Judaism. Religious practice and the sense of spiritual/intellectual community were extremely compelling. At the same time part and parcel of the life were beliefs: that a supernatural God exists, that he revealed the Torah to Moses on Mt. Sinai, and the like. Given that one could not be sure of such things was there something like evidence or a good reason to think that these things were actually true? Doesn't intellectual responsibility require more than just the powerful feeling that attends to the life? Such were my pangs of intellectual conscience.

One could no doubt put these questions in terms of justification, warrant, intellectual duty/obligation and the like. And surely at the time I was not making distinctions between theoretical approaches in epistemology. But the description in terms of virtues like intellectual honesty, integrity, and responsibility seems more in line with my thinking.

Some years ago I was speaking with my then Notre Dame colleague, Fred Freddoso. We were discussing the attempt by our colleague Alvin Plantinga to show that belief in God was rational. Plantinga once commented there were many good arguments for the existence of God, thirty-two if I remember correctly. (I quipped that I knew the five famous ones and they didn't do it.) I believe that Plantinga was thinking of a good argument in a different way than I. When he spoke and wrote about the rationality of belief in God, he

---

[20]For a later reflection on those comments, see my paper, "Forgiveness and Moral Reckoning " this volume.

meant something quite refined, something like—if I have him right—one way one might proceed without irrationality. To establish that belief in God was rational was something like establishing that one had no epistemic duty to reject it. In discussing this, Freddoso, an Aquinas scholar, commented that in St. Thomas's treatment, such a sophisticated (and legalistic) conception of rationality is not at issue. What St. Thomas asks is (something like) "Is belief in God dumb?" The force of that question I can feel.

Thinking in terms of intellectual honesty, integrity, and responsibility may lead in a direction very different from that of the epistemic legalism that has been in vogue for so long.[21] As with other issues in philosophy, switching vocabulary is no guarantee of a substantially different approach. It depends of course, on what one makes of the virtue talk. And of course this is a large topic at which I am merely glancing here.

Justification is the concept from the legalistic framework that I am most concerned with at present. Justification often has a defensive flavor, in philosophy and more generally.[22] In philosophy it is as if a Pyrrhonian homunculus were perched on one's shoulder, repeatedly whispering in one's ear, "How do you know; are you certain?" And providing a non-question-begging answer is a very difficult business even for the most pedestrian beliefs; witness Descartes. This is of course not to say that one cannot theorize about justification without the skeptic in mind. But there is often the scent of skepticism in the air, perhaps especially in discussions of justifying religious belief.[23]

V. Swinburne et al.

I propose that we characterize the religious experiences we have been exploring, neutrally as possible (with respect to what they indicate about God's existence), as experiences "as of God." This lacks

[21]See especially Lorraine Code, *Epistemic Responsibility* (Brown University Press, 1987). My sense is that the recent "virtue epistemology" literature would be a rich source for thinking through these matters. Here I am grateful to a discussion with Linda Zabzebski.

[22]Think about interpersonal strife, or strife between nations or peoples; when a focus on justification becomes paramount, attention wanes about one's opponent's point of view or interests. The idea of justification feels overworked, overemphasized, and overvalued quite generally.

[23]To call attention to this scent is not to say that all attempts to provide arguments for God's existence are responsive to skepticism. See note 1 above.

poetry; but not to worry, it won't come up much in conversation. Richard Swinburne, also in search of a non-question-begging description, proposes that we speak of them as "epistemic seemings."[24] For Swinburne, apparently following Chisholm, "seems epistemically that x is present" means roughly that the agent believes (or is inclined to believe) that x is present on the basis of the experience.

There is one respect in which Swinburne's terminology seemingly fails to achieve the non-question-begging character he seeks. For it presupposes that to have such an experience is to believe (or be inclined to believe) that God exists on the basis of the experience. But as we have seen, on St. Teresa's approach, the experience fails to provide a ground for the belief. The agent's belief is grounded elsewhere. And on the alternative I mentioned above—a further grade of removal from James—the agent can take the experience to be religiously momentous without believing that he is making perceptual contact with God. Again, the experience will hardly provide a ground for his belief.

Still, surely some people do experience such "epistemic seemings," religious experiences on the basis of which they ground their religious beliefs. Swinburne, a super-Jamesian, attempts to extend their justification to the rest of us: given the religious experiences of some people, rationality requires that we all believe that God exists.[25] The following "principle of credulity"[26] is at the heart of his argument:

> It is a principle of rationality that (in the absence of special considerations) if it seems (epistemically) to a subject that x is present, then probably x is present; what one seems to perceive is probably so. (p. 254).

Swinburne argues for this principle on grounds that denying it would "land one in a skeptical bog" about ordinary perception. Here we have not just the scent of skepticism, detected in the emphasis on justification. Skepticism constitutes a crucial link in the argument.

Swinburne's approach to the epistemology of individual religious experience represents an important trend in twentieth-century

---

[24]In *The Existence of God*, revised ed. (Clarendon Press, 1991), p. 254.

[25]This formulation needs qualifications which I ignore here: needless to say, if the percipient in question was notably unreliable, etc. then her testimony could well be ignored.

[26]At first it seemed to me that Swinburne's use of "credulity" was very strange since it suggests credulousness. But Nick Wolterstorff pointed out that there is an older usage—one finds it in Reid—in which credulity refers to a natural tendency to believe in certain circumstances.

Christian philosophy. Respect for skepticism is one important aspect of the trend, but it is not the only one or the deepest.[27] That honor belongs to an idea to which I now turn.

My first encounter with the idea was as a college freshman, overhearing a conversation in a coffee shop. "We all have premises," offered a defender of religion. "These are mine." I didn't know a lot of philosophy at the time, but even then this sort of defense had very little appeal for me. Surely, I thought, we want more than that from philosophy. In such a fashion, one could defend just about anything one felt strongly enough about.

There is another way to take this sort of defense of religious belief. Perhaps the idea is that religious belief does not stand in need of philosophical justification; that religious belief is something with which one comes to philosophy. I myself, while I do not so approach religious belief (at least as it is usually construed—see later), I very much do so approach other matters, for example, our common sense beliefs about the world: that my dog is lying at my feet as I write these words, that he is a dog and I am human, and the like. As I have said, we start with ordinary things; we start out in and with the world.

To maintain that religious belief is something that one brings to philosophy is to give religious belief the status of common sense. But this is to deny a striking intuitive gap between ordinary and religious beliefs; between on one hand the belief that I am a human being and on the other that a supernatural God exists outside of time and space. With respect to the former, it takes some sort of philosophical skepticism to generate concern. Not so for the latter. A normally reflective person, religious or not, will recognize that there is an issue here. Or so we often suppose.

The denial of the intuitive gap is at the heart of the trend represented by Swinburne's approach. It is the meeting ground for James and his contemporary followers. Various philosophic strategies have been utilized to eliminate the gap. The freshman—post-Philosophy 1—comment above was one way. Closely related is the idea that religious belief is in effect (or can have the status of) common sense. Then there is James's: to grant the special "as of God" experiences the epistemic status of sense perception. Still another way to eliminate the gap is by way of skepticism.

---

[27]In James's discussion in *Varieties of Religious Experience*, skepticism does not play any sort of central role in the argument from religious experience.

Here the idea is to place great weight on the skeptic's claims. One begins with the idea that some ordinary belief is in epistemological trouble given the weight of the skeptic's claims. Early along Alvin Plantinga emphasized belief in other minds.[28] Swinburne, in the work cited, speaks more generally of beliefs based on ordinary sense perception. How are we to deal with the skeptic? How might we, in the face of the skeptic's good questions, account for our everyday knowledge? Only by adopting a very strong epistemic principle, for example, Swinburne's principle of credulity. But then, strong epistemic principle in hand, religious belief is no worse off than the most ordinary, pedestrian beliefs. Skepticism levels the playing field.

To the extent that one is moved by the skeptical starting point one will want to scrutinize the idea that something like the principle of credulity is the only way to rescue ordinary beliefs. From my perspective, while I worry about my beliefs being responsible, as discussed above, that constitutes no problem for ordinary beliefs and remains an issue for the religious beliefs in question.

I have explored a number of attempts to eliminate the intuitive epistemic gap I have been discussing. And of course, one needs to have a look at each such proposal in detail. But something seems questionable with the general idea, with the very attempt to eliminate the gap.

Philosophy is notorious for solutions the brilliance of which outshines their contact with good sense. Russell reminded us to maintain our sense of reality "even in the most abstract studies." The intuitive gap I have been discussing is one that presents itself to many religious and non-religious people. Some of our forbears who produced elaborate rational proofs for the existence of God were presumably moved to do so by the sense that their passionately held convictions were indeed controversial, and not only in the sense that some people believed otherwise. Surely a reasonable defense would reveal good reasons to believe without suggesting that the gap was illusory.

VI. Conclusion: Making Sense of Religion

Our modern sensibilities distance us from the ancients for whom God, like the weather, was hardly optional. We have well-known options. And even if one's own way is to take God for granted almost

---

[28] See his *God and Other Minds* (Cornell University Press, 1968).

like the weather, the question of whether this makes sense almost inevitably arises at some point in one's life, certainly in the lives of those around one. In what follows I will sketch an alternative to the approach taken in so much twentieth- and twenty-first-century work, by defenders of religion as well as by critics.

One thing that is striking—and new—in the Jamesian arguments we have been exploring is the idea that the experiential side of religion can serve as the foundation, specifically the epistemic foundation, of religious belief. At the same time, James is hardly interested in religious experience only for its epistemic implications. James called his book *The Varieties of Religious Experience*, and the varieties and their meanings—meanings in the broadest sense—are its main focus.

To thus emphasize the experiential side is to make contact with the mystical tradition, and to diverge from the spirit of medieval rationalist theology.[29] It is also to converge with the approach of the Hebrew Bible with its emphasis on what Buber calls faith, a matter of living a life characterized by an intimacy with God.[30]

The ancients lived their faith without the help of our concept of belief. But this is not to say that there is something illegitimate about the use of our notion to characterize them, although it does require a certain delicacy. Surely there were things in the religious domain that they took to be true: the historical events described in the Bible for example, with God's role in them, as well as that God is good, forgiving, at times angry, and the like.[31] There is no harm in the cautious ascription of belief here.

[29] With its emphasis on philosophically refined doctrine, and the sometime tendency to deemphasize the experiential side. In my own tradition, for example, Maimonides (in *The Guide for the Perplexed*, see especially Book 3, chapter 51 and the following chapters) sees the philosophic contemplation of God as the highest form of worship and sees the more ordinary aspects of religious life as clearly inferior, even if having their own sort of practical utility.

[30] A crucial component of Buber's "faith"—here the emphasis is different than the Jamesians—is the realization of the intimacy with God in all one's relationships and projects. Buber emphasizes aspects of faith like "walking in God's tempo" and "standing firm in one's commitment to God"—is to distinguish this notion of faith, which he attributes to the Israelites and early Christians, from the later Christian, Muslim, and eventually Jewish notion of belief in the doxastic sense. See C. S. Lewis in *Mere Christianity* (Simon and Schuster, 1980 reprint), Book III, "Christian Behavior," Chapters 11 and 12, both entitled "Faith," for what is in some ways a complementary conception.

[31] I steer clear here of attributions that do not seem obviously biblical—at least not when we are discussing the Hebrew Bible—like that of the various perfections or omni-properties that later come to be seen as essential.

Here is one reason for caution: The language in which many of these beliefs are expressed is poetically infused, the way of the Bible. And where not poetic, the language is often anthropomorphic, and so problematic as to its ultimate import. We may speak of belief here, but we are quite far from the philosophers' conception of assent to a well-defined propositional content. Max Kadushin, reflecting on such belief, refers to it as "uncrystallized," an arresting image.[32]

Religious belief can engender philosophical pique from another direction as well, the not inconsiderable inconsistency in the biblical characterization of God, an inconsistency that reflects our own sense of these things. To focus on our own case, we believe passionately in how much He cares—we feel or almost feel His touch—and then, turning a corner, we feel His absence acutely, sometimes almost a sense of cruelty. Or for another dimension of inconsistency, our experience of God, as just described, essentially involves God's feelings, thoughts, and the like. At the same time, we experience God as somehow beyond all that.[33]

The lack of clarity, the anthropomorphism, the inconsistency, these are things that while smoothly accommodated within religious life drive the philosophic mind to drink. Or to purify. When Greek philosophy enters into contact with the Israelite religious tradition there ensues a rationalizing of these earlier modes of religious thought. The literary rendering, so apt for the religious life as it was (and largely still is) lived, is seen as inadequate, as in need of translation into a non-poetic idiom, as in need of a metaphysical foundation and attendant epistemological support. And making sense of religious life comes to be seen as defending the religious metaphysics, in part by supplying a supporting epistemology. Which brings us to proofs of the existence of a God.

What, though, if we maintain our focus on lived experience rather than on any allegedly necessary metaphysical underpinning? Without a religious metaphysics and epistemology we may well be

[32]See *The Rabbinic Mind* (Jewish Theological Seminar, 1952) for an illuminating treatment of religious belief and related matters, including those I discuss in the next paragraph of the text. See especially chapters VI and VII.

[33]I do not mean that we believe, on philosophical grounds, that God is, in principle, beyond anthropomorphic description, that such description belies God's nature. Some of us think such things, but the Rabbis of the Talmud, as Max Kadushin points out, had no such in-principle objection to anthropomorphic description. But their experience of God had the two-fold character. They experienced God's touch and the like, and at the same time it was part of their experience of God that God was beyond all that.

accused of not knowing of what we speak. But is it not a genuinely religious intuition that with respect to understanding God we are over our heads, that central to religious life is an intimacy, the other party to which is as it were seen through a glass darkly?

Making sense of one's commitment to a religious life is not and should not be a trivial matter. But there is a world of difference between defending supernaturalist metaphysics and making sense of the form of life. That the life genuinely speaks to one is, for example, germane to the latter project. An aspect of this, stronger for some participants than others, is a sense of God's presence. And one may reflect that one has more confidence in the wisdom of the life than in any philosophical interpretation of what it all comes to.

The effect of my approach is to reduce substantially the gap between ordinary and religious belief. The gap upon which I have insisted earlier, the gap that we ordinarily feel, is the product of a philosophical interpretation of religion, a metaphysics that we have come to think of as at the heart of a religious orientation. But this is not to suggest that there is no gap, that religious belief is somehow just common sense.

To proceed in this direction is to dethrone philosophy as the provider of foundations in this domain. This is not, however, to deny philosophy the exploration of fundamentals. Here religion provides a rich field. To provide one example, I spoke above of the ancients' (and our) religious beliefs that, I said, drive a philosopher to drink. At the same time, the religious utility of such uncrystallized beliefs is enormous; in that regard we couldn't ask any more of them. Uncrystallized belief is an idea that cries out for philosophical clarification.[34]

We are not the ancients, and philosophy has made its mark on us, one that we do not wish to eschew. But it is one thing to see religious

---

[34]Religious belief, on my conception, may not be as different from some other central beliefs as one might have supposed, e.g., political beliefs, like "All people are created equal," or various beliefs about political rights. In such cases beliefs clearly set out a path for one's life, but what the belief comes to in theoretical terms may be entirely up for grabs. I discuss this matter further in chapter 6, "Against Theology," mentioned in note 4 above.

A related topic—I explore it in my book, *The Magic Prism* (Oxford University Press, 2004)—is the adequacy of the philosophical notion of "propositional content." It may be that "uncrystallized belief" has a more general application, although surely the religious examples, as well as the political one just mentioned, are special and in some ways extreme cases.

life as riding on a metaphysical picture, quite another to view the life as fundamental and the doctrinal side of one's tradition as more like the furniture in the living room, importantly expressive of the specifics of the tradition's sensibility, rather than the foundations of the edifice.[35, 36]

[35]Joseph Almog has made parallel remarks about "the foundations of mathematics." While this latter domain includes topics that are of the first importance, this is not to say, suggests Almog, that the area somehow constitutes or even explores the epistemic underpinnings of mathematics.

[36]This paper is based on my comments on a paper by Yehudah (Jerome) Gellman at the 2008 Henle Conference at St. Louis University. I am grateful to Gellman for virtually introducing me to the topic, and to continued discussions with Jeff Helmreich. Helmreich remarked that in his parents' home talk about God was as easy and uncontroversial as talk about the weather. This proved very suggestive, perhaps especially as an entry point into early Israelite modes of thought. I owe the furniture analogy to one among many helpful conversations with Jack Miles. Finally, I wish to thank Joseph Almog, Yehudah Gellman, John Greco, Charles Griswold, Paul Hoffman, Richie Lewis, Richard Mendelsohn, Calvin Normore, David Shatz, and Nicolas Wolterstorff for comments on an earlier draft.

8

Against Theodicy

I. The Classical Problem of Evil

It has long been urged against traditional theism, very long indeed, that God's perfections—specifically in the domains of goodness, knowledge, and power—are logically incompatible with the existence of unwarranted human suffering. It has almost equally long been urged that the problem is illusory—or at least surmountable; the tradition of theodicy must be only moments younger than the problem. The debate is a philosophical classic, with many ingenious moves on both sides, and epicycles galore. But whatever one's view on the details of the debate, it is difficult—and I think unwise—to resist the sense that evil presents a real and indeed substantial problem for the Western religious tradition.

With respect to theodicy, a Talmudic refrain springs to mind: the question seems better than the answer(s). Such an intuitive sense should never be taken lightly. But in the present case, there is more to be said against the tradition of theodicy. God, at the end of the book of Job, strongly reproaches Job's would-be comforters while He praises Job. What was the mistake of the Comforters? Perhaps their greatest sin was a moral one—to talk so strongly and at times insensitively to the suffering victim. But God's rebuke—and his related praise for Job—had quite a different emphasis: They, as opposed to Job, did not speak the truth about Him. The truth is in question is not specified in the text. But what is most salient about their speeches, what they insisted upon, and what Job denied, was the just reality behind the unjust appearances.[1] We have it on the best authority, then, that their standard theodicy-like responses to evil were mistaken, something we knew from chapter 1 of Job in any case. Unwarranted suffering is no mere surface appearance, but a ground floor phenomenon, not to be explained away.

My suspicion, though, is that it is not only the answers to the problem of evil that are suspect. The question itself is problematic. It presupposes a conception of divinity that does not go without saying. Imagine a dramatic presentation in which the personae are God and a medieval philosopher. The philosopher carefully formulates the problem of evil, and the Master of the Universe yawns. "That should be my worst problem," says God. "After what I revealed about myself in the Hebrew Bible, it is nothing less than amazing that they persist in conceiving me as ethically impeccable, and able to do literally anything. That they should so persist is a tribute to the power of philosophy."

My dramatic fantasy (to be continued below) reflects my sense of a substantial conceptual distance between the perfect-being theology that dominates from the time of the medievals and the religious sensibility of the Hebrew Bible and its development in Talmudic thought (first six centuries CE). This gulf suggests a dissolution of the classical puzzle. Perhaps God simply lacks some or all of the relevant perfections.

II. The Problem of Evil: The Theoretical Side

As one who favors the more ancient conception, dissolution of the classical problem is attractive to me. But to leave matters there is at least as dissatisfying as classical theodicy. For as I said, the sense that evil presents a substantial problem for traditional religion runs deep. The classical problem of evil reflects—in a classical philosophical idiom—a worry (or two) that is (or are) indeed fundamental.

Imagine an episode of *Star Trek* in which the protagonists are about to arrive at a galaxy created and ruled by a just, loving, beneficent deity. We need not assume the perfections, just a good dose of

---

[1] We, the readers of Job, know of God's pact with the Accuser, and so we know that Job's catastrophic situation was not a response to anything untoward on his part. And Job's conversion, as it were, after the speech from the Whirlwind, is also not a matter of seeing the justice behind the appearances. What he sees is something quite different. See below, section I of this chapter, "Job and the Voice from the Whirlwind," for more on my reading of Job. Needless to say, the book of Job is a difficult one, and can be read in different ways.

the classical divine virtues. The protagonists arrive and shudder at a glimpse of the horrors that characterize human history.

The perfections are not the real problem, I want to suggest. It is rather the sheer dissonance of what every plain-thinking person knows to be true about the world and what one would naturally expect from a fundamentally just, benevolent, powerful, creator/ruler.

It is of utmost importance that treatments of this problem respect the dissonance. The question is not whether with enough brilliance one can make for a fit between what we know and the traditional religious picture. Surely this can be done. In philosophy quite generally, the most important question is not whether a theoretical approach can with enough brilliance be shored up. Often, if not always, it can be done. Perhaps it can always be done . . . if one is willing to pay the price. The real question—the place one needs to train one's vision—is rather that of natural fit. One needs to focus not on "One could say . . .," but rather on what is the most natural thing to say.[2] Classical theodicy provides examples of violations, but no more than does contemporary epistemology or the philosophy of language.

The dissonance is only one side of the problem of evil—the theoretical side. I turn now to another, perhaps more urgent, if not more fundamental.

III. The Existential Side

The Western religious tradition advertises, one might say, a certain picture of reality, and recommends an attitude, a stance—including a way of carrying on—appropriate to such a world. The picture is, as noted, that of a world created and ruled by a loving, benevolent deity. The world as advertised is just. It is filled with meaning; a world in which one's actions and character have a kind of cosmic significance. Particularly appropriate to such a world, and at the heart of the religious stance, are the attitudes, if that's what they are, of awe and love. A well-lived life is characterized by awe and love—toward one's God, one's fellows, toward life itself.

---

[2]Cf. David Kaplan in "Dthat," in *Contemporary Perspectives in the Philosophy of Language*, P. French, T. Uehling, H. Wettstein, eds. (Minneapolis, 1979), criticizing the attempt to bring linguistic phenomena in line with Fregean theory writes, "I don't deny that on a phenomenon-by-phenomenon basis we can (in some sense) keep stretching Frege's brilliant insights to cover. With a little ingenuity I think we *can* do that. But we shouldn't." (p. 391).

Let's return to my dramatic presentation: God and the philosopher. God, you will remember, has just shrugged at the classical problem of evil, formulated in terms of His perfections. After admitting the problem of dissonance—He looks thoughtful, somewhat pained, when it is proposed—God proceeds to what is, from His point of view, the most pressing difficulty posed by evil. "The real problem," He urges, "is how to get them out of bed in the morning."

Evil puts us low, sometimes embittering us, sometimes deadening sensibility. Human suffering constitutes a powerful obstacle to facing the world with awe and love, and thus to the religious life.[3]

I have said that at the heart of the religious stance are awe and love toward one's fellows, God, life itself. If we put to the side the theistic member of this triad, we can see that the situation of the traditional religionist, vis-à-vis evil, is not unlike that of his secular fellows. This suggests an interesting generalization at least of the existential side of the problem of evil. Evil, wanton suffering discourages—or makes impossible—one's sense of awe/wonder and love. And this is so for all of us. Thus Robert Adams commented to me some years ago that the problem of evil is a problem for any "religious" view, that is, any view that sees such things as wonder and love as essential ingredients in human flourishing.

IV. Non-Opiate Responses to the Problem of Evil

A. Job and the Voice from the Whirlwind

Marx is justly famous for his remark that religion constitutes (I would say, "can constitute") an opiate, a kind of bill of goods sold to the suffering masses. Their suffering is in some sense unreal, a superficial glitch in the workings of a perfect creation. I want to propose a constraint on responses to the problem, both in its theoretical and existential/practical aspects. Responses, I propose, need to be *non-opiate*.[4]

I said above that in any treatment of the theoretical aspect of the problem of evil one needs to respect the dissonance. But my non-opiate condition is motivated by more than a conception of sound

[3] Of course, suffering doesn't always have this effect. Concentration camp inmates, reports Victor Frankl in *Man's Search For Meaning*, paperback edition (New York, 1984), were often emotionally numbed, spiritually destroyed. But not always. There were the few who could overcome. But one need not think that suffering necessarily obliterates the spiritual life to see that it can and often does.

[4] Whatever Marx was up to, my motivation here is not political. The opiate that is my concern is not administered by anyone in the hopes of keeping down the masses. It is rather a kind of egalitarian opiate. But it is not without its costs.

methodology. There is an ethical dimension that is relevant even to the theoretical aspect of the problem. It is crucial that we not belittle suffering by seeing it, for example, as a mere appearance of some higher form of justice. It is crucial that we call injustice and horror by their right names, as did God's faithful servant, Job.

The non-opiate condition has application to the existential side as well. When we come to think about how it might be possible to live a life characterized by awe and love, our anti-reductionism about evil must remain in the foreground. The aim is to achieve the religious life in full awareness of the dark side.

I will now sketch two sorts of non-opiate responses. Given limitations of space and understanding, a sketch is all that I can accomplish here. I hope to return to these themes elsewhere.

The first response derives from the book of Job, one of the wonders of the Hebrew canon. Let me begin by saying why the book seems outrageous, in the most wonderful sense.

1. Job, a gentile, is said by God to the most righteous man on earth. This bespeaks a certain openness and expansiveness not always characteristic of canon makers, orthodoxies.
2. Impressionistically, the work may be divided into two books.
   a. The first of these includes the first chapter and the last. The first chapter—God's negotiation with the Accuser[5]—has a very distinct mythological feel. It reads as if it could have been written by an ancient Woody Allen, poking fun at God's alleged ethical perfection. And the last chapter—the other component of what I am seeing as the first book—suggests the absurdity that the killing of one's children—never mind the injustice to them—might be rectified by getting some new ones, perhaps children who have a higher IQ or better free-throw percentage. This is not to say that there is no deep message here, for example, as Archibald MacLeish suggests,[6] that part of the point is that Job—post-Whirlwind—is ready to resume living in the fullest sense. But this imagined book—composed of the first and last chapters of Job—has a strange and mythological feel.
   b. The central parts of the book, on the other hand, constitute one of the classical religious treatments of suffering, albeit not

[5] "The Accuser" translates the Hebrew in a way that seems in context more accurate than "Satan," as if the term were a proper name. The Accuser seems to be a sort of heavenly prosecuting attorney, and not Satan of the Christian tradition.

[6] In his "Forward by the Author" to his play *J.B.* (New York, 1958).

on my view an orthodox treatment—about which I will say more shortly. It is a story of great power, of a person who has everything, loses it all, and finds a way to reengage God and life. Indeed, before the last chapter begins, Job has been spiritually transformed, if not materially restored.

3. As noted, God reproaches quite strongly Job's Comforters—who violate my non-opiate condition. As I said above, perhaps their greatest sin is a moral one—to talk so strongly and at times insensitively to the suffering victim. But God says that they have not spoken the truth about Him, and it is certainly tempting to see in this the rejection of standard theodicy-like responses to evil.

4. Most amazing is God's speech to Job from the Whirlwind, to which I now turn.

One thing that is relatively clear, in this book in which little is clear and uncontested,[7] is that whatever it is that God says brings peace to Job. This seems not a matter of simply finally meeting up with God, almost face to face, as it were. The book might have been written so as to suggest that it is the awe attendant upon being in God's presence that does the magic. But Job, as actually written, seems to place enormous weight upon the distinctive content of the speech from the Whirlwind. What Job learns from God seems to be the key, or certainly one of the keys, to his transformation.

The question, of course, is how to interpret the speech from the Whirlwind. My idea is that given God's rejection of the Comforters, it is important that we do not read the Whirlwind as a variation on the classical theodicy of the Comforters.[8] But even without this assistance from the context, the Whirlwind vision is extremely striking in its unorthodoxy.

When Job hits bottom—one of the times that God becomes accessible it would seem—he is, as it were, led by God to the top of the mountain, a perch from which he is allowed, privileged, to gaze upon the creation as God sees it, under the aspect of eternity. The world seen by Job through God's eyes is exquisite, awe-inspiring. But by stark contrast with, for example, Genesis chapter 1, it is a strikingly non-anthropocentric world. It is a wild and violent world, and we are

---

[7]It is striking how many of the key sentences, the ones upon which the book's interpretation hangs, get such different readings. This is in part a matter of the sheer difficulty of the original Hebrew—not because it is Hebrew, but because it is just such difficult language.

[8]Such a reading seems highly undesirable, although it might fit with certain passages in isolation—for example, the famous query to Job as to where he was when God planned the earth.

not its tamers. Most important, it is not teleologically organized with respect to human needs, ends, or values. Indeed, human beings do not figure prominently in the vision. Implicitly, of course, we are part of it, participants in what Stephen Mitchell, in his translator's "Introduction," calls "the sacred game."[9] But we are not the centerpiece, the virtual raison d'être of the creation, in the way that we are so often depicted in biblical literature. At the same time, who else is privileged to accompany God to the mountain top? With whom else does God share His *sub specie aeternitatis* vision of the creation?

How does the Whirlwind vision address our problem? Implicit in the Job story, as I have told it, is a new picture of our relation to God and to nature. Human values, as I am understanding the Whirlwind vision, are not written into the atoms. Justice is not a law of nature of this world, nor does the book speak of any other world in which injustice is rectified. This does not mean that our values cease to be objective; there is no relativism here. Values can remain objective in the sense of objectively appropriate to the sorts of beings that we are, this without their being written into the universe as underlying its non-human structures. It is human—perhaps a condition for human dignity—that we love and seek justice. But it is naïve—even arrogant—to suppose that the universe conforms to our sense of justice. Perhaps this arrogance is one source of the sometimes angry tone of the Voice from the Whirlwind.

Such a non-anthropocentric vision is unusual in the Western religious tradition, unless one counts Spinoza as a member. The more usual anthropocentric picture is so strong in the tradition that one usually thinks of the conception just adumbrated as heretical.[10] The admittedly more naturalistic perspective is, however, as theistic as you like and gives pride of place in its thinking about a religious outlook to the attitudes of awe and love.

The Whirlwind vision yields some peace on the theoretical front—not by denying the reality of injustice, but by giving up on the unreasonable expectation that the universe is ethically coherent. The price has been to complicate the relation between God's goodness/love for justice and the universe's ethical coherence. Not that it was ever simple. Moral faith need no longer be seen as faith in reality of justice, in its instantiation, but rather in its status as an ideal to which, in partnership with God, we are committed.

---

[9] *The Book of Job*, trans. Stephen Mitchell, (New York, 1987), p. xxi.
[10] More heretical than removing the human being from the center is denying the reality of justice.

The existential side of the problem of evil—remains, as it must, a serious human problem. But even a partial glimpse of things from God's perspective, with its attendant awe, certainly helps. Not that it is trivial to incorporate such a vision into one's life. One needs be able to flip perspectives, or to live with more than a single one. One with such a religious outlook—"religious" in the broad sense mentioned above in connection with Robert Adams' comment—lives both as a participant in the ethical life, committed with all one's being to justice, and as one who sees the irony in the expectation that justice prevails. For the traditional religionist, this means sharing both God's love for justice and His privileged vision of things, according to which we are at once puny and little lower than the angels. The sense of irony just mentioned is of great assistance in the project. One yearns for justice, locally and globally, yet sees such things as messianic, a kind of idealizing vision. One lives with the knowledge that among one's most cherished dreams are one's ideals which remain ideal.

This approach to the existential side of the problem puts great weight on the availability and power of awe. A sense of awe at the holy game is variously available and variously efficacious. No doubt it helps some more than others.[11] But it is not awe alone that is supposed to do the work. While it alone seems to have been transforming to Job—he did experience quite a taste of it—for the rest of us the religious tradition provides additional assistance, among other things in the forms of ritual and community. I turn now to still another source of assistance, indeed another sort of non-opiate response. I leave for another occasion the question of how these two responses cohere.

B. One Sort of Rabbinic Response:
God Hyper-Anthropomorphized

Problems of evil become particularly acute during times of catastrophe. Jewish history is littered with such, but the formative catastrophe is the 70 CE Roman onslaught on Jerusalem which issued in destruction of the Second Temple and in the next century (after the failed Bar Kochba revolt) the expulsion of the Jews from Jerusalem. The literature that will constitute my focus here is the rabbinic commentary on the book of Lamentations. That commentary, *Midrash Rabbah* on Lamentations,[12] is a compilation of materials composed

---

[11] As Philip Quinn emphasized in conversation after this session at the World Congress.
[12] The translation consulted is that of the Soncino Press (London, 1983).

over many generations post-70 CE, an attempt by the rabbis of the Talmud to bring Lamentations to bear on their latest and by far greatest tragedy. (Lamentations itself was written some 650 years earlier, in connection with the destruction of the First Temple in 587 BCE.)

One would naturally suppose that the aspects of divinity a literature emphasizes reflect salient features of the community's experience. Subject a community to great trial or triumph, and its way of thinking about God may well alter or enlarge. One has the sense, from the *Midrash* on Lamentations, that indeed the near destruction of the community prompts a new—but of course not historically discontinuous—perspective on God. God is, one might say, hyper-anthropomorphized. The God of the Hebrew Bible, as opposed say to Aristotle's unmoved mover or the Greek philosophy-inspired medieval tradition, was always anthropomorphically characterized. But something very different is going on here.

It is one thing to see God as angry at our antics, even (as in Genesis) as regretful that he initiated the human experiment. But God suffering on our behalf, His mourning our loss, and His weeping and feeling it as His own loss (Proem 24: "Woe is Me! What have I done?") is quite another thing. Sometimes the *Midrash* sees God in maternal terms, like a sparrow bereft at the destruction of her nest (Proem 22). Sometimes paternal: God is compared with a king who, enraged at his two sons, thrashes them and drives them away. The king afterward exclaims, "The fault is with me, since I must have brought them up badly" (Proem 2). More from Proem 24:

> Woe to the King who succeeds in His youth and fails in His old age.
> The Holy one, blessed be He, said to Jeremiah, "I am now like a man who had an only son, for whom he prepared a marriage canopy, but he dies under it. Feelest thou no anguish for Me and My children? Go summon Abraham, Isaac, and Jacob, and Moses from their sepulchres, for they know how to weep."

God, it would seem, needs instruction in mourning from us.[13]

There are related passages from the Talmud according to which, for example, God is said to be in exile after the catastrophe, or to feel bittersweet when his children praise him in prayer—on one hand honored and on the other overwhelmingly saddened by their exile. Nor is the humanizing tendency always related in the Talmud to mourning. God is said, for example, to pray that his nurturing, merciful side dominate his desire for strict justice, apparently not a

[13] As Alan Mintz points out in *Hurban: Responses to Catastrophe in Hebrew Literature* (Syracuse, NY, 1996), p. 60.

trivial matter for Him. He is said to *hurt* when His creatures feel pain. There is much more to be said on this score. But for present purposes, what I have quoted will have to suffice.

Professor Swinburne, in his contribution to the present session, writes, "Theodicy is the enterprise of showing that appearances are misleading, and that (probably) all the world's evils do promote greater good." This is what Job—vs. the Comforters—denies, for which (on my reading) God praises him. The lesson I am taking from Job, that justice remains an unrealized ideal—it seems to me a plain reading of the text—is not a lesson highlighted by the religious tradition. Notice, however, that the post-destruction perspective on God sketched in this section seems, with Job, to emphasize—rather than theorize away—the horrors of our world.

At the same time, the *Midrash* on Lamentations goes to pains to attribute the catastrophe to Israel's sins. To what extent the spirit of that move is coherent with the tendency I have been describing is an open question.[14] No doubt one could—some do—assimilate the tendency I have been discussing to a theodicy-friendly picture. So the implications for the theoretical side of the problem of evil are unclear.

It is on the existential front that the new rabbinic emphasis has immediate impact. Elaboration is here impossible, but the short version is this. What the new emphasis provides—and no doubt the seeds are ancient—is a sort of life partner to the community and derivatively to the individual. Here there are intimations of the Song of Songs, God and Israel as lovers. For God to cry over our catastrophes, to feel great pain over our losses, indeed to feel the pain as shared with us, is to mitigate the loneliness of our suffering. Prayer, seen as communication with a divine partner, transforms bitterness into a potentially healing outpouring of one's pains and disappointments. The new emphasis thus makes for the possibility of nurture and comfort even in the face of a sometimes unyieldingly awful universe.[15]

It is significant that the comforting does not proceed in only one direction. A considerable part of the project in traditional Jewish prayer is comforting, nurturing God, or so the liturgy suggests. One reading of the Mourner's Kaddish—a communal mourning ritual

---

[14]*Midrash Rabbah*, as noted, is a compilation of centuries of rabbinic sermons, stories, parables and like. It is hardly a theoretical work, and so it often proceeds in multiple directions on a single question.

[15]Of course, it is not only our suffering that we share, but our joys and triumphs as well.

that never mentions death or the dead but that glorifies God—suggests that the community is coming together to comfort God for His loss. The liturgy, borrowing from Psalms 22:4, speaks of God as enthroned on the praises of Israel; again pointing to our role in God's flourishing. And then there is a centerpiece of the liturgy, the *Sh'ma*, that emphasizes God's oneness.[16] I have often wondered whether the idea goes beyond numerical unity, whether what is at issue is a kind of coherence that depends in part upon the success of one's projects. Seen in this way, the *Sh'ma* is a messianic dream of God's future, as it were, as in Zachariah 14:9, also highlighted in the liturgy, "In that day, God will be one and His name one."

It is common knowledge that a partner who shares one's life affords considerable nurture and comfort. It seems worth emphasizing, however, that there is also nurture in being nurturing and comforting. The new rabbinic emphasis provides a part of the tradition's answer to how to get them out of bed in the morning.

---

[16]I have in mind here the first line of the *Sh'ma*, the famous call usually translated, "Hear O Israel, the Lord your God, the Lord is one."

9

God's Struggles[1]

I am Y-H-V-H and there is none else;
I form light and create darkness,
Peace is my doing, and I create evil
I, Y-H-V-H do all these things.[2]

—Isaiah 45:7

A person should always stand in awe of Heaven, in private as
well as in public, and admit the truth, and seek the truth in
his heart.

—Jewish morning prayer

Public discussion of [religion] lurches uncomfortably between
overconfident denial ("God" certainly does not exist, and
anyway it's all His fault) and blind allegiance.

—Tony Judt, "Leslie Kolakowski (1927–2009),"
The New York Review of Books, September 24, 2009

---

[1] This paper derives from "Concluding Remarks" I gave at the University of Notre Dame conference, "My Ways Are Not Your Ways: The Character of the God of the Hebrew Bible." I'm told by friendly critics that the written version does not quite capture the oral presentation, available at http://www.nd.edu/~cprelig/conferences/video/my_ways/wettstein1.htm

[2] I use the transliterated letters of the Tetragrammaton name since the usual "The Lord" obscures the fact that the term is a proper name (unvocalized); "The Lord" and a proper name also differ dramatically with respect to distance and formality.

It is important to note that it is difficult to be precise in the translation of the crucial and final word of the penultimate line of the quotation from *Isaiah*, like other key words at focal points in *Tanach*. The word is used in many nuanced ways in *Tanach* (all designating something in the vicinity of evil). See CARM.org, for the reading "calamity," as in natural evil.

The power of our religious traditions is a function, at least in part, of the edifying, morally elevating texts so central to them. Being ancient, however, these texts inevitably reflect—sometimes in shocking ways—the cultural settings from which they emerge. God, for example, is said in *Tanach* to command, or at least to allow slavery, genocide, rape, and other assorted horrors. Critics of religion often seize on these things, paying scant attention to the edifying and elevating; Defenders do the opposite.

The power of the ancient texts is not that of straightforward articulation, the way of many philosophical texts. Rather, their meanings are displayed by way of poetically infused narrative, and dramatic and mythological tropes. As with mythology, one does not want to put the stories through the wringer of the categorical imperative. Better to struggle with the dark side of God's world than to reject such ancient gifts.

How might one even begin to come to terms with divinely mandated moral horror? Given our reverence for these texts there are temptations here, most notably a tendency to minimize the moral awfulness or explain it away. At the Notre Dame Conference on the Hebrew Bible, as in the history of theology, there were many such defenses. Some seemed at the extreme: God, it was said, having granted the gift of life, a temporary gift, can justifiably withdraw it at will. There is, it would follow and it was urged, no issue at all about the death of good people. Being with God in heaven is, for all we know, a superior situation than life on earth, so that even the killing of babies, when divinely mandated, may not represent a morally significant problem. At lesser extremes were variations on familiar modes of theodicy.

Needless to say, and worth saying, not all the contributions by religiously committed contributors were along such lines. But those that were dominated, or so it seemed. Moreover, one had a sense that the Critics and many Defenders of traditional religion agreed on the general idea that some such defense is what traditional religion implicates. For the Critics such defenses provide ample reason for skepticism about the whole enterprise.

My aim here is to provide a very different sense of traditional religion, one that agrees with the Critics on the utter unacceptability of such defenses. The quotation from Isaiah at the head of this paper speaks of a dark side to God's world; a part and parcel of creation, no mere surface appearance. This is less than a happy thought—to all of us, religiously committed or not. But it has the ring of truth.

Peter Van Inwagen points out[3] that *Tanach* is more like a library than a work, indeed one whose ethical ideas are under development, one that represents no single doctrine on many key notions. And this applies to my Isaiah-inspired view of evil and its place in creation. Such is clearly not the only attitude toward evil in *Tanach*, but it is one to which I want to focus attention.

Our problem, though, is not just the dark side of creation, natural evil for example. It is difficult to read the text naively—a good thing in my view[4]—and not come away with a sense of a dark side to God. In the cases of *Amalek* and the *Akedah*, had we not seen such texts we likely would have denied their possibility. For God asks of us what is not only immoral, but a violation of something at the heart of what God presumably stands for, killing children for example.

Indeed, in the case of the *Akedah*—even more horrendous—God commands Abraham not only to violate a moral norm, one that resides close to Abraham's core. God commands Abraham to kill his child, his only child, his beloved child. If asked to do this, the last thing one (other than maybe Kant . . .) would naturally think about is the moral violation. (It helps here to have had children of one's own.) "But it's my boy!," we can imagine him screaming, to himself if not to God. Indeed the very language of the command seems to rub it in, to put it, so to speak, right in Abraham's face.

My emphasis here will be on the *Akedah* and also on the strange story of Job. These stories represent God's treatment not of His (or Israel's) enemies, but rather of His beloved, and so they have a special sting. God considers Abraham one with whom He is intimate,[5] and yet asks of him the unspeakable. God mandates the death of Job's children as an Accuser-inspired[6] test of this person whom God judges to be the most righteous on earth. Why is this not moral monstrosity?

---

[3]In his paper at the Notre Dame conference from which this paper derives. See Michael Bergmann, Michael Murray, Michael Rea, eds., *Divine Evil?: The Moral Character of the God of Abraham* (Oxford University Press, 2011).

[4]Such naïve readings may not prove tenable in the end. And a religious tradition, almost like the courts in our legal tradition, may provide another reading of what, as it were, the constitution meant. But it is important to pay significant attention to what the text *seems* to say, to stay with the naïve reading for a while.

[5]See Genesis 18:19, where God refers to Abraham as (translating literally) one He has known, or perhaps one he has singled out. The verb, *la'daat*, suggests intimacy in biblical Hebrew.

[6]The Hebrew "Satan" is, in context, not the fallen angel of the Christian tradition, but a kind of heavenly accuser, a heavenly investigator/prosecuting attorney, so to speak.

Such a question, admittedly on the edge of blasphemy, seems a religious imperative. Let me selectively choose several biblical texts in support of this idea. I will return below to my selectivity.

In Genesis 18, only a few chapters before the *Akedah*, God approaches Abraham with his plan to destroy Sodom and Gomorrah. Imagine Abraham's reaction; an intimidating situation, even terrifying, not to speak of confusing. For many of us, standing up to social pressure is difficult enough; standing up to God is unimaginable. And yet Abraham challenges God in the strongest moral terms. "Heaven forbid that the judge of all the earth would punish with good along with the wicked." Nor, as God begins to back down, does Abraham hesitate to repeat and renew the challenge.

Perhaps God approaches Abraham in this way to allow Abraham to do just what he does. Perhaps this is part of Abraham's moral training. Nevertheless, Abraham's lack of care for his own safety, for his life after all, his being nothing less than appalled at God and unable to keep quiet about it, these things are no doubt part of why he is so revered by the tradition. And if one can say it, perhaps this is part of why he is revered by God, honored with intimacy.

At the end of the book of Job, God rebukes Job's ironically named "Comforters." They appropriately begin their visit with the bereft Job, sitting silently with him for a full week in the manner of Jewish mourning practices. Silence is difficult to sustain, however, and when the conversation begins, it quickly degenerates. They criticize Job in the manner of conventional religious thinking, ways that are all too familiar. God is just; so Job must be deserving of what has befallen him. He should repent and beg for God's understanding and forgiveness, and the like. We, the readers, know better, having been apprised at the beginning of the book of Job's innocence. What happens does so as a result of a challenge to God from "the Accuser," a representation according to C. G. Jung of God's insecurity about Job's love. Jung's suggestion is irreverent, but hardly out of line with the text.

God's eventually rebukes the Comforters; they, unlike Job failed to tell the truth about God. This, I want to suggest, is an ethical moment of inestimable importance. God appears to be saying that the usual pietisms are false and objectionable, that Job's pre-Whirlwind near blasphemous remarks about God's injustice were well taken.

In selecting the passages from Genesis and Job I am, admittedly, being selective. Religious texts and even more so the larger traditions that house them allow for multiple moral emphases. One could as well pick texts that support a point of view very distant from my own. But this very fact also works against the Defenders, for whom God's authority can justify what looks to us morally horrendous. For it suggests that religious traditions of the sort known to us are too inclusive to provide a definitive foundation for the ethical life. One can cite too many contrary verses; one can cite widely divergent religious authorities. In the end, one is left with one's ethical good sense.

This is not to deny that one's religious tradition may help to form and develop one's ethical stance and character. There are multiple and exceedingly rich connections between religion and the ethical life. In selecting these passages about Abraham and Job, I bring to bear my own substantive ethical views. But those views have in part been formed, enhanced, developed by my contact with those and similar passages as well as by contact with religious models of the ethical life.

The religious perspective I have begun to sketch—it is here that I take issue with the sense apparently shared by the Critics and Defenders—reflects my own Jewish sensibility. This is hardly to suggest that there is a single Jewish view on these matters. Nor is it to suggest something uniquely Jewish. Better still if there are resonances in other traditions. But there is a distinctive flavor perhaps especially to the three passages I am about to explore.

To begin with a passage from the Babylonian Talmud, Tractate *B'rachot* (Blessings),[7] Rabbi Yochanan mentions God's prayer. The interlocutor—as shocked as you or I might be at such mention—immediately poses the question, "And what does God pray?" He prays, we are told, that when his children are at issue, His attribute of mercy/nurture overwhelm his anger and his other attributes—presumably his desire for strict justice. But this is to suggest that it is no trivial matter even for God to subdue His anger, to allow His love to vanquish His demand for justice. In short, God struggles. This is an idea that is difficult to incorporate into the picture of religion shared by Critics and Defenders.

I move now to the book of Hosea, astounding in many respects. Its hyper-anthropomorphic talk of God would be blasphemous if not itself found in the holy text. The book begins with God telling the prophet to marry a whore. The idea appears to be—and this is of a piece with the tone of much of the book—that only in the context of

---

[7]Folio 7a. The translation—really paraphrase—is my own but follows the text quite closely.

such a marriage can the prophet understand what it is like for God to be wed, as it were, to the people Israel.

God, as reported by the prophet, seems to jump between extreme moods, at one moment longing powerfully and painfully for His beloved people; at another furious with her and promising to punish or destroy her and her lovers, the foreign gods.

At one moment (2.16):

Assuredly,
> I will speak coaxingly to her,
> And lead her through the wilderness,
> And speak to her tenderly,
> (2.17) I will give her vineyards. . . .

At another (2.4):

Rebuke your mother, rebuke her—
> For she is not My wife
> And I am not her husband—
> And let her put away her harlotry from her face
> And her adultery from between her breasts.
> (2.5) Else will I strip her naked
> And leave her as on the day she was born:
> And I will make her like a wilderness,
> Render her like desert land,
> And let her die of thirst.

In the 1948 Academy Award winning film, *The Best Years of Our Lives*, a daughter who is suffering through a difficult relationship cries to her parents about the contrast between her own relationship and that of her parents. She remarks that her parents have always had one another; their intimacy was a constant source of untroubled support, this as opposed to her own situation. Her mother looks at her father, turns to her, and replies, "If you only knew how many times we had to fall in love again." The comment applies well to the intimacy between God and His people as depicted in *Tanach* and as understood and experienced in Jewish tradition.

Such is quite a different conception of loving and being loved by God than our usual one: grace on the part of God and adoration of perfection on our side. This is not to say that on the suggestion I am developing God's love for Israel and Israel's for God are one and the same. But the Bible's model moves us closer to a human love relationship. In neither direction does this sort of love presuppose that its object is perfect. God as depicted in *Tanach* is not the perfect being of later tradition. Even before we get to serious moral problems with God, He is spoken of as changing his mind, as angry and resentful, even petty at times, and subject to flattery, and the rest.

It is striking that the Song of Songs (or of Solomon) with its depiction of erotic love, was canonized and used by the religious traditions to model the relationship between God and the people of Israel, or God and the Church, etc. We should, I think, not pass over the eroticism too quickly.[8] What does it mean to model—even as one model among others—the relationship between persons and God in this way? Seemingly important is the central role of our longing for intimacy with God, someone with whom we share our deepest longings, pains, and joys. There is also the suggestion of a certain longing on the part of God, for intimacy with His people, for sharing their love in the context of a transformed world.

I turn now to my final passage, from the rabbinic commentary, *Midrash Rabbah* on the book of Lamentations,[9] an attempt by the Rabbis of the Talmud to bring Lamentations to bear on the destruction of the Second Temple, their latest and by far greatest tragedy. (Lamentations itself was written some 650 years earlier, in connection with the destruction of the First Temple in 587 BCE.)

The aspects of divinity a literature emphasizes reflect salient features of the community's experience. Subject a community to great trial or triumph and its way of thinking about God may well alter or enlarge. The Temple's destruction accompanied by the prospect of an unending exile, certainly qualifies as such a great trial. And the *Midrash* on Lamentations evidences an important theological development, an altered—but of course not historically discontinuous—perspective on God. God is, one might say, hyper-anthropomorphized.

Anthropomorphic depiction was of course characteristic of Hebrew Bible. Early in Genesis, for example, God is angry at our antics, even regretful that he initiated the human experiment. But these were the emotions of a being that was—despite the anthropomorphism—somehow wholly other, the awesome Creator of the universe in whose hands was its destruction, a somewhat remote purveyor of rage, passion, justice and the rest.

It has been said that the Biblical narrative is the history of God's learning that He cannot do it alone, that His plan crucially requires partnership with His human reflections. By the time of the *Midrash*

---

[8] In my own tradition, it is often passed over instantaneously, as if (some actually make this suggestion) the erotic imagery was a mere superficial appearance, not deserving of focus.

[9] Soncino Press (London, 1983).

on Lamentations, and in the perception of its authors, the lesson is well learned. Not only cannot He do it alone, the project is not going well.[10] And God's reaction reveals a new level of affective engagement and self-awareness. He suffers, weeps, even mourns. "Woe is Me!" he cries in Proem 24, "What have I done?"

Sometimes the *Midrash* sees God in maternal terms—or, more accurately, God, as the *Midrash* has it, sees Him/Herself in such terms (Proem 22):

> "Just as when you take away its young a sparrow is left solitary," so spake the Holy One, blessed be He, "I burnt my house, destroyed My city, exiled My children among the nations of the world, and I sit solitary."

Sometimes the imagery is paternal: God is compared with a king who, enraged at his two sons, thrashes them and drives them away. The king afterward exclaims, "The fault is with me, since I must have brought them up badly." (Proem 2). Indeed, not only does God mourn, God, it would seem, needs instruction in mourning from us.

> The Holy one, blessed be He, said to Jeremiah, "I am now like a man who had an only son, for whom he prepared a marriage canopy, but he dies under it. Feelest thou no anguish for Me and My children? Go summon Abraham, Isaac, and Jacob, and Moses from their sepulchres, for they know how to weep."[11]

One aspect of this humanizing of the divine image, interestingly parallel to (roughly simultaneous) Christian developments,[12] is a new emphasis on divine vulnerability. God is, as it were, exposed to the elements to a degree scarcely predictable by what we knew of Him.

Closely related is what we might call divine approachability. God, in Genesis, is available to the patriarchs, and to some extent to the matriarchs. But the *Midrash* on Lamentations (in the continuation of Proem 24) imagines the three patriarchs—Abraham, Isaac, and Jacob—and Moses pleading with God for mercy. God, however, is unaffected; he cannot or will not comply. Eventually, he does promise to restore Israel to its place, but the promise is made not to

---

[10]This is to some extent true of the prophetic literature more generally. What is new here is a matter of degree and sustained emphasis.

[11]Proem 24. For more detail, see my paper, "Coming to Terms with Exile," in this volume.

[12]A key difference of course is that in Jewish thought, there is no suggestion of God becoming—or having an aspect that is—human in some more serious or literal sense.

the patriarchs or Moses. It is only mother Rachel who can move Him. Rachel tells God that she knew of her father's plan to substitute Leah for her in marriage to Jacob. She attempted to foil the plan, but when that failed

> I relented, suppressed my desire, and had pity upon my sister that she should not be exposed to shame. . . . I delivered over to my sister all the signs which I had arranged with Jacob so that he should think that she was Rachel. More than that, I went beneath the bed upon which he lay with my sister; and when he spoke to her she remained silent and I made all the replies in order that he should not recognize my sister's voice. I did her a kindness, was not jealous of her, and did not expose her to shame. And if I, a creature of flesh and blood, formed of dust and ashes, was not envious of my rival and did not expose her to shame and contempt, why should You, a King who lives eternally and is merciful, be jealous of idolatry in which there is not reality, and exile my children and let them be slain by the sword. . . .
>
> Forthwith, the mercy of the Holy One, blessed be He, was stirred, and He said, "For your sake, Rachel, I will restore Israel to its place."

It is interesting that Rachel does not argue on the grounds of justice. Nor does she appeal on the basis of her own merit, as do the patriarchs, Abraham, Isaac, and Jacob (earlier in Proem 24). Her appeal is more personal, predicated on issues of character.

My aim in this paper is not to answer the central questions of the Conference. I don't know how to do that, although I'll say a bit by way of speculation below. Instead I've attempted to alter our perspective in a way that puts those questions in a different light.

I want to return now to the *Akedah* and Job specifically to note some features common to both stories. These stories have a kind of resonance that defies time. We somehow feel that things haven't changed that much. Of course God does not ask us to sacrifice our children. But we, like Abraham, are put in situations that test us, or test our souls, situations—writ large and often small—in which we have to choose between incompatible but truly non-negotiable values. And while the mythological sounding text attributes Job's losses to God's wager with the Accuser, the fact is that awful things happen to people without apparent reason, often pretty obviously undeserved. And so we can feel and share Job's hurt and his eventual outrage. "These things really happen," the texts seem to speak to us; the sense that the universe treats us as if by a whim is familiar.

So there is a kind of truth, or universality, to these stories, right at the outset. I see a certain truth as well in the human heroes' responses. I use "truth" here in a way that I do not have entirely under control. Perhaps it would be more cautious to say that both Abraham and Job, as I read the stories, are moral heroes; they exemplify ethical virtues of the first importance. And in the case of Job, God's revelation to him from the Whirlwind—I will discuss it below—is at once a revelation to us, another measure of the truth I see in these stories.

My reading, though, is certainly controversial; to take the case of Abraham, some see mere obedience—ethically deficient—where I see ethical/spiritual valor. Job is often praised for his patience, actually rather short lived, and not the integrity, even spiritual stubbornness, which I will emphasize. What follows is a quick sketch of my readings of those texts.

Abraham, I want to propose, does *not* decide to obey God; not that he decides against it. Nor is this indecision. Abraham holds in his hands two incompatible non-negotiable loves, two non-negotiable commitments—commitments do not go any deeper than these—toward God and toward his son. Nor does Abraham, I am imagining, have any conception of what it would mean to prioritize such commitments. The idea of making such a choice boggles the mind. There is almost something obscene about it.

The text, strikingly spare, invites us to imagine Abraham's reaction. How could he not have been feeling alone in the universe? It must have been a long and lonely night. As I imagine his response the next morning—all one can do is dwell in the language, letting it seep in—what he does is to proceed, to march resolutely ahead, his eyes fixed, together (the Hebrew *yachdav*, repeated several times, suggests intimate togetherness) with his beloved son.

Abraham's transcendent faith is exhibited in his ability to so march forward, not knowing where the path will lead, but ready to follow it, with confidence that he will know what to do when he has to.[13] To withstand any such an experience must be transformative. And *sometimes*, as the text perhaps suggests, one comes out the other end having survived that ordeal, loves intact, having grown in ways otherwise unavailable. I hope it is clear that I mean this as a comment on Abraham, and hardly a justification of God's command. If I am even roughly on track, there is universal significance here.

Turning to Job, let's distinguish the core of the story from the very strange beginning—God and the Accuser—and the equally strange end—when Job is restored, a new family, riches, and the rest.

---

[13] I see this sort of faith as an important, if rare, human virtue. Attendant to it is the ability not to look too far ahead, not to anticipate the moment of decision.

The core is a classic tale: someone having had everything loses it all, hits bottom, finds God, and through God finds peace.

The peace Job finds seems in part a consequence of his spiritual straightforwardness, his own deep commitments. In his stubborn responses to the Comforters, it is as if he were speaking about a love relationship and said things like, "I don't understand. My love for her was boundless. She understood all that, and she clearly reciprocated. Until today. I am lost."

When Job hits bottom—sitting on a pile of ashes, scratching his lesions with potsherd—God appears and Job is, as it were, taken on a strange journey to a new perception of reality. God, hardly in a soft and comforting mode or mood, somewhat strangely becomes a poet and equally strangely shares with Job the view from above, the view *sub specie aeternitatis*, God's own sense of His achievement. The vision—not to speak of the experience of God—is overwhelming. It inspires awe, and a strange comfort, the latter a consequence of seeing in a new perspective his own pain and the lack of justice in the world. He gets philosophical, one might say.

Whatever one does with the thorny business of God's role in these "tests," there is genuine moral and religious power in these stories. From my own perspective it would be a real loss to overlook that power in favor of an exclusive focus on what is so genuinely difficult—even appalling—God's moral role in subjecting his beloved to such tests, a topic to which I now turn.

The conception of love between people and God that I sketched above finds resonance in these two stories. Prayer experience is at its best an experience of intimacy, of sharing one's longings, pains, joys and the rest. It is, however, a strange intimacy for our experience of the Other is through a glass darkly. There is here a religious idea—I mean one that derives not from philosophic reflection but (in my own tradition) from *Tanach* and Talmudic literature—that in thinking about, trying to understand, God one is over one's head. Intimacy with God tends toward the *sui generis*.[14]

As I read these texts, neither Job nor Abraham knows quite what to make of God. In the case of Job this is easier to see; by the end of the Whirlwind he is overwhelmed, chastened by his lack of understanding how it all works. The text emphasizes no such thing in the case of Abraham. But his notorious silence in response to God's command to kill

---

[14]I say "tends toward the *sui generis*" since it may be that the phenomenon I'm discussing has a reflection in the sense of imperfect connection even with those people with whom we are most intimate. The topic deserves real scrutiny; the eroticism of the *Song of Songs* seems relevant here.

Isaac signals that he knows that this is not the time to argue with God. He knows that God knows that he, Abraham, will not understand; Abraham senses that what is appropriate here—as opposed to the case of Sodom and Gomorra—is to follow the path and see where it leads. And reflecting more generally on the matter of understanding God's ways, we should not forget that Moses—closest of all to God according to the Bible—is sharply rejected in his request to see God's face.[15]

There is a folk fable, perhaps a piece of actual history, concerning the inmates at the Auschwitz concentration camp. As the story goes, they put God on trial for crimes against humanity and against his chosen people. The jury deliberates; God is found guilty. And then the group proceeds to its afternoon prayers. A focus on this story pays dividends for understanding the religious perspective I am trying to elucidate.

A student of mine suggested recently that one would need some doctrinal understanding in order to pray responsibly. "One needs to know to whom one is praying," as she put it. My response was that religious experience may be otherwise. One prays; one achieves (sometimes) a sense of intimate contact. But exactly who or what "stands on the other end" is another question, a matter well beyond us.

Religion, suggests William James, is in the end a matter of the gut rather than of the head. In this spirit, I want to suggest that religion's natural bedfellows are more the arts than the sciences. Religion, wrote Santayana, pursues wisdom through the imagination. It is productive not of a system of the world, a sort of super-physics or metaphysics, but of a way—a literature and set of related practices—to ennoble human life, to give meaning to and make meaning of our deepest hopes, fears, longings, and dreams.

A Speculative Appendix

Anthropomorphism is deeply entrenched in biblical literature, in the Talmud, not to speak of our religious lives. The Rabbinic attitude to anthropomorphism, unlike that of the later philosophers, was dual: on one hand, we experience God in these anthropomorphically describable ways; at the same time, we experience Him as beyond all that. Such "inconsistency," characteristic of the sort of literary theology we find in the Bible and Talmud, is disastrous if one wants a coherent theoretical theology.

---

[15]There is a tradition in Jewish commentary that Moses was asking to understand the problem of evil—the apparent lack of justice in God's world.

But whatever one does with the thorny problem of Biblical anthropomorphism, it is there and very prominent. God so presents Himself, and not always in the best light. Indeed, it is striking how little the Bible seems interested in creating or protecting the image of a perfect being. It is especially striking by comparison with the works of philosophers and theologians.

What then, allowing ourselves speculation, might we make of God's treatment of Job and Abraham? One is inclined to smile at Jung's suggestion that the "Satan," the Accuser in Job, represents God's insecurity about Job's love. At the same time, Israeli religious thinker David Hartman advances a related idea concerning language of Deuteronomy when God is speaking to the Israelites about their forthcoming entrance into the promised land. God, says Hartman, sounds a bit like the parent of a teenager about to leave for college. "We were together from the time of the exodus," God seems to be saying. "I was with you, led the way, protected you. Will you remember me—will you still love me—when you are in your own land, not dependent upon me for sustenance and protection?"

The idea that God is vulnerable is not new, not after the prophets and the *Midrash*, only a bit of which I made mention of above. Might these strange "tests" of Job and Abraham be a function of God's as-it-were humanity? Perhaps.

If one can think of these stories not as history but as parables[16]—so that one does not have to ponder actual deaths and the like—another idea suggests itself. I will introduce this suggestion by way of another similarity between the Job story and the *Akedah*. The language of both stories, specifically, the description of God's initial command to Abraham and his mandates to the Accuser, are, to put it mildly, quite stark. It is as if the reader is invited to extreme discomfort and confusion, perhaps to outrage. It would not have been inappropriate for the writer to warn the reader: "what you are about to hear will make your hair stand on end."[17]

---

[16]Job reads like a parable; the *Akedah* less so. Maimonides, in *The Guide*, announces a highly controversial methodological principle that one might think to apply to the *Akedah*. Strikingly, and unexplained, he does not so apply it. The idea is that when a biblical text mentions an angel, what that text formulates is not a piece of history, but rather the vision of a prophet. So Maimonides, to very mixed reviews over time, interprets the story of Abraham and the three men/angels that visit him in Mamre. To apply this to the *Akedah*—an angel is indeed mentioned in the text—renders it a nightmarish vision of Abraham. It would remain a tremendously interesting vision, one whose messages are hardly mooted by its vision status.

[17]Thanks to Jeff Helmreich here.

Perhaps the reader is encouraged to experience discomfort to the point of moral horror, to join Job pre-Whirlwind, to join Abraham in his reaction to God's plan for Sodom, to inquire about justice, to ask how God can be indifferent to the spiritual torture of his beloved Abraham, how He can be influenced by the Accuser in the face of what God knows about Job. Perhaps these texts are challenging us to ask hard questions that have no answers forthcoming. Why this would be is a speculative matter for another day.

These of course are the merest speculations. Here is another, from a very different direction. The Bible seems to sometimes attribute natural occurrences, the work of God's creation, to God. One quick example: Exodus speaks of God's hardening Pharaoh's heart, perhaps the outcome of natural processes, as when one sets out on a ill-chosen course of action and nevertheless finds sustenance and encouragement for that course. Perhaps then it is the universe that, as it were, tests us, killing our children, removing our riches, nullifying our accomplishments, putting us in a position where we must choose between alternatives, none of which can be abandoned virtually at the cost of ourselves.

I do not have a settled view, or even something that approaches one. Job and the *Akedah*, however, virtually reek of truth for the reasons explored above. Better to suffer in confusion about God, an appropriate state for us if not a pleasurable one, than to forego these stories that, in their own way, edify.

10

Coming to Terms with Exile

"Diaspora" is a relatively new English word[1] and has no traditional Hebrew equivalent. But it seems closely related to the more traditional concept, *"galut,"* exile. Indeed these might seem to be expressions for the same idea. Nevertheless reflection on the two concepts reveals crucial differences.[2]

Diaspora is a political notion; it suggests geopolitical dispersion. It may further suggest—this is more controversial but I think correct—non-voluntary dispersion from a center, typically a homeland.[3] With changes in circumstances like the coming of new generations, new social conditions, movement from one diasporic location to another, a diasporic population may come to see virtue in diasporic life. And so "diaspora"—as opposed to *"galut"*—may acquire a positive charge, as it has for some nowadays. Still, I suspect that we would not think of it as diaspora—"dispersion" itself has something of this flavor—had the shift originally been a consequence of the people simply deciding to leave, say for want of economic improvement or cultural enrichment.

---

[1] According to the *Oxford English Dictionary*, the term first appears in English usage in 1876, and in 1881 is used by Wellhausen, in the *Encyclopedia Britannica*, in connection with Jewish dispersion.

[2] Thanks to Murray Baumgarten, who attributes the distinction to Cynthia Ozick. That there is an intuitive distinction seems clear, but it is much less clear how this is to be spelled out. In the following paragraphs, I attempt to do so.

[3] Carlos Velez-Ibanez suggested this to me.

Galut is by contrast a religious, or almost religious, notion. Daniel Boyarin, in discussion, referred to it as a teleological notion. One of its important resonances is a concomitant of involuntary removal from homeland: dislocation, a sense of being uprooted, being somehow in the wrong place. To view one's group as in *galut*, is to suppose that what is in some sense the proper order has been interrupted. Perhaps the dispersed group has been punished, or perhaps the world is just the sort of place where awful things happen.

I. Normal Dislocation and the Cosmic Jolt

Galut is a pervasive theme—perhaps even the dominant motif—in Jewish history. One might even say that from the perspective of the Hebrew Bible[4] and Jewish religious tradition, human (and not only Jewish) history is a study in exile.

The original, as Arnold Eisen emphasizes,[5] is the mythological expulsion of Adam and Eve from the Garden of Eden. Before their expulsion, Adam and Eve were to carry on in harmony with their world, without pain and suffering. After they are banished, Adam and Eve experience life as we know it, an uncanny constellation of richness, even exquisite beauty, along with all manner of awfulness.

At the surface, the suggestion is that our plight is a consequence of some original misbehavior, of choice exercised in a wrong direction. The story may be seen, however, as making a more subtle suggestion, that such choices are themselves human. Our plight, our condition of *galut*, may then be seen as a consequence of being the sort of creature that we are in the kind of world in which we live, no formula for bliss. It is only in the mythological past—Eden before the apple—and the mythological future—Messianic times—that human existence is not radically troubled and confused.

The human condition is thus one of dislocation—"normal dislocation" I'll call it—as if we were not quite designed for the world in which we find ourselves. To apply the notion of exile to the human condition is thus to allude to the Eden story, but more importantly, it is to call attention to normal dislocation.

---

[4]"Hebrew Bible" and "Old Testament" are not quite names for the same thing. The order of the contained books is not the same, and the former work includes books that were not canonized in the latter. See Jack Miles, *God: A Biography* (New York, 1995), especially chapter 1.

[5]See his seminal work, *Galut: Modern Jewish Reflection on Homelessness and Homecoming* (1986), a book that I have found immensely helpful. I am grateful to Eisen for discussion of the topics of this paper.

A central facet of the religious impulse is the drive to find meaning—even transcendent meaning—in the face of such "exilic" existence. Adversity thus provides raw material for the religious impulse. Even without the well-known horrors of Jewish history, the religious impulse would have an abundance of raw materials. But that history has been supererogatory in this regard.

Ignoring historical detail let us skip to what is, until our times, the catastrophe of catastrophes: the destruction of the Second Temple in 70 CE, the subsequent defeat of Bar Kochba in 135, and the dispersion of Israel. The destruction of the First Temple—in 587 BCE—and the subsequent Babylonian exile was of course calamitous. But that prior exile lasted only half a century; exile could still seem unusual, an exception to the order of things. After Bar Kochba and the expulsion of Jews from Jerusalem, however, with no hope for return in the foreseeable future, exile must have seemed like the rule.[6]

If the dislocation inherent in the human condition counted as a kind of *galut*, we now have the real thing. Temple times—when the sacrificial worship practices were in place and there was at least a taste of the dignity of sovereignty—are seen in retrospect as a kind of Eden. The prospect of living without the foci of national and religious life, and indeed doing so in exile with no prospect for restoration must have been experienced as a grave threat to—if not a violation of—the very conception of a cosmic partnership between God and Israel. The *churban* (destruction), by contrast with normal dislocation, was a cosmic jolt.

Judaism as we know it—"rabbinic Judaism" so-called—is in important respects a response to this catastrophe, an attempt to pick up the pieces, to reconstruct religious and national life in the absence of their central foci. While one should never underplay the enormous continuities between pre- and post-destruction Judaism, the new developments are dramatic. Taking a bit of dramatic license, one might say that the religion as bequeathed to us both by the Rabbis of the Talmud and by subsequent developments—another fifteen hundred years of intermittent persecution, expulsion, and in our times *shoah*—is nothing less than a religion of *galut*. And since the attempt to reconstruct was made in keen awareness of the normal difficulties of the human condition, it is a religion of *galut*, both normal and catastrophic.

The idea that Judaism is a religion of *galut* might be further supported by consideration of the wanderings of the patriarchal families,

---

[6] As Eisen points out in *Galut*.

and the Rabbinic idea that the reported experiences of the patriarchs signify the later history of Israel. But this would take us too far afield and so I will not pursue it here. But even with such additional support for the "religion of *galut*"-idea, that idea is too one-sided. There are many foci of the Jewish religious outlook, and certainly no adequate single formula. *Galut* is one of the crucial ones, and the one under scrutiny here.

II. Coming to Terms with Galut

I said above that residents of a diaspora might come to see their environment in quite positive terms. Post-emancipation Jewish diaspora has been seen in this way, as a condition or situation characterized by liberation from *galut* to a host of newfound freedoms and possibilities. Rebecca Goldstein's novel, *Mazel*, vividly represents such a diasporic transformation in terms of the transition from the *shtetl* to the cosmopolitan city. For some, the State of Israel makes possible a perhaps even more radical and liberating transition, one that involves political sovereignty in addition to the freedoms and opportunities afforded by a liberating diaspora. But Jewish dislocation runs deep; there may be a lingering taste of *galut* in diasporic cosmopolitan life as well as in sovereign Israel.

One reason is the long arm of Jewish history, a mixed history that includes extraordinary and haunting trauma. Equally important is a refined sense of normal dislocation. Different cultures respond to life's customary travails in different ways. A virtue of American pragmatic optimism is that for a wide range of important projects, Americans get the job done with minimum fuss. The cost is at least a tendency toward a lack of serious focus on the travails. A friend—suffering mightily from the death of his mother—commented that what seemed to work best for him was avoidance. This attitude contrasts dramatically with what one is likely to find in cultures that history has made more intimate with suffering. The lingering sense of dislocation may thus have roots beyond national tragedy; it may be due in part to a culturally induced sensitivity to the substantial limitations of the human condition.

Avoiding *galut*—for example, by turning to, or turning it into, a culturally plenteous diaspora—may thus not be a winning strategy for Jews. I want to consider the attempt not so much to defeat *galut* as to engage and come to terms with it, to wrestle with it. In this essay I will attempt to tell part of the story of how rabbinic culture contended with the cosmic jolt. In the course of telling this story, I will comment upon its implications for our grappling with normal dislocation, a struggle of great human significance.

Whatever one's view of the viability of a traditional religious outlook, it is undeniable that the Rabbis took *galut* seriously. For them it was inescapable, a kind of permanently temporary state. What I think of as their distinctive take on human flourishing[7] is heavily influenced by this perception, and by their attempt to find solace, meaning, even salvation while in *galut*. It may be instructive to see how a tradition smitten by *galut*, obsessed with it, develops practices and an outlook to cope with exilic existence.

What I am suggesting may seem paradoxical. For those who see diaspora as a locus of freedom and cultural possibility, the relevant contrast is with *galut*, often seen as the narrow, constricting life led within the four cubits—to use a Talmudic phrase—of the law, of *Halacha*. Now without question there have been and still are narrow and constricting implementations of *halackhic* life. Equally without question, there was a genuinely liberating transition from the *shtetl* to the city, and Goldstein describes with great power the heady engagement of the newly liberated with a whole range of previously unavailable/forbidden new cultural forces. But if diaspora cannot obliterate dislocation, it may be instructive, even if ironic, to have another look at how the tradition contended with *galut*.

This Rabbinic quest might have gone very badly. It would not be difficult, for example, to overemphasize Jewish victimhood—Woody Allen's joke about a Russian rabbi who "developed whining to an art unheard of in the West." This would be stultifying. Alternatively, and more positively, the dislocation might be a sensitizing force. Perhaps, seasoned by *galut*, the rabbis were able to develop a manual, as it were, for the successful negotiation of life experience, even when it goes badly. This is the idea I will explore here.

I spoke above of coming to terms with *galut* by developing practices and an accompanying outlook. Clearly a general exploration would be an enormous undertaking. My emphasis here will be on the outlook, the theological side of the matter, as opposed to better-known post-*churban* developments in communal practice. These include the increased emphasis on prayer, on study of the Torah as among the highest forms of religious practice, and a shift in the locus of ritual holiness from the sacrificial alter to the family table.

---

[7] See my paper, "Awe and the Religious Life," in this volume.

I call the developments that I will discuss "theological" for lack of a better word. This is not a process of refining doctrine, or the adding to/replacing a body of doctrine. Doctrine is not what's at issue; rather developments in what one might call religious sensibility. Indeed, Rabbinic literature until medieval times does not much trade in doctrine.[8] When the concerns of the Rabbis are not broadly legal—or *halackhic*—they are homiletic, parabolic, exegetical and the like. These *aggadic* passages are less authoritative than the legal discussions. This is not to make little of them, or to diminish their significance for the religious life, which is indeed enormous. There is much in Jewish religiosity that operates at the level of religious sensibility, although this is obscured by much of the medieval doctrine-oriented discussion.

III. Theological Developments

My primary focus here will be *Midrash Rabbah* on Lamentations,[9] the rabbinic commentary on the book of Lamentations. That commentary is a compilation of materials composed over many generations post-70 CE, an attempt by the rabbis of the Talmud to bring Lamentations to bear on their latest and by far greatest tragedy. (Lamentations itself was written some 650 years earlier, in connection with the destruction of the First Temple in 587 BCE.)

The aspects of divinity a literature emphasizes reflect salient features of the community's experience. Subject a community to great trial or triumph and its way of thinking about God may well alter or enlarge. The Temple's destruction accompanied by the prospect of an unending exile certainly qualifies as such a great trial. And the *Midrash* on Lamentations evidences an important theological development, an altered—but of course not historically discontinuous—perspective on God. God is, one might say, hyper-anthropomorphized.

Anthropomorphic depiction was of course characteristic of Hebrew Bible.[10] Early in Genesis, for example, God is angry at our antics, even regretful that he initiated the human experiment. But these were the emotions of a being that was—despite the anthropomorphism—somehow wholly other, the awesome Creator of the

---

[8] See my paper, "Theological Impressionism," in this volume.

[9] I will be quoting from the translation of the Soncino Press (London, 1983).

[10] See "Theological Impressionism," in this volume, for an exploration of the contrast between, on one hand, Biblical and rabbinic anthropomorphic characterization, and, on the other, the anti-anthropomorphism of Greek philosophy-inspired medieval theology.

universe in whose hands was its destruction, a somewhat remote purveyor of rage, passion, justice and the rest.

It has been said that the Biblical narrative is the history of God's learning that He cannot do it alone, that his plan crucially requires partnership with His human reflections. By the time of the *Midrash* on Lamentations, and in the perception of its authors, the lesson is well learned. Not only cannot He do it alone, the project is not going well.[11] And God's reaction reveals a new level of affective engagement and self-awareness. Indeed, God has become almost one of us in affect. He suffers, weeps, even mourns. "Woe is Me!" he cries in Proem 24, "What have I done?"

Sometimes the *Midrash* sees God in maternal terms—or, more accurately, God, as the *Midrash* has it, sees Him/Herself in such terms (Proem 22):

> "Just as when you take away its young a sparrow is left solitary," so spake the Holy One, blessed by He, "I burnt my house, destroyed My city, exiled My children among the nations of the world, and I sit solitary."

Sometimes the imagery is paternal: God is compared with a king who, enraged at his two sons, thrashes them and drives them away. The king afterward exclaims, "The fault is with me, since I must have brought them up badly" (Proem 2). In Proem 24 God laments:

> Woe to the King who succeeds in His youth and fails in His old age.

> The Holy one, blessed be He, said to Jeremiah, "I am now like a man who had an only son, for whom he prepared a marriage canopy, but he dies under it. Feelest thou no anguish for Me and My children? Go summon Abraham, Isaac, and Jacob, and Moses from their sepulchres, for they know how to weep."

Indeed, not only does God mourn, God, it would seem, needs instruction in mourning from us.[12]

One aspect of this humanizing of the divine image, interestingly parallel to (roughly simultaneous) Christian developments,[13]

---

[11] This is to some extent true of the prophetic literature as well. Thus, what is new in the literature under discussion here is a matter of degree and sustained emphasis.

[12] As Alan Mintz points out in his book, *Hurban: Responses to Catastrophe in Hebrew Literature* (Syracuse, NY, 1996), p. 60.

[13] A key difference of course is that in Jewish thought, there is no suggestion of God becoming—or having an aspect that is—human in some more serious or literal sense.

is a new emphasis on divine vulnerability. God is, as it were, exposed to the elements to a degree scarcely predictable by what we knew of Him.

Closely related is what we might call divine approachability. God, in Genesis, is available to the patriarchs, and to some extent to the matriarchs. But the *Midrash* on Lamentations (in the continuation of Proem 24) imagines the three patriarchs—Abraham, Isaac, and Jacob—and Moses pleading with God for mercy. God, however, is unaffected; he cannot or will not comply. Eventually, he does promise to restore Israel to its place, but the promise is made not to the patriarchs or Moses. The fact that it is only mother Rachel who can move Him, and indeed by the way that she succeeds powerfully illustrates God's humanity. She tells God that she knew of her father's plan to substitute Leah for her in marriage to Jacob. She attempted to foil the plan, but when that failed

> I relented, suppressed my desire, and had pity upon my sister that she should not be exposed to shame. . . . I delivered over to my sister all the signs which I had arranged with Jacob so that he should think that she was Rachel. More than that, I went beneath the bed upon which he lay with my sister; and when he spoke to her she remained silent and I make all the replies in order that he should not recognize my sister's voice. I did her a kindness, was not jealous of her, and did not expose her to shame. And if I, a creature of flesh and blood, formed of dust and ashes, was not envious of my rival and did not expose her to shame and contempt, why should You, a King who lives eternally and is merciful, be jealous of idolatry in which there is not reality, and exile my children and let them be slain by the sword. . . .
>
> Forthwith, the mercy of the Holy One, blessed be He, was stirred, and He said, "For your sake, Rachel, I will restore Israel to its place."

It is interesting that Rachel does not argue, as did Abraham in Genesis 18:23–33, on the grounds of what divine justice requires. Nor does she appeal on the basis of her own merit, as do (earlier in Proem 24) the patriarchs, Abraham, Isaac, and Jacob. Her appeal is more personal, predicated on issues of character.

These developments are underscored and pushed to still another level with the Talmudic idea that after the *churban*, God Himself enjoys only an exilic existence, that the divine presence resides in *galut*. This is no doubt in part a matter of empathy. To say that God's presence is in *galut* is to say that He is with us, He feels for us. But it is equally an expression of divine dislocation and a constricted existence. Here we approach discontinuity with what we know of God from the Bible, a kind of anthropomorphic quantum leap.

One might argue that there is no quantum leap here, but that the powerful imagery of divine exile is a mere rhetorically super-charged variation on what we have already seen, God in a state of mourning, weeping bitterly, feeling lost, even at times hopeless. But one has the sense that this is not simply a matter of divine affect, that something more "objective" is at stake here. God's project for humanity, His partnership with Israel for *tikkun olam*, the repair and redemption of the world, has been thwarted.[14] The universe is thus dislocated, thrown off course. Israel's political, social, and national catastrophe is thus transformed into a metaphysical cataclysm, a real cosmic jolt. The universe is shaken to its foundations.

So much for the theological developments. What are the implications for the community's struggle with *galut*?

IV. Coming to Terms with Galut, Part 2

Such hyper-anthropomorphism yields new possibilities of relationship. The possibilities for relationship with a more remote Divine Presence, for example as depicted in Genesis, are quite limited—for the people, if not for the privileged few. Quite another matter is a God who is vulnerable in the ways explored, whose range of affective response is not unlike our own, whose self-perception is of one whose fate is tied up with that of the community. Such a God can function as life partner, as it were, of the community and derivatively of the individual. Here there are intimations of the Rabbinic reading of Song of Songs, God and Israel as lovers.

There are then enormous implications for the post-*churban* community's ability to contend with exile, to be effective in the face of exile. For God to cry over their catastrophe, to feel great pain over their loss, indeed to feel the pain jointly with them, is to mitigate the loneliness of their suffering. The increased emphasis on prayer—Jewish prayer is at once individual and communal—makes sense against the background of the new picture. Frequent contact with one's, and the community's, divine partner potentially transforms bitterness into a healing outpouring of pains and disappointments. There is now the possibility of nurture and comfort—for the individual and for the community—even in the face of an unyieldingly awful universe.

As my comment about prayer illustrates, the theological development I have been illustrating proceeds in concert with developments

---

[14] As Eisen expressed it in conversation.

in religious practice. Here as elsewhere, one needs to be careful not to overplay the role of ideas in social developments. In the present case, one should not overemphasize the role of theological ideas in explaining how the community contends with catastrophe. This is especially important given the dominant role of practice in traditional Judaism. Nevertheless, these are powerful developments in religious sensibility.

The cataclysm of *churban* prompts these theological developments. But the engendered religious sensibility has much wider scope. It is relevant to our handling not only of the great catastrophes of human history, but also of difficulties of ordinary life. Indeed, Talmudic discussion of the *aggadic* themes I have been discussing is quite often not restricted to *churban*:

> Rabbi Meir said, "When a man suffers, what expression does the *shechinah* [Divine Presence][15,16] use? "My head is too heavy for me; My arm is too heavy for me." (Tractate Sandedrin 46a).

In Tractate Berachot 7a, the Talmud argues that it is not only we that pray. God prays as well. It continues

> What does He pray? ". . . May it be My will that My mercy may suppress My anger, and that My mercy may prevail over My [other] attributes, so that I may deal with My children in the attribute of mercy and, on their behalf, stop short of the limit of strict justice." [Note: The Hebrew word, *rachamim*, translated here as "mercy" suggests something less Christian in the original. The word seems etymologically related to the Hebrew word for womb, and thus suggests something closer to nurture.]

The passage continues with a remark of Rabbi Ishmael b. Elisha, apparently a priest who performed the Temple service prior to the *churban*. He states that he once entered the Sanctuary whereupon God asked him for a blessing. He replied to God with the formula just quoted as God's prayer: "May it be Your will that Your mercy. . . ." "And," continues Rabbi Ishmael, when the blessing was completed, "[God] nodded to me with His head." There is much that is amazing in this passage, and there are many suggestions that connect with my discussion: God is vulnerable, subject to limitations. God, not unlike us, needs to work at suppressing his anger; achieving the desired balance is something for which even God needs to pray.

Passages like these are important in connection with my hope for assistance with normal dislocation. But in the last passage quoted

---

[15]The *shechinah* is often associated with the feminine side of God.

[16]The comment in square brackets, here and in what follows, are my own.

there is something else as well. The story of Rabbi Ishmael highlights the reciprocal aspect of relationship, specifically, what we
give to God. For in this story God comes to one of us to ask for a
blessing.[17] To this theme of reciprocity I now turn.

In Tractacte Berachot 3a there is a discussion of the recitation of
Kaddish, a prayer that occurs in many contexts in every public service. (The recitation of *Kaddish* requires a quorum.) The *Kaddish* is
typically recited by the person leading the service (or by the mourners
in the case of Mourner's *Kaddish*). Its centerpiece is an enthusiastic
communal declaration: "May His great name be blessed at all
times." God is said in the passage in Berachot 3a to experience *Kaddish* as bittersweet. But it is the positive side that is relevant here:
God is touched, honored, especially by the communal declaration.

> He shakes His head and says, "Happy is the king who is thus praised in
> this house!"

Less relevant to the present point, but worth mentioning in light of
my broader concerns in this essay, God also feels a sense of great
loss. He says,

> Woe to the father (alternative reading, "what is there for the father")
> who had to banish his children, and woe to the children who had to be
> banished from the table of their father.

Mourner's *Kaddish* is constituted by (more or less) the same
glorification-of-God text as other occurrences of *Kaddish*.[18] It is thus
a somewhat strange piece of mourning liturgy, one that never mentions death or the dead. One traditional interpretation begins with
the thought that the loss of each individual is heartfelt by God. God,
like us, does not take well to the loss of His children. The Mourner's
Kaddish—also recited communally—thus represents the community's coming together to comfort God for His loss.

God is thus nurtured by our praise, and comforted by our community effort at comforting Him. The liturgy, borrowing from Psalms

---

[17]This is a striking feature of the story. What to say in the end about a host of
implicated questions is of course quite another matter. What is it to give a blessing?
What exactly does one do for another by blessing her? And so on? These all need exploration. But it remains clear that God is asking us for some sort of important help
or something of the like.

[18]The same core text of the *Kaddish* gets minor variations in a number of its
occurrences. What most distinguishes Mourner's *Kaddish* is the tone in which it is
recited. As opposed to the other occurrences of *Kaddish* that are typically chanted,
the mourner's version is recited in a somewhat sad tone, put to music either not at all
or in a barely discernible fashion.

22:4, speaks of God as enthroned on the praises of Israel; again pointing to our highly significant role in His flourishing. And then there is
a centerpiece of the liturgy, the *Sh'ma*, that emphasizes God's oneness.[19] Perhaps the idea goes beyond numerical unity; perhaps what
is at issue is a kind of unity or coherence that depends in part upon
the success of one's projects, including one's children. Seen in this
way, the *Sh'ma* is a messianic dream about God's future, as it were.
And seen in this way the *Sh'ma* is closely related to the messianic
Zachariah 14:9, also highlighted in the liturgy, "In that day, God will
be one and His name one."

The *Sh'ma* is one of the passages inscribed on scrolls found
inside our *t'fillin*, the phylacteries that Jews wear during weekday
morning prayer. The Talmud, Berachot 6a, asks what passage is to
be found in God's *t'fillin*—as if we would all naturally assume that
God dons *t'fillin*. The answer according to Rabbi Hiyya b. Abin is
the passage from I Chronicles 17:21:

> *And who is like Thy people Israel, a nation one* [or unique] *in the earth.*

The passage continues:

> Does then the Holy One, blessed by He, sing the praises of Israel?
> Yes. . . . The Holy One, blessed by He, said to Israel: "You have
> made me a unique entity in the world [alluding to the *Sh'ma*], and I
> shall make you a unique entity in the world [alluding to the Chronicles
> passage]."[20]

Thus emerges a love relationship between God and Israel. There
are ups and downs, as with human love, and the parties likely need
to fall in love again and again. Such relationships depend upon mutual generosity and often survive the considerable foibles of the
parties. While I have emphasized the comfort afforded in times of
travail, a more complete story would give another central place to
shared joys. Also important, and worthy of treatment beyond the
mere mention I will make, is the nurture afforded by the act of providing nurture and comfort. Generosity of spirit, *chesed*, is a key
virtue of God and His human reflections. So each side, as it provides

---

[19]I have in mind here the first line of the *Sh'ma*, the famous call usually translated (badly, I think) as "Hear O Israel, the Lord your God, the Lord is one."

[20]The *Shabbat* afternoon *amidah* (the standing prayer than constitutes the central moment of every service) places the following text in a prominent place: "You are
one, and Your name is one. Who is like your people, Israel, one (a unique) people in
the land." This *amidah* is chanted in a melody that is sadly sweet, almost melan-
choly. This service marks the approaching end of *Shabbat*, a day which God and
Israel spend together, as it were.

support for the other, expresses its innate *chesed* and so is enriched, fulfilled.

As the Rabbis construe post-*churban* religious life, it is lived if not within the Land, at least within the law—within the four cubits of the *Halacha*. The imagery is both negative—emphasizing constriction, a contrast with life in the Land—and positive—insofar as one sees the law as a source of structure for the enhancement of life. The Talmud also speaks of God living, post-*churban*, within the same four cubits, a similarly mixed image, but with a twist. God's so living certainly conveys exilic constriction—a dramatic contrast with His life in the land, in the Temple, and specifically in the Holy of Holies. But what can it mean that God also lives within the four cubits of the law? I suggest that its import concerns the shared life with Israel. Indeed, perhaps the most significant outcome of the theological developments I have been sketching is this duality: on one hand exile for both parties, and on the other, God and Israel sharing a life of mutual dependence and nurture.

These theological emphases are inspired by cataclysmic *galut*. But if one were to read them with too much emphasis on catastrophe—early or late—one would miss much of the deeper religious significance. The conception of a shared life has powerful implications for our contending with the substantial difficulties of the human condition—normal dislocation.

V. Conclusion

It is acknowledged by foes and friends of a religious outlook that such an outlook affords its adherents comfort during times of trouble. And this is no small matter. At the same time, this comfort is often seen as a bad purchase, the cost being acceptance of false beliefs about all manner of reward, afterlife, and the like. Religion, that is, is often seen as Marx saw it, a dispenser of opiates. I have argued in related other work[21] that even within a religious framework, theodicy should be rejected in favor of non-opiate approaches. And the present essay is an effort in that direction. The theological development highlighted here—notwithstanding the popularity of messianic movements during the post-*churban* period—is distinctly non-opiate. More precisely, the way that perspective facilitates human efficacy in the face of great adversity is non-opiate. We are

---

[21] "Against Theodicy," in this volume.

not provided with a magical solution, or the promise of one. We are provided with, as it were, a Helpmate.[22]

Earlier in this essay, I argued that even a culturally rich and liberating diaspora was not likely to liberate us from *galut*. The question was where we might turn for help. We have now seen one sort of assistance provided by the religious tradition. But even if not tainted as a purveyor of opiates, traditional religion surely does not constitute an answer for all. At the same time, I think there are issues that the rabbinic response brings to the foreground well worth general consideration.

One such issue is that of the stubbornness of our sense of dislocation, both in terms of the long arm of history and what I have called normal dislocation. Such difficulties require considerable attention if one, or a community, is to make headway with them. This is not to advocate an emphasis on victimhood—far from it. But as in traditional Jewish practice, mourning for example, can constitute a way to put one's difficulties in their right place, a way not to be forever mired in them. Related issues concern the power of community and of community-based ritual.

My own interest is not only in the religiously neutral lessons available. For my ultimate aim is to articulate a contemporary Jewish identity at the heart of which is a *galut*-engendered religious outlook. I have taken dramatic license again, since the notion of *galut* is only one of the pillars of such an outlook. But it is one important pillar.

[22]Admittedly, there are promises, e.g., God's remark to Rachel in Proem 24, quoted above, that he will restore Israel for her sake. But there is much to the perspective I have been describing that involves no such promises. And even when one hears a promise, as in Proem 24, it by no means dominate the message. I allow that there may be other rabbinic trends during this period. Still, my aim here is to isolate one important trend.

11

Forgiveness and Moral Reckoning

Forgiveness is no simple matter either to execute or to understand. Charles Griswold explores forgiveness both in its guise as a virtue—I will call it "forgivingness"—and as something that is more difficult to categorize, something like an act or process. Griswold's *Forgiveness* provides a classical philosophical analysis of the act or process, "a theory of paradigmatic forgiveness—of what forgiveness would have to be in order to be perfectly accomplished." Griswold's is a fine book, one that serves as at once an able introduction to and an accomplished advanced treatment of a set of difficult and important questions.

One of Wittgenstein's legacies, one emphasized by Kripke, is an approach to philosophic criticism that attends both to the details of views under discussion as well as, perhaps even more significantly, the underlying conception, what Kripke refers to as the picture of the domain. I will initially focus on a number of my hesitations concerning Griswold's analysis of forgiveness, the act or process, his concern in the central portions of his book. I will raise matters of detail that at the same time signal the need for a very different underlying conception. Afterward, I turn to the virtue, some of whose features make this need even more dramatic.

I. Hesitation: Moral Anger and Resentment

Griswold, along with much of the literature, sees forgiveness as, to some large extent, a matter of overcoming the offended party's "moral anger," "moral hatred," and like phenomena. The adjective "moral" draws attention to itself here. There is a tradition of the use of the term, "moral," according to which morality is not implicated; modern philosophers speak of the moral sciences, where "moral" means something like "concerning human nature" or "concerning human mores." Griswold's use of "moral anger," "moral hatred," and the like seem, however, part of a conception of the domain which sees it as highly moralized, beginning with an unjustified moral intrusion. Forgiveness, on Griswold's view, pivots on the offended party's moral reckoning.

Are the offenses for which apology and forgiveness are appropriate always, typically, or paradigmatically moral offenses? Are all significant breaches in human relations moral breaches? Arguably even highly offensive personal affronts are not always moral wrongs. Examples are plentiful: breaches of courtesy, speech that is a bit too harsh, various kinds of presumption, a pattern of behavior that while disturbing is too close to the line to be remarked on but that persists over time. Or consider the distribution of goods and attention within a family, where without ill will someone is hurt, perhaps lastingly. Or self-absorbed, someone fails to attend adequately to another's pain or joy. It is difficult to see all such examples as involving moral wrongs. Clearly the question of delimiting the scope of morality is beyond my reach here. But Griswold's locating forgiveness in strictly moral terrain is, I think, very significant, and I will return to it below.[1]

Griswold sees "moral anger" as a justified consequence of personal offense; he speaks similarly of "resentment." It is not altogether clear from the text whether these are precisely the same concepts. But clearly they are close, and perhaps the same. The idea seems to be that there is in the well-functioning moral agent's response to offense something relatively uniform, in Bishop Butler's terms "a species of moral hatred . . ., a retributive passion that instinctively seeks to exact a due measure of punishment." (p. 39).

Why suppose any such uniformity? Our reactions to offense—moral, personal, or however one thinks of them—vary widely and along myriad dimensions: with personalities, contexts, social stratification, expectations, and the like. Anger is only one among many reactions. A sample of others are revulsion, sadness, depression with

---

[1] There is a large question concerning the scope of the moral, perhaps independent of what I am raising here, but at least reminiscent of it. Bernard Williams and Harry Frankfurt, perhaps inspired by Nietzsche, distinguish the moral from the ethical, a much broader domain that includes our values, loves, and the like. Forgiveness may provide an interesting terrain to contrast such an approach like Griswold's that sees the category of the moral as overriding.

the state of things, annoyance, even relative indifference. And why presume that the desire for revenge is ubiquitous? Such an urge is no doubt a deep and primitive feature of human responsiveness to injury. But a deep feature is not necessarily a universal feature.

I mentioned indifference as one possible response. It is not a response that Griswold and others in this literature afford much respect. Griswold speaks as if such a reaction bespeaks most likely a lack of self-respect, or else, much less likely, a kind of sainthood. Sainthood aside, there are those no doubt who fail to react to offense (or who overreact) out of a lack of self-regard. However, many people at least some of the time refuse to take others' untoward behavior to heart, and there is no simple story to be told about why. Indeed, sometimes it may be a function of psychological health and perspective. If one proceeds through the world with a well-developed sense of irony, perhaps grounded in a strong sense of self, all sorts of things become possible.

And when there is anger, even at an uncontroversially moral offense, is one's reaction *moral anger*? What is moral anger? Is it a species of anger, one with a different phenomenology than other sorts, or rather one with different sorts of accompanying thoughts, or a merely different etiology? Assuming for a moment that there is some distinctively moral anger, it must be very difficult to tease it apart from a more personal anger. Such clarity would seem to be the last thing on the mind of typical victims. And need one add "moral" to the other reactions mentioned: moral depression, sadness, and the rest? What would be the point of such an addition? What work does "moral" do in talk of moral anger, hatred, and the like?

II. Griswold's Analysis of Forgiveness: The Offender

I turn to the heart of Griswold's analysis. Griswold formulates six conditions that must be satisfied by the offender, in paradigmatic cases of forgiveness.[2]

1. There are two parts to this first condition: the offender must first acknowledge that she was the responsible agent. And second, she must demonstrate that she no longer wishes "to stand by herself as the author of those wrongs."
2. She must repudiate her deeds and disavow that she would author those deeds again. This, Griswold explains, is a step toward showing that one is not simply the "same person" who did the

---

[2]Paraphrases and quotations are from pages 49–51 of *Forgiveness*.

wrong. One thus, in Griswold's words, "repudiates the self that did X."

3. The wrongdoer must both experience and express regret—not simply acknowledge the wrongness of the act—and the regret must be expressed to the wronged party.
4. The offender must commit to becoming the sort of person who does not inflict injury, and that commitment must be shown through deeds as well as words. ("Then," comments Griswold, "her repudiation of her 'past self' would become credible, and it is her task to make it so, for the 'burden of proof' is hers and hers alone to shift.")

These first four steps constitute a "contrition" condition. There are two additional conditions:

5. The offender must show that she understands, from the injured person's perspective, the damage done by the injury.
6. The offender needs to offer a narrative account of "how she came to do wrong, how that wrong-doing does not express the totality of her person, and how she is becoming worthy of approbation. She needs to make herself intelligible by offering up an account that is neither fiction nor excuse making, and that puts the wrong-doing as well as the self that did the wrong in context."

III. Hesitation: What Did I Do?

When I first studied these conditions, I, one who regularly asks for forgiveness, felt as if I was losing touch with the project. Repudiation of the self? A full narrative that reveals that my offense does not represent the "totality" of my person? On the countless occasions I apologize, were I to issue any such full narrative or self-repudiation, I would likely be looked at quizzically and be told to lighten up.

I will turn in a moment to Griswold's conception of these conditions as necessary only with respect to paradigm cases; this might be seen as blunting my concern about the conditions being overly extreme and dramatic. But I do want to register the sense that some of these conditions have purchase only with respect to severe, even heinous offenses. This threatens to skew any general account of forgiveness. Even if what is at issue are paradigm cases, it is not clear why the focus should be the most heinous offenses.

It took me some time to see what Griswold was after in his talk of paradigms, since I took the term to refer to classical or typical cases. One learns the meaning of terms, one might suppose in the spirit of Wittgenstein or psychologist Eleanor Rosch, by acquaintance with paradigms, typical cases, rather than by the intellectual mastery of definitions. And if one uses paradigm in this Wittgensteinian way, Griswold's talk of paradigms and the analysis he proposes for them is indeed very difficult to assimilate.

Attention to the beginning of chapter 3, however, revealed that I had missed Griswold's intention. Griswold's "paradigm" talk derives not from Wittgenstein but from Plato: paradigm as perfect exemplar. Griswold's view is that the sort of extreme cases of moral breach that he emphasizes and the forgiveness that is appropriate to them constitute a sort of perfect example of the phenomena in which he is interested.

Still, the connection between extreme cases and perfect ones remains obscure to me. In what way are the extreme cases perfect examples? And why assume that the human resolution of heinous moral offenses somehow models for us the resolution of everyday hurts and indignities? In what way, to speak with Plato, are the ordinary examples reflections of the extreme ones. My own contrary, Wittgensteinian instinct is to make a study of our actual practices of forgiveness focal. Wittgenstein's advice was that we "look; don't think," that we scrutinize actual practice rather than theorize about what it must be like by our theoretical lights.

I vacillate between two ways to thinking about Griswold's contribution here. At moments, it seems to me that he has provided an analysis not of forgiveness in general but rather of what it comes to in cases of heinous offenses. My dominant tendency, though, is to suppose that even in such cases, forgiveness is not captured by Griswold's net.[3] Perhaps Griswold's discussion does illuminate the domain, but in an unexpected way. Griswold's conditions have natural application not so much to forgiveness as to reconciling, reconstructing a relationship that has been damaged or broken by a quite serious, even grievous, moral wrongs.

IV. Griswold's Analysis: The Side of the Offended Party

There are three preliminary conditions on the side of the forgiver: the forswearing of revenge, the moderation of resentment, and a commitment to letting go of all resentment. The idea is that unless one has put aside revenge, the process is not well underway. When

---

[3]This reflects my reaction in the next sections to Griswold's requirements on the side of the offended party.

one has gotten past the vindictive urge, and has begun to moderate one's anger, forgiveness is in process.

The completion of the process, complete forgiveness, has two requirements on the side of the offended party. First, the *resentment must be no more*. And second, the offended party must *reaccept* the person. Griswold sometimes describes this as a change in belief: the offended party no longer thinks that the offender is a bad person with whom one should not consort.

There is an important proviso on the first of these conditions: it not sufficient that the resentment is gone, even gone for good. Instead the passing of resentment must occur for moral reasons, because it is the right thing to do. Once the offender has fulfilled the conditions specified above, the victim's resentment, says Griswold, is no longer morally warranted. A consequence is that the offended party is "morally obligated to forswear resentment."

V. Hesitations: The Two Requirements

Griswold's "change of belief" requirement: This seems to have application only to the most heinous offenses. Except for very serious offenses, such an initial harsh judgment by the offended person—this is a bad person with whom I should not consort—would bespeak an inappropriate judgmental character on the part of the injured party. Nor is it not easy to construe this condition as a suggestion of something weaker but analogous for more pedestrian offenses. The condition thus raises the issues I raised above about conditions that apply only to extreme cases.

Griswold's forswearing resentment idea: This presents a new problem and from a different direction. To suggest that forgiveness is not complete until resentment is eradicated, virtually obliterated, seems too idealized to have purchase in actual cases, even those that involve heinous offenses. But if the condition is unrealistic even for the extreme cases, this militates against the equation of extreme with perfect cases, Platonic paradigms. To begin with the cases of heinous offense, total eradication of resentment is virtually impossible for most people, and perhaps not desirable. Only a saint would be capable of a total elimination of her resentment toward those who, for example, performed a genocide that included her loved ones. And in ordinary cases of personal, forgivable offense, forgiveness involves "getting past" one's resentment. But this usefully imprecise expression hardly suggests that under no conditions might any resentment arise again.

I apologize, you forgive me, and our relationship no longer bears the burden of that offense. I am forgiven. But if I do it again, the former offense may reemerge in your thinking with renewed resentment. Alternatively, you may have forgiven me, but on the occasion of a book you are reading, or a movie you are watching, or another incident with another person, or on many other sorts of occasion, the old offense may come to mind and there may well be the taste of resentment. In some such cases it will be natural to say that the forgiveness had its limitations, that it was not complete. But certainly not in all cases. A certain amount of lingering, hardly noticed, resentment is natural, unremarkable, and compatible with having forgiven.

VI. Hesitation: The Moral Environment of Forgiveness

I called attention earlier to Griswold's emphasis on *moral* anger. In fact, Griswold's picture of the entire domain is a highly moralized one. A potential forgiveness situation paradigmatically begins with an unjustified moral intrusion. This typically results in a justified moral anger on the part of the offended. But the justification comes to an end when the offender fulfills the conditions specified, 1–6 above. These conditions both involve the moral repair of the offender, and the reaching out to the injured party to repair the moral damage. She asks the offended for forgiveness. And the offended, if he is to do his moral duty, must grant the forgiveness that only he, with his unique moral standing, is in a position to grant.[4] That is, he must forswear resentment; he must "swear it off" as we might say, since it is no longer morally justified. If, as is often the case, that resentment lingers—if his duty cannot be accomplished at once—then the forgiveness is not complete. When resentment is finally forsworn, we have forgiveness, full, complete, perfect.

As noted, Griswold requires not only that the resentment be permanently eliminated, but that this happen for moral reasons, namely the offended party recognizes that her resentment is no longer warranted. This seems to me to make forgiveness too much a matter of moral calculation and reflection. When you apologize to me in a heartfelt way, I am *moved* to forgive, resentment recedes, etc. Perhaps I am touched by your reaching out. The wound is healed. In other cases perhaps there was no deep wound; no real resentment to speak of. Your sincere apology is all that I need to put what happened behind us. In many such cases, I forgive, but not because I am motivated to do so by moral thinking or calculation. That would be the

---

[4] Griswold writes that the moral community has ceded exclusive standing to the offended party to grant forgiveness.

proverbial one thought too many. Instead, my resentment lifts; I no longer resent, period.

Contrast this with a case in which the wound is unhealed. Perhaps you have done your part to apologize in a heartfelt manner, but the offense is one to which I am particularly sensitive. At a certain point, I make a conscious, deliberate effort to overcome my resentment. I do so—it takes a special exercise of the will and of conscience—because it is the right thing to do. The latter situation is also part of human experience. But it is hardly the norm. Why make it so?

Indeed there are examples that take us far from Griswold's model of these things. Perhaps you have injured me; perhaps it really stings. But perhaps I know you, and care about you; I know your history, and some of the difficulties you faced earlier in your life, perhaps as a child, perhaps in a first marriage. I am ready to forgive without an explicit apology. Perhaps we look in each other's eyes and that is more than enough. Or perhaps I do not even need that much in order to let the resentment go. I am hardly here forswearing resentment because it is no longer warranted. Perhaps resentment is indeed still, technically speaking, warranted; surely another who did not approach the situation as I am doing would be not offending any moral norm if he still felt resentful. There was, after all, no apology. But given how I am approaching the situation, the question of warrant simply drops out as irrelevant. Notice that my willingness to forgive in such cases in no way exhibits any sort of lack of self-respect; nor is it condoning untoward behavior. It is uncontroversial that what you did was offensive. Griswold's analysis seems insensitive to the ethical realities in such cases.

Something I felt to be particularly jarring about what I am calling Griswold's moralizing of the situation is Griswold's (and others) bring to bear legal terminology on the ethical life. The question is whether concepts like *justification, warrant, obligation* and *moral duty* are the pivotal ones in potential forgiveness situations. A really striking example was Griswold's idea that the moral community cedes to the offended party the *moral standing* to be the sole purveyor of forgiveness.[5] That, and the role of *justification* and *warrant* throughout Griswold's discussion.

---

[5] *Forgiveness*, p. 52. On page 48, Griswold writes that "the victim alone owns the moral right to forgiveness." On pages 118–19, Griswold discusses *standing* in connection with "third-party forgiveness." For politically inspired vocabulary in addition to the legal, see Pamela Hieronymi, "Articulating an Uncompromising Forgiveness," *Philosophy and Phenomenological Research*, 62, no. 3 (May 2001), who sees the resentment and anger as expressive of moral protest.

Bernard Williams and others have objected to what they call *scientism*, the (mis)application to various domains of philosophy of modes of thought and explanation that derive from the sciences. Parallel to such scientism is legalism, the imposition of legal categories on the ethical domain. The matter is of course quite controversial.[6]

VII. Secular and Religious Approaches to Forgiveness

When the APA approached me to comment on Griswold's book, Charles expressed interest in my articulating a religious perspective that might contrast with his secular perspective. The topic of secular and religious perspectives on forgiveness, and on ethical matters more generally is of great interest to me. While I am skeptical of religion's ability to provide a logical or philosophical foundation for ethics, I do think that a religious outlook provides important perspective on the ethical life, forgiveness an important case in point. The topic deserves much more discussion, but here is a sketch from my own religious orientation.

It is characteristic of the Jewish religious sensibility (first emphasized in the prophetic literature) to see God and the people as bound in a quasi-marital relationship. Our love for God, and God's love for us, are thus modeled on human love relationships, more than they are in say in various strains of Christianity (and to some extent also in various strains of Jewish and other traditions), where a person's love for God is something like the worship or adoration of perfection, and God's love for persons is a matter of undeserved grace.

Given the intimacy, intensity, and domesticity of the relationship between God and the people, it is not surprising that frictions are engendered. We often fail to live up to our responsibilities to God, sometimes in how we treat Him per se, often in our relationships with one another.[7] On his side, God is angry and vengeful, silent, absent.

It is characteristic of the Hebrew Bible and Jewish religious sensibility to be blunt about the mutual failures. God tells the prophet

---

[6]See my paper, "The Significance of Religious Experience," in this volume. I note there the same legalizing tendency in epistemology, specifically in philosophical theorizing about the justification of religious belief. The key notions are again warrant, justification, and obligation. In both domains, ethics and epistemology, the matter is controversial and to many the legalistic turn will seem perfectly natural. In the epistemic realm, my own view is that we would do better to worry about whether we are being epistemically responsible than whether we are justified, the latter connected with granting too much respect to the skeptic, or so I argue in that paper.

[7]When one fails to treat another appropriately, an evil in itself, one at the same time violates trust with God.

Hosea to marry a prostitute; perhaps to convey to him a sense of what it feels like to God to be intimately associated with Israel. At the same time that book powerfully expresses God's commitment to the people; even his longing for them. On the other side, there is a folk story about a group of inmates at Auschwitz who put God on trial for crimes against humanity, find Him guilty, and then proceed to their afternoon prayers.[8] And just as God longs for His people, we think of him as flawless, for example, (sometimes) in *Psalms*. Real love relationships are like that. At one moment one is intoxicated with one's lover and her virtues; at other times, one can feel estranged, alienated and the like.[9]

Forgiving one another and the virtue of forgivingness, it should go without saying, must play an enormous role in such relationships. I will focus here on God's forgivingness, for the Bible one of God's cardinal virtues. God is said to be long-suffering (absorbs many stings), quick to (stands ready to) forgive, does not let his anger consume (it consumes neither him nor us).[10] We are told to be like Him in these ways, and further (like Him) not always to hold one's tongue but in the right context to rebuke one another for wrongdoing. This among the commandments is one of the most difficult to get right since it amounts to pointing out the foibles and wrongdoings of another with love and sensitivity, and without condescension. None of this implies that anger is never appropriate; for one sufficiently ethically developed, some sorts and degrees of anger are compatible with love, sensitivity, and a lack of condescension.[11]

My interest in a religious perspective and specifically the biblical perspective just sketched is not because I think that religion

---

[8]Even if it is only a folk story, its existence tells us something about the cultural/religious outlook of the folk. See Elie Wiesel, *The Trial of God* (Schocken Books, 1995).

[9]In the 1948 Academy Award winning film, *The Best Years of Our Lives*, a wife of many years says to her daughter about her husband and their to-all-appearances very successful and happy marriage, "If you only knew how many times we had to fall in love again." Such is the fate of God and Israel.

[10]These remarks prompt questions about how God's fierce anger in the Bible comports with his being long-suffering and with his anger not consuming. Also pressing is the problem of injustice in the world, the problem of evil. For my approach to the latter see my paper, "Against Theodicy," in this volume.

[11]So I sum up my sense of the matter. But there is a truly extensive rabbinic literature on anger, much of it concerned with the perils of anger. Unlike the philosophic literature I have been discussing that sees moral anger as appropriate, justified, as the correct reaction to injury for a person morally and personally well-situated, the emphasis of the rabbinic literature is on the ideal exemplified by God's forgivingness. Perhaps there is the suggestion here that what forgiveness overcomes is not always anger; offense creates rupture, and forgiveness reestablishes harmony.

makes possible some special and perhaps superior kind of forgiveness, one that is unavailable to a purely secular outlook. Rather it sheds light on what we humans are up to in forgiving one another. One point of special interest is the Bible's domesticating of forgiveness, the quasi-marital relationship mentioned. Focusing our thinking about forgiveness on situations of intimacy seems salutary, for as noted, proximity engenders friction and forgivingness becomes an important virtue. I turn now to a rough and ready account of the virtue, one that is inspired in part by the discussion of the biblical perspective.

VIII. The Virtue of Forgivingness

As a preamble, I want to mention a remark of my colleague Larry Wright, a remark that I alluded to above. Wright suggested that we human beings would do well to forego some of our anger in favor of an increased sense of irony, a kind of cosmic irony. I took this to be a remark in the spirit of Spinoza; one with a refined sense of human limitation and some ability to see things "under the aspect of eternity" may be less surprised and less angry at the human foibles that come in one's direction. This is no matter or making excuses or condoning injurious behavior. One remains committed to being a certain sort of person, to teaching this to one's children, etc. One who has internalized something of this perspective seems to me on the road to becoming a more forgiving person.

My sketch:

- A forgiving person is likely to absorb more stings (for lack of a better word) than an unforgiving person, and not because of a lack of self-respect or anything of the sort.
- She is also more apt to forget such stings as have occurred, at least the minor ones, and even not so minor ones, again not at the cost of self-respect, etc. Forgetting, in the right context, to the right extent, comes to seem like an important aspect of the virtue.
- Crucially, she also knows the limits, at what point it is important not to hold one's tongue, to protest wrong, and the like. This is of course related to self-respect.
- In contexts where apology is owed her, she is unlikely to require a full narrative of the sort discussed by Griswold (major moral breaches aside of course).
- Her interest in not humiliating the other similarly makes it entirely natural that she not be much interested in any repudiation of the self that did the damage (again major breaches aside).

- In contexts where apology is owed her and done in the right spirit and to the roughly right degree of detail, she finds herself spontaneously less angry. She does not *forego* her anger (since it is no longer warranted), as one foregoes things one might still desire.
- She is not apt to reduce the other to less than he is, to one who is "just an offender" even while the offense still hangs in the air.

My characterization of the virtue of forgivingness makes strong contact with a number of my earlier hesitations about Griswold's analysis of the act or process of forgiveness. At the level of detail, many of Griswold's central foci just do not figure in the virtue I have been describing, for example, Griswold's emphasis on the duty-motivated foregoing of resentment.[12] But perhaps more important—this at the level of the picture of the domain—the moral reckoning so central to Griswold's account violates the spirit of what I am suggesting. We need to shift attention, or so my sketch suggests, from questions of justification and the agent's sense of his duties to affective matters like love, generosity of spirit, and the desire to bridge the gulf that hurt creates.[13]

To thus comment on the need to shift direction is not yet to articulate an alternative picture of forgiveness, something I cannot yet do to my satisfaction. What exactly is it to forgive? Is forgiveness a single thing—an act or process—subject to some sort of analysis? Are terms like "act" and "process" adequate? Of course, there are examples where forgiveness seems to consist in an act; I ask for forgiveness; you respond that I am forgiven, and the issue never arises again for either of us. Sometimes "process" seems just right; one works for some time on forgiving a dead parent and at some point the process seems to have taken hold. But there are examples that seem to involve nothing of these sorts; my friend asks for forgiveness for

---

[12]I have been describing a virtue of character in a rough and ready way. Needless to say, there will be all sorts of variations in actual cases. A person who is virtuous in the respect in question may, if very sensitive on a certain topic, have to forego her desire to hurt back. She may have to work at letting go of her anger because it is no longer fair, etc. These are, of course, some of the features that are emphasized by Griswold. But where he makes them internal to the nature of forgiveness, I see them as reflecting special circumstances, human foibles, and the like.

[13]I am grateful here to (my recollection of) a comment of Tom Olshewsky at the APA symposium, which expanded my focus to include generosity of spirit. His point was that forgiveness might be related (perhaps even etymologically) to givingness. Jeff Helmreich, in a related comment, emphasized what I think is a Levinasian perspective according to which forgiveness paradigmatically derives from a departure from the stance of the moral judge and the taking up of a very different stance, one that reflects empathy and love.

something that took place a while back, and I respond that I forgave him for that a long time ago, this despite the fact that I never explicitly, in some mental act or verbal remark, did so. What transpired was the gradual passing of bad feeling. In many such cases forgiveness seems bestowed *en passant*.

Perhaps what we have is a non-uniform array of cases—examples of forgiveness—that resemble each other in complicated ways. Sometimes, the offended party's anger is understandable and something to be overcome. Sometimes, anger is hardly present or not present at all; nevertheless, the offense created a rupture. Sometimes the forgiveness is a more or less datable act or event. Sometimes it is more like a lingering process, one that is only more or less complete. Sometimes the offender is forgiven but not by way of some intentional act. Sometimes forgiveness requires elaborate apology, sometimes with a detailed accounting of how such a thing could happen; sometimes not at all. . . . Perhaps we have here what James and Dewey suppose about religion, and what for Wittgenstein became a central analytical tool, the idea of a rough assemblage that for good reason have come to be thought of, and so in an important sense have come to be, a single phenomenon.

Let me conclude by saying again how much I appreciated and learned from Griswold's book. Philosophical differences aside, I particularly appreciated many of its insights and emphases, for example, Griswold's distinguishing between, and his sustained attention to, the relevant virtue of character and something else that is difficult to be clear about, something that we bestow on one another. Moreover, the granting of forgiveness, as Griswold explains, is no simple bestowal; it involves ethical commitments that are extended over time.[14]

[14]This paper derives from my Pacific APA comments in Pasadena, March 2008, in a symposium on Griswold's *Forgiveness*. I am grateful to Charles Griswold for discussions of these matters, and to Michael Goerger and especially to Jeff Helmreich for helpful discussions both of the Griswold book and of what went into this paper.

12

Ritual

I. The Ethical Import of Ritual and Traditional Judaism

Ethical theory, as we have it, seems unfriendly to ritual. For the Kantian, what distinguishes moral norms is their applicability to all rational agents. Rituals, however, are owned by communities in whose highly particular and idiosyncratic idioms they speak. Indeed, rituals are sometimes optional even within the community. Nor does ritual come to mind when utilitarians reflect on behaviors that contribute to human betterment. Finally, engagement with ritual does not suggest itself to us, nor did it to Aristotle, as a trait that figures crucially in flourishing.

To explore our question, it will be helpful to examine a tradition or cultural setting in which ritual is taken seriously, in which it has a weighty, even a central, role. We will focus upon traditional Judaism, a highly ritualized, comprehensive system of practice, indeed an inclusive legal system in which ritual permeates areas like torts, contracts, and divorce law. Ritual is pervasive, and since communal customs attain something of the status of law, the domain of ritual increases over time. How are we to think about the ethical status of ritual in the Jewish context?

A striking and suggestive feature of Jewish ritual is its essential role in the tradition's distinctive approach to human flourishing. Flourishing, of course, is the pivotal ethical notion, at least according to Aristotle and his followers.

Aristotle himself did not see ritual as essential to flourishing. Different cultural settings and traditions, however, may yield different ideas about human flourishing. And while not just anything should count as flourishing, a broadly Aristotelian view will want to allow for some latitude. The Aristotelian project as understood here—the empirical study of flourishing, and of the traits of character that contribute to and partly constitute human flourishing—thus becomes applicable to a wide range of cultural settings. Carried out in connection with traditional Judaism, the project yields the conclusion that ritual observance is ethically of the first importance. It is noteworthy that Mencius, in the Confucian tradition, counted *li*—often translated as "propriety," a trait that centrally involved engagement with ritual—among the virtues.

What is the distinctive approach of traditional Judaism to human flourishing, and how is it that ritual is essential? At the heart of that approach is the conception of developed religious character. Ritual plays an essential role in the growth and sustenance of religious character.

II. Developed Religious Character: The Role of Awe

We begin with a (partial) characterization of the religiously developed person, and return below to the role of ritual. We are apt to think of a deeply religious person as a "true believer." However, there is no expression in biblical Hebrew that corresponds to our term, "believer." The phrase that comes closest is "*Y'rei Adonai*," which means "one who stands in awe of the Lord." (The Hebrew expression "*yirah*," translated here as "awe," also means "fear." As A. J. Heschel notes, the term and its cognates are used in the Bible primarily in the sense of awe.) This suggests an emphasis on affect, orientation, responsiveness, rather than the cognitive. Specifically, this Hebrew expression suggests that awe plays a central role. "Awe rather than faith is the cardinal attitude of the religious Jew," writes A. J. Heschel. (p. 77).

One can see why awe might be of special interest by an examination even of quite ordinary—not religiously charged—awe experiences. Particularly important is a curious duality. In the grip of awe, one feels humbled; in the extreme case, overwhelmed. At the same time, remarkably, one does not feel crushed or diminished, but rather elevated, exhilarated. This duality—humbled yet elevated—is of great importance for the religious orientation at which Judaism aims. (Needless to say, the features of awe experiences highlighted here and below vary in intensity and relative prominence from experience to experience.)

Awe experiences, perhaps as a consequence of the elevation-cum-humility, characteristically engender generosity of spirit, lack of pettiness, increased ability to forgive and to contain anger and disappointment. The tradition notably associates just such affect and behavior with God. Turning to the cognitive, awe experiences engender a godlike perspective, the ability to see things, or almost see things, under the aspect of eternity, as Spinoza put it. One often also feels a powerful sense of gratitude.

Reflection on awe provides an entry point into the concept of holiness, a concept that is as important to Judeo-Christian (as opposed to Greek) thinking about flourishing as it is difficult. In the grip of powerful awe, one often feels oneself to be in the presence of something sacred. To destroy the object of such an experience—say, the Grand Canyon—or to allow it to be destroyed, would be sacrilege. If "holy" and "sacred" have any natural application for non-theists, it is in connection with such moments. It is sometimes suggested that such reactions on the part of non-theists reflect the lingering presence of a religious upbringing, or an earlier time in our history. Instead, such reactions might be taken at face value, as shedding light on the concept of holiness by providing a beginning point for reflection: Awe seems to engender a sense of the holy.

These considerations provide a sense of what we might call the religious content of awe, and thus provide motivation for Heschel's making awe pivotal. At the same time, powerful awe experiences are relatively rare and then transitory. How can such uncommon and fleeting experiences bear so great a weight?

It is here that the concept of the *y're Adonai*, one who stands in awe of God, comes to the fore. What is distinctive about such a religiously developed person is not only the object of awe. Perhaps even more important is the habitual quality, the steadiness, of awe. The *y're Adonai* is one who has made awe a regular, albeit not a constant, companion. And with awe comes its concomitants: the sense of being humbled and yet elevated, the Godlike tendencies to thought, feeling, and behavior, the perspective *sub specias aeternitas*, the gratitude, the sense of being confronted by the holy in all sorts of unlikely places. "Ordinary" experiences, interactions with other human beings, for example, or with nature, become encounters with the holy. It has been said that close to the core of the Jewish religious attitude—and this perhaps represents an important contribution of Judaism to culture—is the idea of the sanctification of the ordinary. If so, then awe goes to the heart of the Jewish religious attitude.

To say that awe goes to the heart of the religious attitude is not to say that there are no other important aspects. A more complete treatment than is possible here would need to explore other such features, for example, the love of God, an aspect of the religious attitude that seems related, but not reducible to, awe.

III. Developed Religious Character: The Role of Ritual

To attain the heightened responsiveness of the *y're Adonai* is of course quite a feat. What is called for is a substantial change of orientation, a heightened responsiveness, a deepening of wonder, of appreciation and of one's character. Effecting such change is intrinsically difficult, and external factors often make it more so. The frailties and limitations of one's fellows often inhibit their support for such development. And the distractions, discouragements, frustrations and sufferings of the human situation only increase the difficulty.

How then is such character development and sustenance possible? What are the tools by which the tradition means to effect its exceedingly ambitious plan? The tradition employs a multiplicity of such tools. One often said to be the most fundamental is study of the tradition. Indeed, "study" is not adequate, for it fails to convey the intensity of intellectual engagement. Jewish liturgy highlights an adaptation of Deuteronomy 30:20, "For they [the words and teachings of the Torah] are our lives and the length of our days, and with them we are engaged [or we meditate] day and night." Saintly personalities throughout post-biblical Jewish history are paradigmatically giants of scholarship, those who quite literally are engaged day and night.

Ritual plays a major role in effecting and sustaining the transformation. Consider the practice of saying blessings: on eating and drinking, on smelling fragrant spices, herbs, plants, on seeing lightening, shooting stars, vast deserts, high mountains, a sunrise, the ocean, on seeing trees blossoming for the first time of the year, on seeing natural objects (including creatures) of striking beauty, on meeting a religious scholar, on meeting a secular scholar, on seeing a head of state, on hearing good news, on hearing bad news.

Heschel suggests that the practice of saying blessings is training in awe. One develops the habit, before so much as sipping water, to reflect and appreciate. In addition to the blessings' training function, blessings also function as reminders. Ordinary experience is distracting, and the tradition has assembled reminders to assist in maintaining focus.

In addition to occasion-related blessings, Jewish practice includes thrice daily, fixed prayer. Whatever one thinks of the practice of saying occasion-related blessings, the thrice daily fixed prayer is likely to appear highly constricting. The blessings, at least, are appropriate to one's current experience.

We should remember, however, the magnitude and ambition of the tradition's project. While fixed prayer can degenerate into mechanical, unthinking, unfeeling performance, it offers great opportunities. Some of the usual translations notwithstanding, Jewish liturgy is a compilation of passages of literary magnificence. That such literature, *Psalms*, for example, has survived the ages is a tribute to its expressive power, its ability to articulate and illuminate religious experience. To engage regularly with such literature—not merely to read the words but to declare them, to wrestle with them—is to occupy oneself with the tradition's project. Encounter with literature of such power, first thing in the morning for example, encourages the regularization of attitudes to which the literature so ably gives voice. Indeed, ritualization turns out to be a great virtue: the agent need not wait until the appropriate experiences present themselves.

Ritualized prayer has another distinct advantage over spontaneous prayer. Spontaneous expressions, for example, of awe—and who would deny that these have a place?—are limited by the expressive capacities of the agent. How many among us are up to the challenge of summoning words adequate to powerful experiences and their concomitant thoughts and emotions.

Ritualized prayer does indeed present challenges of its own. The challenge is presented not by the repetition, but rather by the difficulty, the sheer hard work, involved in summoning up the thoughts and feelings appropriate to such literary magnificence. The founder of Hasidism, the Ba'al Shem Tov, is reputed to have said that it would be easier to deliver two advanced Talmudic lectures than to offer a single *amidah*, a fixed prayer of a few pages.

IV. Rituals: Linguistic and Nonlinguistic

The examples of ritual we have been exploring all involve ritualized speech. Rituals need not involve linguistic performance, however, even in the context of the highly word-oriented Judaism. Some may involve non-linguistic behavior that accompanies speech, as in bowing at appropriate times during prayer. Some may involve pure behavior, that is behavior that is not an accompaniment of a linguistic performance, for example, the donning of a prayer shawl, or of phylacteries, or the burning of the leaven before Passover. These performances are accompanied by blessings (expressive, inter alia, of appreciation for the opportunity to perform the ritual), but the blessing accompanies them (and not vice versa). This is distinct from examples in which the action is a mere adjunct to the linguistic performance, for example, in bowing during prayer. Still other non-linguistic rituals may involve no overt behavior, as in the practice of hearing the searing call of the ram's horn every day during a month of the year devoted to reflection on the direction of one's life.

Ritualized prayer is ritualized engagement with dramatic representation, literary representation. It might seem that non-linguistic ritual is distinctive in that it involves the actual performance of a dramatic representation, as opposed to merely engaging with one as in prayer. There is, no doubt, something to this. Dramatic representations of ideas, for example, have a power considerably beyond mere discursive articulations of the ideas themselves. It would be difficult to find a verbal equivalent of say, wrapping oneself in a prayer shawl (where part of what this may mean to the agent is the wrapping of oneself in the tradition). Similarly the call of the ram's horn is simply not to be equaled by any discursive substitute. Still, we should not forget that to engage in the prayer of Jewish tradition is not simply to read the text. It is rather to declare it, to make it one's own in speech and thought.

For the stranger to ritual, ritual will seem like rote performance, constricting rather than expansive, mechanical rather than expressive. One of the things lacking in such an attitude, according to the advocate of ritual, is a healthy respect for repetition. One who regularly engages with prayer, for example, not only can come to take comfort in the familiar, but can also come to see, in the repeated sentences, new depths. Since we are speaking of great literature, it will inevitably be that difference sentences, or different turns of phrase, leap off the page, as do different emphases, different meanings and levels of meaning. And what is true of prayer is also true for the non-linguistic rituals.

For the stranger to ritual, multiplication of ritual forms will seem like a burden. But for one's day to be sprinkled with such dramatic representations, is for one's day to be sprinkled with powerful expressions of the attitudes and ethical motifs in question. It is also to be in possession of a multiplicity of reminders, mechanisms by means of which one may retain one's focus.

V. Conclusion

Our look at traditional Judaism suggests that in the right cultural setting, ritual can figure importantly in human flourishing. Having come this far, we can extend the point: Whether ritual is ethically relevant for the utilitarian depends upon what counts as well-being. A different sense of what counts as flourishing may indeed yield a different sense of well-being. Even for Kantians, community-based ritual might well come to be seen as ethically relevant, as conducing, say, to an increased respect for persons.

The foregoing suggests that ethical relevance is not a purely formal matter, but depends upon the particulars of the culture or tradition. One might conclude that although ritual may indeed be ethically relevant, it is not so in our cultural setting. One may wonder, however, whether ritualized ways of acquiring, sustaining, and celebrating values might play a more useful role than we have allowed.

13

Concluding Remarks: Religion without Metaphysics

During my first sojourn in religious life, I dreamed that religion and I would part ways and I would be bereft. It brought to mind a line from our evening prayers in which we implore God not to remove his love from us. (The line, in turn, regularly brings my dream to mind.) At some point afterward, I left religious life, but certainly did not feel bereft. Now that I am back, I feel profoundly enriched. I have the sense that my religious life puts me in contact with deep truths and equally deep perplexities.

Since returning to religious life, I have had my eye on a set of targets; the project is at once personal and philosophical. The targets come into and drop out of focus; they sometimes seem relatively clear, but often recede. The essays collected here represent my attempt to articulate and clarify the vision, which is at once (and perhaps strangely) both (seriously, I hope) religious and naturalistic. I close this volume with a sketch of how the matter looks to me now.

I have written a good deal here about religion in the absence of metaphysics. If the reader is anything like my usual interlocutors, the issue may not be entirely resolved. . . . I have a friend, an Israeli academic, who thinks I must be cheating. He left religious life roughly when I did, and he now both longs for it and cannot stand the thought of it. (Would he agree? I'm not sure.) My sense is that I drive him nuts since I seem to be seriously in touch with religion, and yet I get it on the cheap: without metaphysical commitment.

For some years now, we regularly talk about the issues, poking gentle fun at one another about our differences.

Some years ago I shared my early essay, "Awe and the Religious Life" (chapter 3 in this volume) with another American-Israeli friend in Jerusalem. I did so not knowing what sort of reaction I would get; in the last section of that paper, I argue for an unorthodox understanding of what look to be appeals to the supernatural. My friend's religious orientation was (seriously) Orthodox.

My friend appreciated the paper's discussion of awe in the earlier sections. To my surprise, he was not so sure how far apart we were even on questions of basic theology. The reason was, he said, that he is not at all sure what he is speaking of when he speaks of God, and not at all sure to whom he is speaking when he speaks to God.

But how is that possible? "One must have some idea of the theological basics; otherwise to what exactly does one pray?" So argued a student of mine recently. I responded in the spirit of my Jerusalem friend: Perhaps. But my own prayer experience suggests something quite different. In prayer (when it goes well), I have the sense of the presence of the divine, of making contact. But ask me about the party on the other end and one of two things will happen: either I will beg to be excused for not having too much to say, or else we will have a very long talk about how difficult a matter it is that is in question.

Such an approach, unconventional as it might seem, coheres with one strong trend in religious thought: that in thinking about God, we are over our heads, we have outrun our conceptual competence. Ironically, my approach even makes contact with one theme in medieval theology. The medievals wrestled with religious language: many of the things we want to say about God utilize concepts that in the first instance pertain to human experience—concepts like "goodness," "power," "knowledge." Such concepts, Wittgenstein might have said, reflect our form of life. How can we apply them to God? What does it mean to say that God is, for example, good? Among the variety of proffered answers is Maimonides's anti-anthropomorphism, the idea that God is so "other" that we cannot grasp what it might mean to apply any such term to God. We can at most know what God is not, the famous *via negativa*. Again, our conceptual competence is inadequate to God.

Still, philosophically indigestible (at least undigested) contact, even intimacy, with God, as in my prayer experience, may well seem an unstable resting place, perhaps especially strange for one seeking philosophic understanding. I want to approach the topic of understanding with caution. Philosophy's contribution to our understanding of religion is in my view very different from that envisaged by the medievals and their followers. For the latter, philosophy and theology were bedfellows; theology was a philosophic project. I want to begin with prephilosophic sort of understanding, one that in my view, philosophy needs to respect, even to begin with.

In the spirit of Wittgenstein, we might distinguish two kinds of understanding. First, there is the kind that accrues to a person in light of her engagement with a set of practices or a practical ability, a culture, an institutional arrangement, a craft or art form, or the like. This is a kind of understanding from the inside as it were; she knows her way around. It is not necessarily articulable by the agent. The understanding that emerges will vary in degree, range, and articulation depending upon the participant's degree of reflectiveness, knowledge, and so forth.

Second, there is a more "from above" theoretical understanding. There may be many forms of such understanding. One involves the articulation of the rules of a practice or the rules of the various forms mentioned (practical ability, culture, etc.). Various kinds of philosophic understanding apply here as well, for example, the discerning of metaphysical and epistemological underpinnings of a practice or the recognition that a particular practice needs no such underpinnings.

Here is an example from mathematics, but the point is quite general: the competent or even expert mathematical practitioner, completely at home in the practice, may not be very articulate about what exactly is involved in the practice; he may be quite good at the mathematics but a bad teacher. Perhaps he is even a fine teacher, but conveys the technique by exhibiting it, appealing and contributing to students' intuitive apprehension. About philosophical concerns, he may be naive, even insensitive to them. Think about questions of realism about mathematical entities—whether they exist in a realm of abstracta. Or think about Wittgenstein's discussion about rule following in mathematics, the sort of thing mathematicians may or may not understand or care much about.

Richard Feynman, the great physicist and mathematician, allegedly remarked that he lived among the numbers, this by contrast to merely proving theorems about them. His contact with the numbers and their relations was almost palpable. At the same time, he was not given to queries about their metaphysical or epistemological status. If one were to ask Feynman about the reality of numbers, I imagine him unhesitating in his affirmation. If one were to ask, in a philosophical vein, about their existence as abstract entities, I imagine him scratching his head in wonder about what exactly was in question.

Parallel points apply to understanding religious culture. In the case of Jewish religious culture, practitioners vary widely in their "from within" understanding of the life and of the traditions, including traditions of study, ritual practice, and ethical practice. With respect to the "from above" sort of understanding, appreciation for example of the relevant philosophic issues the degree of variation is even more dramatic.

I have known people with a genuinely deep grasp of religion "from within"; only some of them have any taste or feel for philosophy. Another Jerusalem friend, a rabbi who seemed to live in an exceptionally pure relationship with God, might be seen as the Feynman of religious life. He denied that anything as cerebral as belief had much to do with it; he was highly impatient with philosophical worries. The remarks I made about Feynman's imagined differential reactions to questions about the reality and the existence of numbers apply equally to my friend's reactions concerning the parallel queries about God. God was as real to him as the weather; His existence in a supernatural domain was another thing, not to speak of the questionable proofs.[1]

While there is, as I see it, much room for philosophical illumination of religious phenomena, respect for the autonomy of the institution-under-study requires attention. If I am correct that our notion of belief was not at the heart of biblical and Rabbinic religion, then the medieval tendency to make belief focal is an example of a kind of philosophic imperialism. Indeed, it is precisely of the sort Wittgenstein warned of: reconceptualizing the practice to make it amenable to the philosopher's preferred methodological or substantive ideas.

Maimonides furnished an extreme and wonderfully pure case at the end of his philosophical magnum opus, *The Guide for the Perplexed*. In those last chapters, Maimonides advanced the unorthodox idea that the focal religious moment is not constituted by traditional modes: prayer, religious ritual, or Talmudic learning, but rather by solitary philosophic reflection on God and identification with the "active intellect" of Aristotelian fame.

From my perspective, the tendency to make belief focal—not to speak of this more radical Maimonidean idea—is to bring in

---

[1] The comparison to the weather is double-edged. Does the weather *exist*? Are we sure that the concept of existence is quite the right idea here?

philosophy too early. It is to give philosophy power to alter the subject matter, the substance of the practice. The truly considerable intellectual power of philosophy is limited—a strange word, not without irony, given the considerable power—to providing illumination "from above."

Here are some examples of that power, potential areas of illumination. The sort of reflection that philosophers practice might be useful in exploring what our religious institutions have done with the domain of the sacred. Raising the question in such a general way may prompt reflection on aspects of the sacred that are ignored or undervalued. Related are the relations between religious value and aesthetic and ethical value, or between the domains of the religious, the aesthetic, and the ethical.

More specifically, there is the question of belief. It is extremely important and suggestive that the Bible had no such word; but is our word, our concept of belief applicable to religion, and how? I have claimed that religious life of a traditional kind is coherent without special metaphysical commitments. This is, as we know, quite controversial and in need of further discussion.

And what of the deep truths that I claim to be put in touch with by religious tradition? How do we (and do we?) distinguish such truths from metaphysical claims on one hand and, on the other, from mythological elements?

Concerning the abundant poetry and other literary tropes with which biblical and Rabbinic literatures are so rich, how do these figure both in the power of religion and the truths that underlie? It seems important that religious language is born, historically, not in theological theory, but in poetry, narrative, and the like. What implications do such questions of origin have for our understanding of theological concepts?

These are examples of what might issue from philosophic attention to religion. But such illumination from above is compatible with a philosophically naive engagement with religious practice. An analogy is provided by the remark of a mystic in the *Shulchan Aruch*, the code of Jewish law, to the effect that while he had spent his life exploring profundities about God, when he prayed he adopted the stance of a twelve-year-old. This is no doubt a matter that needs elaboration, and I will do so elsewhere.

A return to the topic of anthropomorphic language will allow me to illustrate further my perspective. The Bible speaks of God—and so do we—in terms appropriated from human experience. We speak as if God were a kind of super-person: supremely good, just, loving, and so on. And yet there is the sense that somehow God is beyond such characterizations, that concepts that are apt for human motivation and character are not appropriate to God.

For medieval philosophy, the inappropriateness of such characterizations is an "in-principle" matter. God simply cannot instantiate such properties. The character of the principle involved is another matter. Perhaps it is that the attribution of these human-like properties to God constitutes a kind of category mistake, like attributing weight to the number 2. Or perhaps while God can be good in some way that is analogous to our being good, the divine analog is one that we can never grasp. Or perhaps even the idea of analogy brings God too close; perhaps we can have no idea what terms like "good" mean in connection to God. Or perhaps, as Maimonides suggested in the spirit of neo-Platonism, God's unique and extreme sort of unity excludes the possibility of Him instantiating properties at all, any properties; properties per se violate God's unity. And no doubt there are other possibilities. So medieval philosophy (and its aftermath, until the present time) struggles with what to make of biblical anthropomorphic attribution.

Maimonides's philosophical magnum opus, *The Guide for the Perplexed*, constitutes a purification project, to systematically explain away biblical anthropomorphism. And yet, when one thinks about religious experience—in daily prayer, at times of grief and illness, at times of joy—experiencing God in anthropomorphic terms seems internal and essential to our experience. To eliminate anthropomorphic thinking and feeling about God would be to eliminate religious life as we know it.

The elimination of anthropomorphism, and with it much of our ordinary religious perspective, does not rule out any and all religious perspectives. Maimonides's approach at the end of *The Guide*, certainly does not rule out love and awe of God, as Maimonides rightly insisted. But the sort of love in question is the adoration of perfection; it might rightly be called "worship." But it is hardly the gritty, real love of which the Bible speaks, both in recommending our love for God and in its depiction of God's love.[2]

The attitude of the Rabbis was hardly eliminativist in the fashion of the medievals.[3] Indeed, one should not see the Rabbis as reacting

[2] What I am calling gritty, real love is a commonplace in the Hebrew Bible. For its perhaps most dramatic appearances, see the Song of Songs (the Song of Solomon) and the book of Hosea.

[3] Here I am grateful to Max Kadushin's seminal work, *The Rabbinic Mind* (reprint: Global Academic Publishing, 2001).

to the idea of anthropomorphism per se, as if that idea was inconsistent with something about their concept of God. They had, Max Kadushin argues, no such "concept"; they had instead conceptually undigested experience of God.[4]

Nor was that experience suited to easy conceptualization. The Rabbis experienced God both as if He were a person and as if He were radically other. On the anthropomorphic side, they had a vivid sense of God's nearness,[5] of intimacy with God, and of His abundant love. There are also less positive if still personal religious experiences, the sense of God's being distant from us, a sense of His anger. But, and here is a crucial point, internal to their experience was a sense of God's radical otherness.[6] Distance and otherness are, of course, very different. The first is classically anthropomorphic—modeled on the sometime painful experience of distance between friends or loved ones.

To remain true to these perceptions is to refuse to deny some in favor of others. It is to live with a kind of unresolved tension. That is key to an important sort of Rabbinic sensibility. Add to this the sense that anthropomorphic characterization of God threatens to portray God as too much like us, and thus to be "speaking out of turn"; anthropomorphic characterization is both true to our experience and on the edge of a kind of human arrogance. Finally, there is the general and overriding Rabbinic sense that in all of these comments we are speaking in a context where we are over our heads. Speaking of God in these ways—confusing, anxiety-provoking, both right and wrong—was to the rabbinic mind hardly dispensable.

As with my earlier discussion of conceptually undigested contact with God in prayer experience, we have here again what might look like a sort of irrationalism—a failure to even try to make philosophic sense of something that might well be seen as crying out for a rational approach. From where I sit, the charge of irrationalism again yields to the idea of sensitivity to the subject matter. Were we

---

[4]The notion of "concept" is sufficiently flexible so that one could maintain that there is also a sense in which they indeed had such a concept. Still, Kadushin's point seems well taken, that their approach is experience-based; this as opposed, for example, to Anselm's famous definition of God as the most perfect being, understood in terms of the classical omni-properties.

[5]For example, the Rabbis emphasize that the central prayer in Jewish liturgy, the *Amidah*, should be whispered, as if God is that close. (This is a comment of Kadushin.)

[6]The experiential duality reflects itself, maintains Kadushin, in the standard form of Jewish blessings. One speaks to God as "You," and in the next phrase refers to Him in the third person.

dealing with a theoretical take on the world—the project of medieval philosophical theology—we would not and should not be satisfied with such inconsistency. On the other hand, it is hardly a liability of, say, love poetry that it does not portray one's love in entirely consistent ways. If religion is more like the poetry of one's life, if it is prompted by a unique kind of responsiveness to life—related but not reducible to aesthetic and ethical responsiveness—then it is predictable, even plausible, that it involves tensions that are not to be resolved.

Index

CPSIA information can be obtained at www.ICGtesting.com
Printed in the USA
BVOW08s0047020716

454314BV00002B/3/P